DANCING IN THE VORTEX

Choreography and Dance Studies

A series of books edited by Muriel Topaz and Robert P. Cohan, CBE

**Please see the back of this book for other titles in the Choreography and
Dance Studies series**

DANCING IN THE VORTEX.

THE STORY OF IDA RUBINSTEIN

Vicki Woolf, ᵛ·

harwood academic publishers
Australia • Canada • France • Germany • India
Japan • Luxembourg • Malaysia • The Netherlands
Russia • Singapore • Switzerland

Copyright © 2000 by Vicki Woolf. Published by license under the Harwood Academic Publishers imprint, part of The Gordon and Breach Publishing Group.

Amsteldijk 166
1st Floor
1079 LH Amsterdam
The Netherlands

British Library Cataloguing in Publication Data
Woolf, Vicki
    Dancing in the vortex: the story of Ida Rubinstein. –
    (Choreography and dance studies; v. 20)
    1. Rubinstein, Ida, 1885–1960   2. Ballet dancers – Biography
    I. Title
    792.8′092

    ISBN 90-5755-087-3

Cover illustration: Ida Rubinstein as Europa, by V. A. Serov.
By kind permission of Mr and Mrs N. D. Lobanov-Rostovsky.

add 7/04

CONTENTS

Contents

INTRODUCTION TO THE SERIES

Choreography and Dance Studies is a book series of special interest to dancers, dance teachers and choreographers. Focusing on dance personalities, dance composition, its techniques and training, the series will also cover the relationship of choreography to other components of dance performance such as music, lighting and the training of dancers.

In addition, *Choreography and Dance Studies* will seek to publish new works and provide translations of works not previously published in English, as well as to publish reprints of currently unavailable books of outstanding value to the dance community.

Muriel Topaz
Robert P. Cohan

LIST OF PLATES
(Between pages 92 and 93)

ACKNOWLEDGEMENTS

To Annmarie Fox, my excellent translator and interpreter. A dear friend who made our work in Paris so memorable and such fun.

To Charles Butler, with his vast fount of knowledge, who was always at the end of the telephone to assist me.

To Professor Vitya Borovsky of the University of London for his generous help.

To Count Chavlomov for his advice and kindness.

To Dr Roger Nichols whom I met in the archives of the Paris Opera House and who was of such unfailing assistance back in London.

To Madame Renée de Monbreson, together with her daughter, for the delightful time spent with her in Paris listening to stories of her cousin Ida and the family.

To the late 2nd Lord Moyne for his kindness and contribution of further information about his father.

To the charming Roland Leblond with whom I spent an emotional afternoon in Menton whilst he regaled me with stories of the Free French and his memories of Ida.

To the staff of the British Library reading room.

To the late William Chappel, a kind and beguiling gentleman, with whom I spent delightful times whilst he told me about his life with the Ida Rubinstein Company.

To the late Keith Lester who also danced with Ida and who allowed himself to be "interrogated".

To Madame Soretto, Ida Rubinstein's housekeeper, for sharing with me memories of her illustrious employer.

To the staff of the London Theatre Museum.

To the Bibliothèque Nationale de France.

To Madame Kahane and her assistant Madame Kerhoas at the Archives of the Paris Opera House.

To Jean Mouraille, Curator of the Vence Museum, and to his wife Janine Mouraille for their hospitality and assistance, and for valuable time spent well beyond my expectations.

To Lee Norman, a man of great courage who convinced me to write this book.

To Francis and Lionel Davidson for their advice and kindness.

To Pat Butler, a dear friend who has always been there when needed.

To John Zieger for his friendship and invaluable legal advice.

To Christina Gallea and Alexander Roy, of the Alexander Roy London Ballet Company, friends who were generous with their time and enlivening suggestions.

To Sonya and Louis Marks for setting me off on the trail of Ida, and for their enduring and special friendship.

To Irene Carter-Milhan, Katy Gardner and Pat Hare-Baker for being such beloved and wonderful friends.

To Chris Naylor Smith for his encouragement, enduring loyalty and loving support.

To Bonnie and Tony Tabatznik for being family and allowing me to write in the splendid tranquility of their island home.

To dearest friend and writer Alix Kirsta whose love and support has sustained me throughout the writing of this book.

To Bronwen Belcher for being my wonderful daughter.

Finally with love to David Belcher, my husband and confederate, for holding me and the book together.

Vicki Woolf

FOREWORD

There have been many scholarly books written about Serge Diaghilev and the phenomenon of the Ballets Russes, as well as finely detailed biographies and meticulous records of the company's seasons and tours. The personality of the "private" Diaghilev remains enigmatic and, whereas we know much of the lives of his famous collaborators, Cocteau, Stravinsky, Picasso, et al., no one has yet dared to pry closer into Diaghilev's own social behaviour and the influence, not just professional but personal and, above all, sexual as a result of his liaisons with so many, on succeeding generations of dancers and choreographers.

Beside the mainstream of classical ballet there have been the great "individualists"; those who chose an independent or separate path, both professionally and in their lifestyles. Isadora Duncan is, of course, the best known of those independent dancer-personalities and no doubt her own writings have helped to support her legend. But there have been others and, amongst those, some have been sadly neglected. One such was the extraordinary Ida Rubinstein. Virtually untrained as a dancer, her qualities as a performer warranted her a place in the first triumphant Parisian season of the Ballets Russes and her charisma and creative energy attracted collaborators of the quality of Debussy, Stravinsky, Ravel, Cocteau, Bakst and Benois. Yet virtually nothing of her lengthy and innovative career remains. Benois writes that Pavlova was so incensed by the adulation by the Parisian audience for Ida Rubinstein that she refused to join the Ballets Russes for the following season. We have little to judge this by – a sensuous portrait by Serov and a few dim photographs. However, there is no doubt that Ida Rubinstein was a "superstar" in all its meanings: as extravagant as her friend Sarah Bernhardt (with whom she shared a penchant for collecting wild animals as pets) and as revolutionary in her lifestyle and performances as Isadora. The fact that she was extremely wealthy is also intriguingly unusual in artistic circles notorious for impecunity.

We therefore welcome any new light shed on Ida Rubinstein – particularly on her origins and her personal life – that helps us understand how she inspired so many great artists, choreographers and composers to collaborate during her long career as performer and as director of her own ballet company. Vicki Woolf gives us this long-awaited insight into the life of a remarkable woman and illuminates an especially fascinating chapter of artistic activity in Paris in the early twentieth century with the emergence of a number of wilful and artistic women, as divergent as the Comtesse de Noailles, Gertrude Stein and Misia Sert. We are grateful to Vicki Woolf for bringing all this to life.

Christina Gallea and Alexander Roy

*To my beloved mother, Basila Sieff
and in memory of her mother, Anna*

"This is a fabulous being. We are
blessed to have her amongst us.
I might love the whole of humanity,
every living being like a flower
of the Lord, but she I adore
like a beautiful tulip, insolent
and dazzling, proud of herself
and shedding pride around her."

Léon Bakst

PROLOGUE:

RUINS AGAINST THE SKY

"Last month Ida Rubinstein died in Vence.
Her death was ignored by the whole world."
Le Figaro, October 17, 1960

On September 29, 1960, Ida Rubinstein was buried in a neglected corner of a cemetery on a hilltop in Vence, close to Nice in the south of France. Apart from the country priest there were only two mourners: her housekeeper, Madame Soretto, and her long-time companion and secretary, Madame Olivier, who has never been seen or heard of again. Since then the grave has been desolate, blown and buffeted by the mistral, yet another forgotten plot. Once a year, on All Saints' Day, November 1, M. Roland Leblond, Commandeur de la Légion d'Honneur and holder of the British Distinguished Flying Medal, travels with his wife from Menton to Vence to lay flowers on the grave.

The Rubinstein tombstone is stark and frugally plain, just a slab set into the ground on which is etched simply her name, the day she died and a small plain cross. The plaque was added later, organized and arranged by Roland Leblond. Translated into English it reads:

"Godmother through the War,
from the Alsace Regiment."

Otherwise the grave is deserted, and the only music is birdsong in the wind.

Nothing. No hint. No breath that there lies a woman who danced and entranced all the courts of Europe; who danced with Nijinsky; who had not only her theatre costumes and sets designed by Bakst but also her houses and her gardens, those same gardens whose flowers were changed whenever she entertained to match the colour of the clothes she wore. This was the woman who commissioned Ravel's *Boléro* and Debussy's *St Sébastien* and danced naked on the Paris stage years before Josephine Baker, the woman whose audience was threatened with excommunication from the Catholic church.

This was no ordinary woman: she was a chameleon, a diva who lived many lives. This was a Jewess who overcame the endemic, fashionable anti-semitism of her times to enchant and captivate the highest of societies. She touched the sun and lit flames all over Europe, only to disappear into complete obscurity. Here was the aristocrat who drank champagne out of madonna leaves and had two great loves, one woman, one man. Here was a woman who scandalized society from Paris to St Petersburg, whose charisma attracted people from Marc Chagall to Sarah Bernhardt and Jean Cocteau to the first Lord Moyne; here was a woman who for a quarter of a century dominated centre stage, her own gala firework display, her own festival, a gilded being touched by the Gods.

Finally, here was a woman whose pious craving for obscurity matched her youthful passion for celebrity. As notorious as Isadora Duncan, Rubinstein was Sarah Bernhardt's chosen heir and successor. She lived her life as though it were a legend, straddling eras from *La Belle Epoque* through the carnage of two world wars to the height of the Cold War. Yet, by the time of her death, her star was extinguished:

"How has she the temerity to alter so mercilessly the image we had of her? To us that image seemed unforgettable, but she has erased it for ever. Nothing is left but the debris, which does not even have the usual beauty of ruins silhouetted against the sky."

Serge Lifar

This is her story.

1

ST PETERSBURG

"Society is composed of two large classes:
those who have more dinners than appetite
and those who have more appetite than dinners."
Nicholas Chamfort (1741–1794)

Ida Rubinstein was born on 5 October, 1885. Very little is known about her
mother and father who died in a typhus epidemic when Ida was two. She
and her older sister were sent to live in St Petersburg with their aunt,
Madame Horwitz, a fashionable and cultivated woman. Her family was
successful and wealthy, extremely unusual for Jews in Russia. The
Rubinsteins were closely connected by marriage and business interests
with the Raffalovich and Poliakoff families, all of whom dealt in interna-
tional finance and the construction of railways. They mixed with the
cream of the Russian community.

These privileged families ceased overt practice of their Judaism in their
eagerness to enter into and be accepted by the elite of Russian society.
They were cushioned against the anti-semitic feelings which were particularly rife during the reigns of Alexander III and Nicholas II. They
adopted a lifestyle which made them indistinguishable from the Russian
aristocracy of the time.

Only two years earlier (or later, as he deliberately obscured the date)
Marc Chagall was born to a poor Jewish family in Vitebsk, a chief
provincial town studded with Orthodox and Catholic churches as well as
synagogues. "But like the rivers which in spring would burst their
covering of ice and inundate the banks, so the human calm was
sometimes broken! A wave of pogroms would hurl itself against the
Jewish villages and then, like a storm, would pass" (Sidney Alexander).
The Jews were confined to their ghettos, their Pale of Settlement.
Residence or travel outside the Pale was only permitted in exceptional
circumstances. They earned their livings as hotel keepers, moneylenders
or in the commercial occupations; the professions were banned to them.
They were disliked by landowners and peasants alike, a hatred and
distrust based upon mediaeval Christian tradition; inevitably they
became the convenient scapegoats when times were hard.

The poverty and hunger at the time was so acute that outside the Pale of Settlement there were many stories of Russian peasants resorting to cannibalism. The horrendous activity of the flesh eaters lasted throughout the 1890s and cases were still being reported in 1903 when butchered torsos, arms, and legs were being sold secretly deep in the Causasian woods.

Meanwhile Ida lived in a luxury that today is hard to imagine. In her Aunt's house on the Angliskaya, the most fashionable street in St Petersburg, the child would roam the beautiful grounds, amongst the delicate scents that hung in the leaves of the apple trees, the peaches and the cherries in the orchards. Lilac, acacia and wisteria bloomed around the house; violets grew in the shade and wild strawberries ran riot on the slopes on the edge of the grounds. Grapes hung on huge vines which grew along the walls. She would watch the exotic vegetables and fruits growing in the greenhouses and dip her toes into the River Neva as it flowed at the bottom of the gardens.

The family would regularly dine on a variety of smoked and pickled fish, black oysters and all sorts of smoked meats, thirty different varieties of mushrooms and exotic candied fruits, but when her Aunt entertained there would be a feast of spectacular extravagance.

Her guests were served countless flavours of vodka and a selection of magnificent wines to accompany the meals, imported from France at such great cost that one bottle equalled the cost of living for a year for a family in the Pale. There would be rich, dark red borscht, mounds of caviar, blinis filled with more caviar, cream cheeses, puréed duck pâté; twenty different kinds of fish would be served at the same meal. Countless different types of poultry and game, stuffed smoked swan and the more popular cygnet, bear, pheasant, quail, and grouse were all put on the table. Pickles and salted cucumbers surrounded the huge platters of meats and sausages; desserts of such artistic confection as to compare with the creations of Fabergé would appear. Oranges, lemons, pears, apples, melons and grapes were displayed in huge piles on silver platters six feet in diameter and on gold platters encrusted with semi-precious stones. Everything was served by red, blue and gold-dressed servants who pampered and cossetted the guests in the ways to which they were accustomed.

Ida was given the name Lydia, which comes from Greek meaning 'the cultured one', but almost immediately it was shortened to Ida which, strangely enough, is not a diminutive of Lydia but comes from the Teutonic and means 'happy'. The name comes from Mount Ida in Crete where Zeus is supposed to have been hidden. Both names seem to fit perfectly the life of this beautiful child, encompassed by the artistic and cultured talents her aunt entertained. Ida was surrounded by paintings and objects of the period. There was a massive library of thousands of books and, in her salon, the finest musicians of the day would play their most recent compositions. Apart from her sister, Ida had numerous cousins who, like all children, would make up plays, dress up, and perform in the gardens of the house. They would play hide-and-seek amongst the bushes and flowers, and race pieces of twigs down the River Neva. It was a carefree and happy time where, cushioned from the harsh realities of life beyond the Angliskaya, Ida, the birdlike child, was starting to grow into a swan.

Ida had a French governess and a Russian teacher. The formal side of her education was extensive and well-rounded. She was taught many languages simultaneously, which she was unusually quick to learn, including English, French, German and Italian. The English dancers, William Chappell and Keith Lester, both recalled Ida's ability to speak many languages fluently. William Chappell remembered that she could also speak Czech, Hungarian, Romanian, Spanish and Greek:

"We had been made aware of Madame Rubinstein's impressive fluency in many languages because, being such a caring person, and being so polite to everyone – the dancers, the stage hands, the lighting people – she spoke to each and every one in his own language. She would always enquire after each person's health, or that of their family, in their mother tongue."

This young, beautiful, Jewish, strangely angular girl was in the unusual situation of being brought up in the high echelons of St Petersburg society. In this haven of sophistication she was formally educated to a level of high academic achievement. A sharp intelligence and an enquiring mind made her an excellent scholar. Her aunt, who took her responsibilities as a guardian seriously, was delighted in Ida's academic progress. Her niece, whom she had grown to love as if she were her own child, was, happily, a great credit to her. Ida's keenness for knowledge was matched by a fierce determination and diligence, which she used in pursuit of her goals throughout life.

Ida's interest in ancient Greece was encouraged by the employment of a scholar to instruct her in the Greek languages, ancient and modern, as well as Greek history and classical antiquity. Her passion for the classics was to spread to French, Russian, German and English literature in which she became extremely knowledgeable. In later years she would enjoy outraging her friends by arguing that Dostoyevsky was a greater genius than Shakespeare, and infuriate them further by being able to demonstrate the academic logic of her argument.

Through air heavily scented by the exotic perfumes and Turkish cigarette smoke of her Aunt's guests, Ida's education roamed over vast areas and seemed particularly geared towards the arts. Madame Horwitz widened Ida's curriculum to include the more aesthetic elements of education suitable for a young woman of Ida's background. She was taken to all the best theatres in St Petersburg. Without intending to do so, Madam Horwitz was preparing Ida magnificently for a theatrical career.

Had she realized this, Madame Horwitz would have changed course immediately. Whilst it was quite acceptable to lionize, patronize and be entertained by theatricals, it was most definitely not acceptable to become a member of the theatrical profession itself. Madame Horwitz did not realize that she was encouraging Ida in what she, herself, would have considered a most unsuitable ambition. She even allowed the girl to have dancing, singing and drama lessons with the best teachers, most of them attached to the Imperial Theatres. From the Maryinsky Theatre Nijinsky, Kschessinskaya and Pavlova all gave dancing lessons to the rich and titled of the St Petersburg elite.

"Only dancing lessons to the wealthy made it possible for us to live and have pocket money, so society people rejoiced in engaging ballet artists as private instructors and nurtured a cultural understanding of themselves through ballet… .

"Hence it was as 'Konchensky' that I taught the titled class in Petersburg… . I was the dancing master chosen to teach, among others, at the homes of Count Tolstoy, Princess Ourusov, the Narishskin family (which once disputed the Russian throne with the Romanovs)… . Prince Hilkov, Princess Bieposelsky, Princess Orlov, Countess Zoubov, Prince Schinsky…"

Anatole Bourman

Ida was soon delighted to find her aunt joining her private classes. Amongst the fashionable matrons of Petersburg society, dance classes were taken to help with deportment and graceful movement as well as to keep weight in check despite their sumptuous eating habits. The perfect figure was appreciated in Russia years before the health fetish and body beautiful became a religion in America. Gymnastics and athletic training were never considered elegant enough for the ladies of St Petersburg; they were much too rough and uncouth. However, ballet barre work and dancing was the perfect combination of strenuous exercise, grace and elegance of movement and weight reduction.

Madam Horwitz quickly became a devotee. After the lessons she and Ida would bathe and change and entertain their dance teacher to tea, serving it in the finest bone china cups, eating pastries, tiny cakes and honey biscuits, putting back on more weight than ever was lost. Madam Horwitz and Ida enjoyed the cultural discussions on art and literature and the backstage secrets they learned about the ballet and the theatre.

At the time it was the court that sponsored the art of dancing and advised the Imperial Ballet and its school to nurture and encourage the creative imagination and inspiration that dancing properly enbodies. The ballet became a vital part of St Peterburg society and Madam Horwitz became a regular visitor, even though she did not have her own seats. The seats at the Maryinsky Theatre were like the rarest of pearls and held only by those who had originally sponsored the art. Most had received them in a legacy and they would be passed down in the families as a most privileged possession. From a social point of view it was very useful as the same people sat in the same seats for every ballet; thus one could see at a glance if Princess Ourusov, Prince Hilkov, Countess Zoubov or Princess Orlov were present.

Performances were important social occasions. Gowns of the finest materials were worn with matching jewels. Full evening dress was essential; tuxedos would have brought severe reprobation. Tuxedos were only for the smoking room, most certainly not the theatre.

Ida was encouraged to take as many lessons as possible to equip her for the salons of the day. She was taken to the opera and ballet and afterwards to sumptuous restaurants where she would meet the principals from the theatres.

St Petersburg enjoyed several elegant, French-style Russian restaurants of which the "Cubat" was the favourite. There the patrons and the stars of the ballet would meet for luxurious dinners after the show. It was more like an exclusive club than a restaurant, every doorman and waiter not only knowing each customer by name but also his or her family history and social standing. Strangers, however persuasive, however affluent in appearance, found it virtually impossible to get into the magic inner sanctum of the Cubat. Cajoling or bribery were to no avail; there had to be a specific invitation from a regular patron.

Almnure Cubat was in charge of the Tsar's cuisine, which lent him added prestige with Petersburg society. They danced and made merry to music by Oki-Albi, a Romanian virtuoso. Not a table was to be found without a choice of the rarest imported wines ranged on it. Mumm, Roederer, Monopole and Pommery were preferred although Mumm enjoyed the mightiest sale, for no matter how inebriated, the most capacious customer could always manage "M-M-mm-."

The Cubat drew the brilliant parties staged for every ballerina after her success or her benefit. There the famous Svehov sat and wrote his criticisms of whatever presentations he had witnessed, and woe betide the star who tried to influence him! He had been known to sit at the same table with a premiere ballerina, laughing and joking good naturedly and chatting most amiably with her at the moment he was scribbling out a vitriolic criticism for his paper *Novoye Vremia (Petersburg New Times)*. It was impossible to buy Svehov.

Kschessinskaya and Pavlova knew and loved the Cubat. The bills ran into thousands of roubles when they entertained or permitted themselves to be entertained. Russia adored her ballerinas passionately, and paid tribute with such a wealth of floral bouquets that trucks would have to transport the bowers of roses which engulfed a Maryinsky favourite after a first night.

A girl like Ida had to be well-versed in all aspects of life for the salons of the day and therefore be able to dance, sing and play some musical instrument. Ida excelled over the whole range of all her lessons except one: ironically, dancing. Perhaps this was one of the reasons why someone with a will as strong as Ida's, a determination to conquer any hint of limitation, chose such a career. In order to master dancing, to tame the art, she began practising for hours in front of the huge cheval mirror in her bedroom, posing and articulating all her emotions through movement, fascinated by this exotic, angular stick insect she could see in front of her. This eventually began to irritate Madame Horwitz who forbade Ida to do any more posing. She found this to be too frivolous, too narcissistic and unbecoming in a young lady of Ida's background and breeding. When it was discovered that Ida was still posturing and admiring herself in front of the mirror there were great family ructions. Many times Ida would be caught in some dramatic gesture by an angry aunt who would be equally dramatic in condemnation of her niece. Ida's frustration only accentuated and magnified her interest in her own willowy body and its capacity for instilling fascination for that body in others. The time was soon to come when audiences all over Europe were to become slaves to its "fluidity and plasticity."

At this time only Ida herself had any idea of its effect. Hers was a narcissistic pleasure which she was to indulge and be governed by for most of her life. Here was her first hurdle: she had to perfect that which did not come easily to her. Perhaps the type of dancing which she was taught was too formal, too confining for someone of her soaring imagination. To find her own style she had to experiment and constantly change, to spend hour upon hour in front of that mirror, although this was forbidden. It would take more than the wrath of Madame Horwitz to stop Ida from getting exactly what she wanted. Already, through all her studies of the Greek, an idea was beginning to germinate.

2
ANTIGONE

"The heart has reasons which reason knows not of."
Blaise Pascal (1623–1662)

Outside the Angliskaya and the cosseted community of the highest society, Russia was on the point of revolution, ravaged by need, poverty and hunger. It was a revolution which stemmed from a Tsar whose one obsession was to invade Manchuria and Persia in order to add to his already huge empire, a Tsar whose police were always ready to arrest anyone, rich or poor, for the crime of speaking out against his regime. This was a Tsar and his court who lived the sumptuous lifestyle which only those like Ida, who experienced the excesses of Imperial Russia, could picture in its extravagance. This was a Tsar who covertly supported the Black Hundreds, an organisation of hooligans and thugs, mostly uneducated, who roamed the cities in gangs of xenophobic fervour, waylaying Jews, odd students or striking workers. At demonstrations they would create a counter-revolution, watched by the police who, out of boredom and bloodlust, would aid and abet them.

It was a time of fear, a time of terror, when the fuse of revolution was being lit. It did not take long to ignite. On "Bloody Sunday," January 22, 1905, the Tsar's soldiers fired on a delegation of working men who had assembled to petition the Tsar for a redress of grievances. About a thousand workers were killed in an incident which aroused the sympathy of many waverers.

At one iron plant approximately 1400 people went on strike. The strikes spread like an epidemic from machine shop to factory to building works to textile plant. All at once the employers found themselves dealing with a serious strike situation and it was too late to do anything about it. Even the small shops were coming out on strike; each day more closed. Large groups of the working class gathered together and marched for the first time, openly and defiantly, calling for all workers to join the strike. Their taunts and accusations of betraying the people of Russia were not as instrumental in gathering converts to the cause as the fervour and excitement surrounding it. They could almost smell the excitement as it spread through the crowds. The down-trodden could at last feel, even taste, power and freedom as it coursed through the hordes. Those who had never dared to question the lowliness of their station, their desperately poor and miserable way of life, suddenly began to envisage a life equal to any man, even the Tsar!

Workers of every type and in every stratum of the working community marched together in an unending show of the power of the many against the few. It has been said that Vaslav Nijinsky and Anatole Bourman were part of these marches and witnessed the shooting on Bloody Sunday. Students marched alongside dustmen, craftsmen alongside butchers, the dancers of the Maryinsky corps with the shop girls. Even streetwalkers joined in, as did the intelligentsia alongside the illiterate. The aristocracy may well have been better armed and protected but the proletariat had the numbers and the might behind them. Gradually even those who were guarding the upper echelons turned their guns around and attacked those whom they were supposed to be protecting. Eventually the turn-around was completed; by October the strike stretched right across Russia.

With success, the strikers became even more confident and began to loot weapons from the shops. They made bombs and fashioned other weapons however they could. They fought the hooligans of the Tsar's Black Hundreds with gusto and a new gallantry, born out of years of fear and oppression and united in their single cause. They then set about organizing themselves even more efficiently, setting up committees and councils. Representatives of each committee banded together into a "Soviet." St Petersburg was the heart of the revolution and the "Soviets" were the valves which pumped the lifeblood of the revolutionary cause.

On October 12, 1905, after a meeting with the Tsar, General Trepov told his soldiers not to spare cartridges and to use no blanks. Russia, which had become a gigantic nation through its warring and acquisitive nature, was turning inwards and tearing itself apart.

Against the backcloth of this initial agitation for the 1905 revolution, Ida Rubinstein had appeared unannounced at the studio of Léon Bakst, an artist and designer of considerable renown. He was a portrait painter whose sponsor was the Grand Duke Vladimir. Well respected in St Petersburg for his book illustrations and interior decoration, Bakst also designed for the Maryinsky Theatre. He met Serge Diaghilev through his friend Alexandre Benois and all three worked on the magazine, *The World of Art (Mir Iskusstva)*, which Diaghilev had founded in 1898.

As he had no prior notice of Ida's arrival that day he was completely unprepared for this apparition of androgynous beauty who stood before him, chaperoned by her governess, as was the custom for young ladies in society at that time. They had a mutual acquaintance in Count Benkendorf, the Tsar's Court Chamberlain. What was not customary for an upper crust young woman was the reason for her visit. Léon Bakst gazed at her in awe. Not for one moment would this well-bred girl have shown any surprise at the extraordinary-looking Léon Bakst. His pale eyes and pink skin were made to look even more strange by the orange-red hair which hung down in curled locks above his ears in the style of a Hasidic Jew.

He was immediately enchanted by this unusually self-confident, willowy girl who began explaining to him her ideas for a production of Sophocles' *Antigone*, which she wanted him to design. Bakst tried to dissuade her from the venture. One of the sounder reasons, apart from Ida's total lack of any experience, was that the Alexandrinsky Theatre in St Petersburg had just finished a cycle of plays by Sophocles and Euripides. But Ida could not be persuaded to change her mind.

Thus, in 1904, we have in embryo the woman she was to become, already strong and immensely determined, totally in control and supremely confident. Her belief in herself and her ambition were unassailable. She knew what she wanted, why she wanted it and how she was going to achieve it.

Bakst gently questioned her choice of play. It was a mountain, whereas Ida should start with a nursery slope. He tried to make her change her mind and suggested other ideas and other plays, but Ida was adamant; it was *Antigone* and she knew, unquestioningly, exactly how it should be done. She had done an impressive amount of homework: she had taken herself to Greece to imbue herself in the atmosphere of *Antigone*; she had travelled to Athens with only her Greek tutor and personal maid. In Athens she stayed several days, steeping herself in its ambience when it was possible for tourists to walk around the Acropolis itself. Ida would stay until nightfall, immersing herself in Ancient Greek history with the guidance of her tutor. He answered her countless questions, conversed with her in Greek and stayed at her side whilst she breathed the Athenian night air and enveloped herself in the city's greatness and history. Ida did what thousands have done before and after her. She threw a stone from the top overlooking the amphitheatre and listened to the wonderful acoustics as it fell onto the stage. Here she visualized the performances thousands of years before. This was what she had come for; she went down to the stage and stood quietly, a sponge absorbing the artistic heritage of the ancient Greek theatre.

By the time she returned to Russia she had formed her ideas for an entirely new and original production of *Antigone*. These she presented in glowing detail to Bakst who, though logically still very much against the idea, was slowly being mesmerized by the fervour with which Ida stated her case. After more argument and much passionate discussion, Bakst persuaded her to to use only one act of the play rather than the whole

thing which would have been much too long. Ida eventually agreed. She
was too astute to be completely immovable or unapproachable in her
ideas and she had too much insight not, in the end, to be guided and to
use the experience of those she employed.

Bakst then persuaded her to mount the show privately, leaving her
professional debut in the commercial theatre for a later date. She must,
after all, think of her social standing. It was most unusual for a young
lady of Ida's background to mount a production in which she was to
appear. Performing on stage was still tantamount to being a courtesan
and she had years ahead of her. At sixteen, she could wait, she could
afford to be patient. Her hour would come, but one step at a time. Ida
acquiesced, but she never told Léon Bakst that she was really nineteen,
not sixteen as he thought. She never corrected this mistake throughout the
whole of their working relationship.

Their relationship would last until Bakst died in December 1924.
During those years they would work together many times. Together they
would touch the pinnacle of success and become the toast of Paris. He
was her original 'cavaliere servente' and was to become possibly the
greatest stage designer of the twentieth century. After *Schéhérazade* in
1910, Bakst's designs and choice of colours would dominate fashions and
interiors throughout Europe. Bakst alone dared to mingle oranges and
crimsons, in sensuous drapes inviting wickedness. Future taste was
entirely influenced by Bakst: women began wearing clothes that looked
vaguely oriental, turbans on their heads and skirts with freer waists,
colours all became much brighter; highly-coloured cushions were strewn
in the homes and ornate lamps appeared everywhere. Almost single-
handedly Bakst changed the taste of European society.

Ida threw herself into her production with all-consuming determination and zeal. It took two months to rehearse, day and sometimes
night as well. The sets and costumes were lavish. She had very strong
ideas, as usual, about whom to invite to the show. Bakst had advised her
of some of the more useful people to include. The elite of St Petersburg
society vied with each other to obtain invitations to this extraordinary
event and there were far more people than seats available. The final list
was still too large for the venue and the room was grossly overcrowded.
Many were there not because thay had artistic or cultural interests in the
production but because, as Bakst was to say:

"In the room there were a good number of sceptics who would ask for
nothing better than to pass comments on the audacious young thing in
the event of her falling flat on her face. But ... her success was immediate
and decisive."

André Levinson, the critic, recalled the event:

"I remember this unique production. And I see again the proud maiden as she is wrapped in the numerous and complicated folds of her black mourning robe. In working out this conception, Bakst had drawn his inspiration from a tombstone or else had deciphered the clever pattern on a Greek vase.

"This young woman with her disconcerting and mysterious beauty, this mysterious virgin, voluptuous yet frigidly cold, with a will of iron underneath a fragile frame, possessed of a haughty and cold intelligence … became one of the muses of our artist (Bakst). Hers was the gift of driving his imagination to exasperation. She held for him the all-powerful attraction of the strange, of the unreal, of the supernatural. His muse, perhaps that is not the right term, his friendly demon."

At nineteen years old Ida's first venture as impresario, producer and star, albeit a private performance, was a huge success and the audience applauded her triumph. She had made her point and achieved her realization, her fulfilment. Those seeds sewn in front of her cheval mirror were beginning to blossom. Most important of all, amongst all those people in the crowded hall that evening, was one who would have a huge bearing on her future: Serge Pavlovich Diaghilev.

Diaghilev, who was to create the Ballets Russes and, against all odds, hold it together for twenty years, was a man with extraordinary vision. From the start he saw the world through fresh eyes. On arrival in St Petersburg he showed his fellow countrymen the delights of Russian painting. His taste and total belief in himself enabled him to select the best examples of Russian paintings for exhibition in the west. He was to introduce Paris, Berlin, Monte Carlo and Venice to the glories of Russian art. He brought Russian music and ballet to the west with a company which became the most famous in the world for the two decades it existed. His 1909 and 1910 seasons in Paris were a turning point in the history of ballet. They were not only great social occasions, because of Diaghilev's great publicity talents, but also demonstrated that ballet could stand on its own, for the first time in European history, as a great theatrical art, rivalling opera and drama. Many of his ballets are still performed today in much the same form in which they were originally created, spanning an astonishing eighty years and more.

In 1895, at the age of twenty-three, he had written to his stepmother:

"I am,
1. A charlatan.
2. A great charmer.
3. An insolent man.
4. One who possesses much logic and few scruples.

5. A being afflicted with a total absence of talent, but I believe I've
   found my vocation.
I have everything I need except money, but that will come."

His appearance, which served him to good effect, belied his poverty.
He was huge, with a head which hatters had trouble fitting, an astrakhan-
collared overcoat which he slung around his shoulders and an
extraordinary lock of white hair that hung over his forehead, his hair
parted down the middle to segregate white from black. He was
nicknamed 'chinchilla', and 'silver beaver' by his associates. He looked at
you with the "hooded eyes of a hawk". His personality and strong will
made him a charismatic figure.

At the time there was nothing to show that his future lay in the ballet.
In his *Reminiscences of the Russian Ballet* Alexandre Benois wrote:

"Diaghilev showed no interest whatsoever in the ballet during his first
years in St Peterburg and if he did, from time to time, attend ballet
performances with us, it was only for the sake of Tchaikovsky's music. It
was not until considerably later that Diaghilev became attracted towards
the ballet, which was not surprising for one who spent his childhood in
Perm and had never seen a ballet before his arrival in St Petersburg. At the
beginning he even looked upon the ballet as something alien and slightly
unworthy …

"How great, therefore, was my surprise when, on visiting me in
Brittany in 1907, Diaghilev suddenly confessed to me that he had become
interested in the ballet during my absence."

Diaghilev was to use Ida in his 1909 and 1910 seasons in Paris and take
her to the zenith of her success on the stage. Equally quickly they were to
fall out and the rift between them was to turn them into the bitterest of
rivals for the rest of their lives. But at the start Diaghilev saw a definite
potential in the girl Ida as Antigone.

"There never was anyone with quite his genius for recognising and
encouraging talent, and more than anyone else of his generation he
understood the importance of bringing to the service of the ballet,
painting and music and poetry at the highest level."

                                                         Léonide Massine

A star was about to be born.

3

SALOMÉ

"After all, the world is but an amusing theatre,
and I see no reason why a pretty woman
may not play a principal part in it."
Comtesse Du Barry (1746–1793)

Almost before that heady applause died down Ida was planning her next production: Oscar Wilde's poetic drama *Salomé*. She would have the best of everything, sparing nothing. By employing the most talented people she could only enrich her own performance and production. She was to work in this way for the rest of her theatrical life. She might have been eccentric but she also had great style and dignity and was never penny-pinching. Everything she did was thoroughly researched and meticulously planned and she used the best people and materials she could find.

First, she found the best and most experienced translator to render *Salomé* into Russian without losing any of the excessive or extravagant language. Bakst again would design the sets and costumes. The incidental music would be composed by Alexander Glazunov, Director of the St Petersburg Conservatoire, a man with a formidable reputation although he was an alcoholic with a furious temper who did not suffer fools gladly; nevertheless, he was one of Russia's leading composers, regarded as being the man to fill the shoes of Rimsky-Korsakov. To even approach him, Ida must have had supreme confidence. For an untried and untrained young woman, having not even gone through the Maryinsky school, it would have appeared an act of folly: the shrew parading before the eagle; the undaunted confronting the daunting. To everyone's surprise and disbelief, he accepted.

Once this was all organized, Ida turned her attention to improving her acting and dancing ability. She took private lessons in dance from Mikhail Fokine. They had been working together for over a year when, in the summer of 1908, Fokine interrupted work to set off to Switzerland for a holiday with his wife. Not only did most of St Petersburg society leave the city for the summer, but the roads were crowded with ordinary folk on their way to the estates and parks of the south. Ida was not at all happy to let her work with Fokine be interrupted, so she followed him to Switzerland. None too happy at being pursued in this way and wanting the privacy and relaxation of a family holiday with his wife, Fokine nevertheless agreed to continue working with her. Perhaps these feelings were apparent when he said:

"She was anxious to play the role of Salomé... and to perform the "Dance of the Seven Veils." This resulted in her working daily with me and devoting a great deal of effort to her work. When my wife and I went to Coux for our vacation, she followed us there. One had to give the artist credit, I have seldom seen such energy and persistence."

She must have fired his imagination:

"The work on the Salomé dance was unique in my life. I had to teach Rubinstein simultaneously the art of dance and to create for her the dance of Salomé.... Before this she had studied dancing very little.... Her energy and endurance were of great assistance, as was her appearance, I felt it would be possible to do something unusual with her in the style of Botticelli. She was tall, thin and beautiful and was interesting material from which I had hopes of molding a unique scenic image."

So Ida Rubinstein learned the rudiments of her art. With a ruthless diligence and endless capacity for hard work she trained towards her goal, and when she had a goal there was nothing and no one who could stop her. After all, she had the world to conquer. She had Bakst's preliminary designs for the sets and costumes for *Salomé* and she also had the first script which she took with her to Paris in 1908. There she could research and further study *Salomé*.

Her sister Irene and Irene's husband, the celebrated Docteur Professeur Lewinsohn, lived in Paris and mixed in a very arty world. Two of Ida's aunts, Julia Cahan d'Anvers and Marie Kahn, also lived in Paris and they too were passionate about anything artistic, particularly the fashionably avant-garde. They were branded with their friends the Baronne Gustave de Rothschild and Ernesta Stern as the 'Jewesses of Art' by the writer and anti-semite Jean-Louis Forain.

Ida immediately felt at home in Paris where she mixed in a circle of people as passionate about art as she, and with relatives who were also notorious for their interest. She felt relaxed and understood and completely at ease; so she told them of her theatrical ambitions.

Instead of the support and encouragement Ida expected, Irene and her husband were at first amazed and then horrified: this was an impossible decision and must not happen. They tried to explain that someone in her position, from their sort of family, could not become an actress or dancer. They would all be made laughing stocks. One could "dally" with the artistic world as a hobby, as an amateur, but certainly not professionally, under any circumstances whatsoever. It was not done.

Ida was adamant. She had brought the script of *Salomé* to Paris to conduct further research on the project. This she still intended to do and she saw no reason to change her mind. The arguments continued for days with both sides immovable. When Irene and Docteur Lewinsohn discovered Bakst's costume designs for Ida, things came to an extraordinary and dramatic head.

Dr Lewinsohn was so incensed by the obvious fact of Ida's nudity at the end of the "The Dance of the Seven Veils" that he coldly informed Ida he had no option but to protect her against herself. Oblivious to the splendour of the designs, he told her that he intended to use his medical standing to protect not only her, but the reputation of the entire Rubinstein and Horwitz families. In his professional capacity he would have her pronounced mentally unstable and committed to a mental asylum. With his eminence and reputation he could do this with ease. This was the prospect with which Ida was threatened until she changed her mind.

Ida would not budge. She held fast to her beliefs and could not believe the threat. Her sister would stop him. Her brother-in-law would surely never do this. She had trained for over a year specifically for this. She had already employed a translator, a designer, a composer. They had all been working on it for months. She could not and would not surrender now. Irene begged her to reconsider. The idea was ludicrous. For the umpteenth time Ida explained her triumph in *Antigone* and the strength of her muse. It was a calling which she had no choice but to follow.

Dr Lewinsohn did just as he threatened; Ida was committed to the asylum at St Cloud as mentally unstable. There are no details of how she was transported to the asylum against her will. The beautiful, willowy, thin creature could not physically have fought for long. Perhaps she was sedated or, more likely, her supreme belief in herself and her pride allowed her to be taken in the most dignified way possible, dressed in her most sumptuous finery, haughty, walking alone into this tragic turn of fate. How she was treated in the asylum, how she behaved, how she coped, we shall never know. It certainly did not dampen her ardour or curb her resolve.

News of her predicament reached the family in Russia within a few weeks and Madame Horwitz immediately arranged for Ida to be freed and allowed to return to St Petersburg. Her situation was still not easy. Her relatives in Russia agreed with the Lewinsohns: the theatre was not a career for a woman of Ida's background; it was a phase she would grow out of, a momentary whim. They discouraged and hindered her in every way they could, but did not go so far as to incarcerate her to stifle her ambition.

In non-feminist, pre-revolutionary Russia, a young unmarried woman was not independent. Ida, although quite wealthy, was not entirely free to use this wealth. So far as her ambitions were concerned, she was just as confined in Russia as she had been in the asylum in St Cloud; to control her massive fortune herself she must marry.

Her choice of husband was applauded and Ida's aunt gave a sigh of relief. He was to be Vladimir Horwitz, her cousin, a very personable young man who was madly in love with her. She had known him all her life and Vladimir had adored Ida since they were children growing up together. He had always wanted to marry her and now his dream was to be realized, as if someone had waved a magic wand and granted his greatest, most impossible wish. But, as he was to learn, life is rarely as simple as that.

Ida had found a man who would comply with her every wish. She insisted upon a white wedding, white in every respect. Her conditions were that the marriage would not be consummated and that she could pursue her career without any hindrance. She wished to have no responsibility as a wife to him in any way. The poor man was so besotted he acquiesced to everything. Ida was free at last. The marriage in St Petersburg in 1908, after the brutal suppression of the 1905 revolution, appeared to be normal. It was a grand affair with all the ostentation and pomp befitting the wealthy Russian elite. Ida actually enjoyed this part of the marriage, which had been stage-managed with the bride taking more than the usual interest in the arrangements. It was another performance, another production to be mounted.

Her wedding dress was designed and made by one of the best dressmakers, specially chosen by her aunt. Unbeknown to anyone, and especially Madame Horwitz, Léon Bakst had been called in at the last minute to make a few changes to the bridal gown. The result was a wedding dress which was to be the talk of St Petersburg for many weeks to come.

The young couple moved into an enormous and sumptuous apartment on the fashionable Angliskaya, within walking distance of the house belonging to her aunt. The compliant Vladimir no doubt believed that once they settled down to married life together he would be able to seduce his sensual young bride into a more normal and accepted form of married life. He underestimated the new Madame Horwitz.

Within a few days of her marriage, Ida returned to her first and, at that time, only love, the theatre. She immediately became immersed in mounting her production of *Salomé*. Such a production about such a sensual and exotic character raised immediate questions about Ida in the leading role. Ida's research was no less exotic. At twenty-two years old, having been married for a few days, she crossed the Syrian Desert in order to reach her destination, Palestine. Vladimir remained at home at Ida's request, another of her conditions. Her only travelling companions were a few servants, including her faithful maid, an elderly relation as chaperone and her hairdresser. The party would make camp at nightfall in the desert and Ida would dine under the stars in the splendour to which she was accustomed. The fine lawn and linen table cloths would be unpacked and a table laid with the finest crystal and china. She ate sparingly but enjoyed her champagne, a predilection which would last all her life. Even during her final, reclusive days in Vence her staple diet would be one trout in aspic each day and pink champagne.

Before dinner her hairdresser would deal with the ravages of the desert wind and sand, so that by the time she sat down her flowing hair would be immaculate. Then she sat in the light of an oil lamp under the stars, pale, beautiful and mysterious. A Syrian Prince was so captivated by the sight that he approached her chaperone with a proposition: he had to have this apparition he saw before him and no expense would be spared. He was willing to give anything! He offered in return any number of women, young Syrian beauties personally chosen. He was bewitched and determined to have this Goddess. No! Then he would offer the ultimate; he would give his gold watch and chain! The offer was graciously declined and the prince was invited to dine with the group; what he devoured with his eyes made up for the little he ate.

The story of this incident only added to the scandalous gossip about *Salomé* already flying around St Petersburg where the production was the talk of the town. A society lady to appear in the nude? She had lain with a Syrian Prince alone in her tent only days after her marriage? The tongues wagged. The St Petersburg elite could not wait to see this play.

Their appetites were not to be satisfied. Perhaps because of the gossip and wild publicity or the scandalous nudity and lascivious sensuality that surrounded *Salomé* from the start, it was stopped. After the dress rehearsal the production was suppressed by the censor.

4

CLÉOPÂTRE

"Celebrity! What is it but the honour
of being known by those who do not know you?"
Nicholas Chamfort (1741–1794)

Whilst Ida was totally absorbed in building a career and artistic reputation for herself there were many rumblings in Russia. The Tsar's love for his family was already entering the downward spiral in which the Romanovs were to sink. Empress Alexandra's love for her haemophiliac son led her to encourage her guru, Rasputin, to gain great influence at court. This was to add more fuel to the hatred and revolutionary zeal already rampant in Russia. Whilst Ida was working on perfecting her balletic movements, her fellow Jews were frantically striving to avert further pogroms. The nobility protected their vast estates and abundant lifestyles with tougher, more repressive laws. Unfortunately no law could protect them from the deep loathing which the poor and starving people had for their weak Tsar and his regime. When he knew he was to be the next ruler of Russia Nicholas had complained:

"I am not prepared to be a Tsar, I never wanted to be one. I know nothing of the business of ruling. What is going to happen to me, to all of Russia?"

The contrasts between the lifestyle of Ida Rubinstein and that of her fellow Jews living in the shtetls of the Pale of Settlement, and between the lifestyle of the Russian aristocracy and that of the starving peasants, would soon help answer his question.

Meanwhile the ballet which first captured the public's imagination was *Cléopâtre*, first presented under the title of *Nuit d'Egypte* on March 8th, 1908, at the Maryinsky Theatre in St Petersburg. The Maryinsky is a great and beautiful opera house which is located in Theatre Square. Tsarist splendour was at its height in these doomed years and the exquisite Maryinsky Theatre was the perfect setting for a glittering, bejewelled audience. Named after the Empress Marie, the theatre, built in 1860, became the home of the Imperial Ballet in 1889. Inside the white, gold and turquoise-blue auditorium, five tiers of seats, huge crystal chandeliers and tiny twinkling lights were part of the opulence. Facing the stage in the middle of the first tier was the vast Royal Box with its heavy blue draperies and gilded surroundings. The magnificence of the scene, when officers bedecked with decorations and their richly gowned ladies promenaded through the foyers, rivalled the fantasies on stage.

"An invitation to attend a performance with the loan of a box was enough to cancel the most pressing social obligations of any consequence!

"Grand Duke Nicholas Nicholaievitch was likely to arrive tardily, surrounded by his imposing staff of generals. We could tell the exact moment of his arrival, for his Romanov voice trumpeted through the theatre unfailingly and, if anything displeased him, it thundered a stream of the most priceless and extraordinary oaths that ever fell on the ears of man or woman. If the Tsarina herself was there the oaths lost none of their colour, for the Grand Duke Nicolai was not only the Tsar's uncle, he was commander-in-chief of the Russian armies, and he feared neither God nor devil!

"We called the Grand Duke Nicolai 'the Trumpet of Jericho,' with his sunburned face, his short curly beard, his blue Hussar's uniform, brilliant with gold braid, and his red officer's cap jauntily askew while he toyed with his silver cavalry stick. He often strode onto the stage after the show and talked informally with the artists in the same cordial and friendly manner as that of his nephews; only his eyes portrayed the dissipations that were a byword..."

Anatole Bourman

In 1895 the Maryinsky was chosen to be the Imperial Ballet Theatre instead of the Bolshoi. Both theatres, however, answered directly to the Tsar. All those employed were very much subject to the whims of the Tsar but, in exchange for this, they had a state pension at the end of their working life.

Nuit d'Egypte, starring Nijinsky and Anna Pavlova, was mounted by Fokine with music by Arensky and soloists' costumes made after sketches by Bakst; the other costumes were borrowed. The set was a backdrop from one of the operas in the repertoire which had been retouched by the Maryinsky stage designers. Even though it was well received, Diaghilev had his doubts about Arensky's music which, although quite pleasant, was not in the least memorable. It was very ordinary and reminiscent of a small town drawing room. Diaghilev, a gambler with extraordinary vision, would make many changes and include it in the legendary 1909 "Ballets Russes" season in Paris. Apart from the music, one of the changes he made was to cast a wealthy socialite Jewish amateur as Cleopatra. It was a gamble which made the Ballets Russes the toast of the season and turned Ida Rubinstein into one of the most famous people in Europe.

The casting of *Cléopâtre* was fraught with difficulty and caused a huge furore in the company as Matilda Kschessinskaya, the principal ballerina of the Maryinsky Theatre, automatically expected to be offered the part. She was a traditional dancer and a great favourite in St Petersburg, but Fokine was not looking for a traditional dancer; he was looking for a new concept, a new type of movement entirely. He was looking for a sinuous, tall, sensuous, almost treacle-like plasticity, something to change the image of ballet at a single stroke. As far as Fokine was concerned, although admirable, Kschessinskaya was from the old school of dancing and did not fit his vision of the ballet of the future.

It was he who suggested Ida to Diaghilev. Having coached her privately for the part of Salome, he knew that her tall, thin, strangely androgynous beauty fitted his idea of Cleopatra perfectly, for behind her image lay an inherent danger that was both immensely cruel and charged with sexuality. She was as far away from the traditional image of the ballet as a journey into space; Fokine was dreaming of the stars. Diaghilev, who was always bewitched with anything new, needed little persuasion. Ida should have the part. The only problem was Kschessinskaya. She was the mistress of the Grand Duke and, as such, was one of the most influential women in Russia. It was directly through her that the Grand Duke gave the theatre such a generous subsidy. She must be handled very carefully. Diaghilev persuaded Fokine to cast Kschessinskaya in *Le Pavillon d'Armide*. Although Fokine was not enthusiastic about the idea, he realized it was an excellent compromise.

Kschessinskaya, however, did not. When she discovered that it was to be the only role she would dance in the whole of that first Paris season, she was furious. She immediately persuaded the Grand Duke to withdraw his subsidy, a massive 100,000 roubles. This virtually bank-rupted the Ballets Russes before it had even begun. The company, which had been able to use the scenery and costumes of the Imperial and Hermitage Theatres, suddenly found this privilege also withdrawn. They were not allowed to rehearse in the rooms that the theatres had gener-ously provided. At a stroke, on a single command from a slighted and hurt Kschessinskaya, the newly formed Ballets Russes was penniless and on the street. It was a blow which would have destroyed most people but Diaghilev was not to be thwarted. His dream of taking Russian culture and Russian ballet to every nation would not be vanquished. Within days he had found a place to rehearse in a small room in a run-down building. It was a quarter of the size they were used to, almost totally inadequate for the numbers of the company, but there was a roof over their heads and it was somewhere to work. They were confined but at least they could dance.

Finding new financial backing was much more difficult. After a great deal of upheaval and travelling all over Europe, Diaghilev, with his charismatic charm and massive determination, eventually found backing through Astruc in Paris, from Henry de Rothschild and countless smaller subsidies from artistically-minded businessmen. That he suceeded at all was a small miracle: in lesser hands the Ballets Russes would have died at birth. But there were more hurdles to clear.

General Besobrasov, who was on the board of the Maryinsky Theatre, objected very strongly to Ida Rubinstein being cast in the role because she was then an amateur. He was to go on objecting to her inclusion in the company for quite some time after she had joined them. She was, in fact, the only outsider; the rest of the company were from the St Petersburg and Moscow theatres.

With hindsight it is clear how close the Ballets Russes was to disaster. By insisting on having Ida Rubinstein play the role of Cleopatra, Fokine risked not only his reputation as an Imperial choreographer but the entire venture. With no subsidy and no suitable place to rehearse, the Diaghilev season was already on the edge of a precipice. Fokine was compounding the situation, apart from casting Ida, by introducing a whole new style and concept of ballet. The outcome could so easily have been dangerously different. As it was, Ida became the canvas on which he was to design his most extravagant masterpieces. The theatre, music, ballet, design, decor, interior design, fashion and an entire mode of social mores would never be the same.

Even though Fokine was to break with Diaghilev in the most bitter circumstances, at the beginning of his career his work was extraordinarily progressive and his contribution to the success of the first two Ballets Russes seasons in Paris cannot be understated. That Diaghilev would leave Fokine an exhausted artist, that his imaginative vein wore thin and proved incapable of development at the same rate as Diaghilev's constant search for novelty, is another story. But the discovery of Ida and the monumental acclaim of those seasons in Paris are almost entirely because of the genius of Fokine and Léon Bakst flowering under their ringmaster, Diaghilev.

As a child Fokine had had no encouragement to enter the world of ballet. In fact, any leanings in that direction had been positively discouraged. His father most certainly did not want him to study as a dancer: "I do not want my Motchka to become a jumping stick."

But he was not to be dissuaded. He was such a success at the Imperial Ballet School that he did not need to have to pass through the corps de ballet. By twenty-two he had not only studied drama, but also was a first-class artist and a teacher at the Ballet School. He wanted to change ballet by making the dancers express themselves through the whole of their bodies and, as a dancer and choreographer, he was able to begin to put his ideas into practice. His dictum was:

"If it were necessary to read a libretto before the ballet was understood, the choreographer had failed."

He laid down his main principles for the production of ballet, which were, briefly:

1. To invent in each case a new form of movement corresponding to the subject and character of the music, instead of merely giving combinations of ready-made steps.
2. Dancing and gesture have no meaning in ballet unless they serve as an expression of dramatic action.
3. To admit the uses of conventional gesture only when it is required by the style of the ballet, and in all cases to replace the gestures of the hands by movement of the whole body. Man can and should be expressive from head to foot.
4. The group is not merely an ornament. The new ballet advances from the expressiveness of the combined dancing of a crowd.
5. The alliance of dancing on equal terms with other arts. The new ballet does not demand "ballet music" from the composer, nor tutus or pink satin slippers from the artist; it gives complete liberty to their creative powers.

These five principles became evident in the production of *Cléopâtre* and also in the choice of Ida for the title role. Looking at his principles now, they appear merely common sense, a statement of the obvious, but at the time they transformed ballet from the traditional rut of the 19th century to the boundless, unconfined spectacles of today. Paris would be taken by storm and the legend of the Ballets Russes would be born.

Diaghilev prepared carefully, only too aware of the extraordinary talent he had in his company. He could not paint or design, neither could he dance nor sing nor compose nor choreograph. He had no artistic skills at all; his ability was in discovering talent and then channelling that talent in the right direction. He had great taste and an almost psychic vision of what could be achieved by those with talent. Jacques-Emile Blanche, a devotee of the Ballets Russes, wrote:

"If he signed no work, he was the 'Deus ex Machina', the professor of energy, the will that gave body to others' conceptions. He draws out the best of everyone; he knows how to extract gold from the earth surrounding it."

Months previously, Diaghilev had spoken of his visions for ballet and Russian art when Count Tyszkiewicz, the richest magnate in Poland, had introduced him to Nijinsky and Anatole Bourman in one of the elite restaurants in St Petersburg. Anatole Bourman recalled the scene:

"Whenever I glanced at Diaghilev, his monocle in place, his voice vying in culture with those of his nobles about him, I realised that before me was a man in whose veins flowed the essence of aristocrats and gentlemen, whose heritage was culminating in a brilliant mind and a grand manner. A moment's foresight linked his name to Nijinsky in an eerie vision of fame that faded as swiftly as it had come. He had the head of a Roman patrician, and his coal black hair was marked by a broad white forelock … The Silver Beaver was a name on which he was quick to capitalize. It was the Silver Beaver who was recognized in crowds wherever he went, and won fame throughout Russia as 'A man of Art'. He was saying:

'I dream of carrying Russian Ballet into every nation. I long to astonish the whole world with the talent, grandeur and the beauty we Russians, alone, have as our own. I shall lay to rest forever the ghost of Russian Barbarism that haunts Europe. And I plan to do exorcism with the proof of a culture so mighty in Russian hearts that it overshadows noble-born and peasant-born alike with ardour and reverence in the presence of Art!

'I have succeeded in extracting promises of help from Stravinsky, Raouch, Alexandre Benois, Léon Bakst, Golovin,' his voice dropped to a whisper, 'soon now I shall talk with the artists I have chosen – and with my ballet master who will make my dream of cultural conquest a triumphant reality! … only the cream of Russian greats will be in my ballet – not one from Moscow will find a place. My dancers will come from St Petersburg and Warsaw! Everyone in my ensemble will have been a soloist in Russia.' "

But now his vision was on the threshold of reality. The first Ballets Russes season was about to be born and he set to work. First, the name was changed from *Nuit d'Egypte* to *Cléopâtre*. Two new dances were added, one with music by Glazunov, and the other by Glinka; the finale was changed to have music by Mussorgsky, and the disrobing of Cleopatra took place to the beautiful and haunting music of *Mlada* by Rimsky-Korsakov.

Diaghilev now played his trump card. The gamble he had taken in engaging Ida Rubinstein would be played to the full. Diaghilev could not possibly be sure about this young artist; he was going purely on the recommendation of Fokine and Bakst, but he knew her background and he was going to capitalize on it. With his unerring genius for publicity, he intrigued the public of Paris with stories of a mysterious society woman of striking beauty and animalistic attraction who would appear in the title role of Cleopatra. They were enthralled. Rumours were rife. The Paris audiences were being enticed by these tales of Ida, masterminded and manipulated by Diaghilev.

Apart from Ida the company was made up of young Russian dancers who, until then, had seen nothing of the world. They only knew the disciplines and artistic flavour within the walls of the Maryinsky Theatre and the Imperial Ballet School. One can imagine their excitement as they arrived for this season in Paris. A new world greeted them: new smells; freedom they had never known; strange fashions; a completely different diet; an entirely changed life. They were all lodged in hotels near the Châtelet Theatre, particularly in the Latin Quarter of which some of them would have had a shadowy idea through the novels of Dumas and Paul de Kock. From there, beyond the roofs and chimneys, they could glimpse the legendary towers of Notre Dame Cathedral. They arrived in the spring of 1909, with Paris in all her glory and at her most seductive.

These young dancers were seeing a new, glorious, freer life than they had ever known. It is a great credit to their characters and their passionate commitment to the ballet that they threw themselves into their rehearsals and worked harder than they had ever done before. One reason might well have been that here the eyes of the world were upon them. They were in a dazzling spotlight, under close scrutiny. They worked with a discipline and enthusiasm which they had never achieved in St Petersburg, where their standards and discipline were already the highest in the western world. Their director, Fokine, was more than aware of their responsibility. He was a hard taskmaster, training them with considerable severity, demanding from them, from his aide, Serge Grigoriev, and from himself a one hundred per cent effort. Except for official receptions and the official party given for the company by Briand at the Quai d'Orsay, when they performed Russian dances, Ida, Karsavina and Nijinsky were the only dancers among them who went out in society. The rest of the company seemed to prefer to socialize among themselves. Perhaps they were too shy and unsure of themselves to venture socially beyond their own boundaries or perhaps they just did not get the same opportunities. "Paris never recovered from the fact that when they were not dancing these lovely girls were just honest misses, with apparently no taste for banknotes and spiced meats."

Arnold Bennett

Time was short and there was still much to be done. Tempers were frayed and fights broke out as dancers snapped under the pressure of rehearsals. Everyone was on tenterhooks but underneath the outward turmoil there was an undaunted enthusiasm and company spirit. They were possessed with a fervour, as if it were a war to be fought, each one going into battle as a crusader fighting for a sacred cause. This first Russian season in Paris, which originally had seemed like an excellent public relations exercise in showing Russian Art to the West, had now taken on the mantle of a general offensive.

Money continued to be Diaghilev's major concern; even though he had the sponsorship of Astruc and Rothschild, it was not enough. It was almost essential, in Imperial Russia at this time, to have some kind of Tsarist backing. Diaghilev however was no favourite of the Tsar, who was known to be mistrustful of personalities with strong wills and great talent and power, even if it was only in the artistic field. By the time Diaghilev first saw the highly delapidated state of the theatre in Paris he had totally lost the backing of the Grand Duke; this coming as a great shock to his financial manager.

The Châtelet was a theatre dating back to the time of Napoleon III. It was slightly run down, and 'elegant' would have been the last word to describe it. It did not suit Diaghilev's dream at all. The magnificence of the artistic feast he was about to offer Paris could not be served up on a bread-board. He decided in a moment, without a second thought of the cost, to renovate the theatre almost entirely. It needed to look gorgeous; its appearance had to be no less than brilliant. He went to extraordinary expense. First, he had the auditorium, the foyers and the boxes totally spring-cleaned, and then in many places entirely repainted. He took out the first five rows of the stalls, losing, of course, a precious part of his take; he extended the stage forward and had it totally refloored with best-quality pine. He had two fountains of real water installed on the stage, even though he had been told it was impossible. But his *coup de grâce*, which was financial madness, was to re-upholster much of the seating and carpet the aisles in a sumptuous ruby-red material. He would not listen to any protests about economy. It caused a monstrous hole in the budget but Diaghilev tossed it aside as merely a slight nuisance. His lordly temperament served him well as he steamrollered every objection into the ground. The decor and setting would add to the brilliance and elegance of the performance. Great art is always complemented by a fine frame. Diaghilev had his way even though most of the purchases for the theatre renovation were made on credit. All his life Diaghilev was to be dogged by debts as he struggled to pay for his grand and costly productions, but his seductive charm always managed to pull him through.

Meanwhile word was beginning to circulate that something unusual was being created at the Châtelet. Apart from the rumours about the dazzlingly sensuous society woman, Ida, it was said that the theatre was being totally refurbished, that something unusually beautiful was being prepared. A circle of fanatical worshippers, "Les Fervents des Russes," grew bigger every day as Diaghilev let out *soupçons* of news and information about the rehearsals. More interest was aroused through word of mouth than any advertising campaign or reviews in the papers. French critics, writers, artists, theatregoers and Paris society found themselves speculating and talking about this 'thing' that was being created by these Russians at the Châtelet.

For the opening the audience had been carefully assembled. The French Foreign Minister and his wife escorted the Russian Ambassador and his wife; the Ministers of Foreign Affairs, Finance and Education and the British and Greek Ambassadors were all present. The arts were well represented: Auguste Rodin, Isadora Duncan, Yvette Guilbert, Gabriel Fauk, Claude Debussy, Maurice Ravel, José-Maria Sert, Gabrielle Réjane, society hostesses, critics and designers all attended the gala occasion.

Astruc, one of the chief sponsors, dreamed up a publicity idea which was both simple and brilliant:

"It was always my principle to devote as much thought to my preview audiences as though they were themselves part of the production. In May 1909, the night the Russian ballet was first revealed to the public, I offered the prettiest actresses in Paris front-row seats in the balcony. Fifty-two were asked, fifty-two accepted. In the seating I was careful to alternate blondes and brunettes; they all arrived on time, they were all very pleased and the sight of this row of smiling beauties caused the rest of the house to burst into applause. That most serious of newspapers, *Le Temps*, devoted a front page article to this innovation, referring to it as my *corbeille*, my flower basket, and since then the balconies of all new French theatres have been called not balconies but corbeilles!"

Bakst had reworked the set, retaining the archaic Egyptian style of the first presentation of *Nuit d'Egypte* whilst giving a completely new appearance with strikingly different colours and designs. As the curtain opened, the orange-russet hues of the Egyptian stage setting, bathed in a steamy African sun, perfectly suggestive of a hot, sultry evening, astonished and enchanted the spectators. Huge Egyptian columns and massive statues of pharaonic gods framed glimpses of the Nile in the violet dust. It was a spectacular background and an ideal foil for the purple costumes, the brilliant gold and the elaborately-plaited, oiled, jet-black hair. It immediately created a powerfully sensuous impression on an unprepared Paris; it launched a new age of exoticism. It was against this background, with its overtones of heat and sand and dust, that Ida made her extraordinary professional debut. Jean Cocteau describes the moment:

"The unforgettable entrance of Mme Ida Rubinstein must be recorded for all time. I shall merely transcribe a few notes I jotted down during the course of the performance. May that feeling of immediacy which memory cannot recapture, excuse their disorder.

"A ritual cortege was seen to appear. There were musicians who plucked long, oval-shaped citharas, their tones richly resonant yet as soft as the breathing of serpents. Flautists, their arms raised in angular poses, blew from their sonorous pipes spirals of sound so piercing, so sharp, ascending in turn, that one's nerves could hardly endure them. There were terracotta-complexioned fauns, with long white manes, pointed elbows and flat eyes. Finally, borne on the shoulders of six colossi, there appeared a kind of ebony and gold casket, which a young black watched over diligently, touching it, clearing the way for it, urging the bearers.

"The bearers set the casket down in the middle of the temple, opened its double lid, and from within lifted a kind of mummy, a bundle of veils, which they placed upright on its ivory pattens. Then four slaves began an astonishing manoeuvre. They unwound the first veil, which was red with silver lotuses and crocodiles; then a second veil, which was green with the history of the dynasties in gold filigree, then a third, which was orange with primatic stripes; and so on until the twelfth veil, a dark blue, which, one divined, enclosed the body of a woman. Each veil was unwound in a different fashion; one called for a melange of intricately-patterned steps, another for the skill needed to shell a ripe nut, another for the casualness with which one plucks petals from a rose; the eleventh veil, in what seemed the most difficult moment, was peeled off in one piece like the bark of an eucalyptus.

"The twelfth veil, dark blue, Mme Rubinstein herself released, letting it fall with a sweeping circular gesture. She stood leaning forward, her shoulders slightly humped like the wings of an ibis; overcome by her long wait, having submitted in her dark coffin, as had we, to the intolerable and sublime music of her cortege, she wavered on her high pattens. She was wearing a small blue wig, from which a short golden braid hung down on either side of her face. There she stood, unswathed, eyes vacant, cheeks pale, lips parted, shoulders hunched, as she confronted the stunned audience. She was too beautiful, like a too-potent oriental fragance."

Thus Ida appeared to an amazed and dazzled Paris. Even the original sorceress of the Nile would have had difficulty matching the ravishing beauty of Ida Rubinstein as she was slowly and breathtakingly unveiled. Here indeed was a woman for whom wars could be fought and empires lost, who at a glance could bewitch her hapless subjects.

Her body was not that of a conventional beauty. She was very tall and very slim and the etched lines of her limbs gave her an extraordinary, angular individuality. Her whole body, her incredibly long legs, her face and hands were covered with a light turquoise-green paint which gave her an astonishing, androgynous sensuality. She looked out at the audience, her grey eyes elongated by make-up to give her an Egyptian snake-like gaze. Here was not just a beautiful actress appearing naked, having been divested veil by veil, but a real, fatal enchantress.

Such was the power of that first entrance. Her favourite slave, Nijinsky, stayed close to her, crouching at her feet like a black panther ready to pounce if danger threatened.

"While defending his queen, Nijinsky would snarl and bare his teeth like a dog. It was one of those character roles that allowed him to act out his latent aggressiveness.

"His animal-like ferocity, the pent-up violence and killing instincts alluded to by his gestures, were elements that drove audiences to the point of hysteria."

Peter Ostwald

Prior to the performance of *Cléopâtre*, Pavlova was to be the undisputed star of this production. Nijinsky, although in a smaller role, was quite expected to shine in his inevitable way. But the fact that a previously unknown, unconventionally trained, more or less non-dancer should steal most of the thunder was a revelation.

"Even the admirable Pavlova was eclipsed by the triumph of Rubinstein. Pavlova arrived at the end of our season and found no role that was truly to her advantage. She kept her old part in *Cléopâtre*, but she did indeed seem relegated to second place by the majesty and beauty of her rival."

Boris Kochno

The climax of *Cléopâtre* was the bacchanale when, in a daring and highly-sensual, passionate scene, the Egyptian Queen gave herself up to the ecstasy of love before the eyes of the whole audience. She had allowed Amune, played by Nijinsky, to make love to her on the condition that after the orgy he should take poison. Imagine this divine body, omnipotent in its beauty, this tall, angular, strangely dangerous creature, gliding very slowly downstage, the poisoned chalice in her hand, with Amune cowering on the floor downstage, whimpering and begging her to stop. Not an emotion crosses Cleopatra's face. That extraordinary blue wig, her flesh an almost translucent, death green, shining with sweat after her writhings and couplings with Amune. She forces him to drink the poison and watches him die. Then this most beautiful but dangerous and violent enchantress simply walks away, not a flicker of emotion crossing her face. The body of Amune lies on the stage where his real love, his true love, played by Pavlova, finds him and weeps heart-rending tears over the corpse.

Cléopâtre made Ida a star, *the* female star, of the Ballets Russes in that legendary 1909 season. The same season made Diaghilev and Nijinsky household names. Even today people who know absolutely nothing about ballet will recognize the names of Diaghilev and Nijinsky. None remember Ida Rubinstein, but in 1909 and for many years afterwards her fame was equal to both of theirs. *Cléopâtre* carried Paris by storm. It was a *feu de joie*, a bonfire of elation.

"Words cannot describe the reception given to this first night. Success? Triumph? The words convey nothing of the exaltation, the religious fervour and ecstasy, which took possession of the audience. 'Success' or 'Triumph' may be appropriate in describing the reception afforded to some remarkable, unusual performances, better than most; but here no comparison was possible, for nothing like it had ever been seen before. Suddenly, unexpectedly, a new, marvellous, totally unknown world was revealed; a world, whose existence not one of those Parisian spectators had even suspected, and which so intoxicated, so overwhelmed them that for a time all else was blotted out completely. A sort of psychosis, a mass delirium, seemed to sweep over the spectators which the press re-echoed the following and many a succeeding day."

Serge Lifar

Hyperbole followed hyperbole. Jean Cocteau was so swept off his feet that he offered his services backstage to help with the production:

"It is a wonderful experience to assist at the draping of Madame Rubinstein before the curtain rises. Silent stagehands and 'helpers' form a respectful circle around her, and melt gradually away as she disappears beneath the wealth of veils.

"One night I had the honour to escort Madame Rubinstein for the process, for she cannot walk alone upon her pattens, and, as I felt the light weight of her trembling palm in mine, I thought of Fanbert's Cleopatra with blue hair, her rapid breathing, her delicate discomfort. Disposed as I already was to admire Rimsky-Korsakov's music, Madame Rubinstein has fixed it in my heart as a blue-headed pin might impale a moth with feeble fluttering wings."

The praise grew more and more extravagant. For six weeks the frenzy continued unabated, six spellbinding weeks in which opera and ballet alternated. The Châtelet was sold out every evening. It was like a Gala every night, a heady cocktail which intoxicated the cast not only during performance but throughout their working hours. Even Diaghilev described the atmosphere: "as though enchanted in the gardens of Armide. The very air around us seemed as though it was drugged."

Critics and public alike fought for even grander superlatives. Reynaldo Hahn, in a masterly understatement, wrote:

"The elders of Troy were content to accept all the horrors of war without a murmur because theirs had been the joy of seeing Helen. So I too find consolation for what is happening around us, since I have seen *Cléopâtre* on stage."

The last word about that first Ballets Russes season may be left to the Countess Anna de Noailles (1876–1933), one of the extraordinary characters of Paris high society at the time. She wrote poetry and gave parties at which everything was required to focus on her. "She glided through her lovely rooms in long white floating garments like the ghost of something too beautiful to be real. She did not trouble much about her guests, merely smiled upon them when they arrived and softly sighed when she saw them going away."

The Countess wrote:

"No one thought that in the realm of art there might be something utterly new under the sun when, in instant splendour, there appeared the phenomenon of the Ballets Russes. In the spring of 1909, every capital in Europe had a Ballets Russes premiere. I attended the one in Paris. It was as if the creation of the world had added something to its seventh day. When I entered the loge to which I had been invited – and I arrived a little late, for I had not believed the several initiates who promised me a revelation – I understood I was witnessing a miracle. I was seeing something that had never before existed. Everything that dazzles, intoxicates and seduces us had been conjured up and drawn onto the stage. There it flowers as naturally, as perfectly as the plant world attains its magnificence under the influence of the climate."

Anna de Noailles became the darling of the salons. She loved dancing, reading her poetry and conversation. Once in a discussion with Jean Cocteau on theology she was heard to say: "It's as simple as this: if God were to exist, I should be the first to be informed."

Apart from *Cléopâtre* the other productions in the first Paris season were *Le Pavillon d'Amide, Prince Igor Scenes, Polovtsian Dances* and the dance-suite *Le Festin*. Diaghilev, with his incredible foresight and confidence about most things artistic might have been a little aware of what a sensation his company was to be, but one wonders if even he realized the extent to which it would affect the artistic world, not only then but for the future, not just in the confines of the theatre but in the worlds of design, interior design, and haute couture.

Even with this huge acclaim (or because of the notoriety), Ida's sister, Irene, and her brother-in-law, Professor Dr Lewinsohn, never attended a performance of *Cléopâtre*; in fact they did not attend any performance of the Ballets Russes in which Ida was involved or any other performance mounted by Diaghilev. They were never to see any performance of Ida's throughout her long theatrical career. Indeed a rift between the Lewinsohns and Ida's aunts, Julia Cahan d'Anvers and Marie Kahn, occurred when both aunts insisted on attending every performance of the Ballets Russes, including those in which Ida was involved. Their great passion for all that was fashionable, artistic and avant-garde was to over-rule family loyalty.

The rift did not affect Ida. She was to publicly humiliate her stage-struck aunts when they attempted to congratulate her backstage after her performance. They were kept waiting only to be given a very cursory acknowledgement by Ida as she swept out of the theatre.

The reports of Ida Rubinstein being uncaring, unkind or even cruel are rare and relate only to her dealings with her family. One could presume that had she had more to do with them, the more often would she behave in a way contrary to her otherwise acknowledged kindly, well-bred and well-mannered behaviour. Ida, the woman whose considerate, benevolent and ever-thoughtful good manners were much known and discussed, was to turn into an unfeeling, inconsiderate barbarian whenever any of her family were concerned. The contrast of such behaviour with that of Ida Rubinstein the patriot, the benefactress, public spirited and charitable recipient of the Légion d'Honneur, is another paradox in her total enigma. Knowing such a woman seems only to lessen the understanding. The rift between Ida and her family lasted all her life.

At the end of the Ballets Russes season Ida did a gala performance at the Paris Opera House in aid of the city of Messina which had suffered a disastrous earthquake, sharing the stage with Nijinsky, Karsavina, Sarah Bernhardt, Sacha Guitry, Réjane, Felicia Litvin and George Robey. She then went on to make music hall appearances performing dances of the *Cléopâtre* genre. She scored a great success at the Olympia in Paris and in September 1909 she came to the London Coliseum to take part in an all-star music hall programme. Ida was so delighted and impressed with Sir Edward Moss she wrote to Count Montesquiou:

"Sir Edward Moss, who is a cultivated and very kind man, attended my rehearsal last Monday. He was so impressed by the music and the dance that he begged me to delay my debut for a week to allow time to change the whole programme, to obtain a larger orchestra for me and to prepare the public through the newspapers, he said, 'for the most beautiful thing that London will have ever seen.' This is extraordinary for an administrator and even more extraordinary is that they send me my money every day as if I were dancing."

Moss took all this expense and trouble for just eight performances, twice daily from September 27th to 30th, 1909. Ida was lonely in London, however, despite her joy in the way she was appreciated by Sir Edward. She confessed to Montesquiou to "feeling very alone and almost lost," as she waited at the Grand Hotel in Trafalgar Square. As soon as her engagement was concluded she returned to Paris.

5

SCHÉHÉRAZADE

"Pretty women are like kings; one flatters them only through self-interest."

Madame de Staël (1766–1817)

Paris had become notorious, the naughty lady of *La Belle Epoque*. Throughout the 1880s and 1890s the city had danced, sung and shocked with a lack of restraint which attracted free spirits (and would-be artists) from all over the 'civilized' world. Artists flocked there, played their tunes amongst the bars and music halls, and left a history of the time on canvas unparalleled before or since. Toulouse-Lautrec, Renoir, Van Gogh, Degas, Utrillo: Paris attracted everyone from the highest to the lowest, anyone who dreamed beyond the confines of society, who found himself chained by the laws and conventions of the time. Prostitutes, homosexuals, acrobats, wrestlers, poets and pimps all flocked there; Oscar Wilde, the Prince of Wales (later Edward VII), Russians, Italians, Romanians, fled from the boredom of their own societies into the arms of the dissipated but exquisite mistress that was Paris.

The mood was electric. It had persisted into the new century. It was as if the world came to the City of Light to frolic without perpetual complaint and inhibition. Both Frenchmen and foreigners spent money freely. They wined and dined their wives and mistresses at expensive restaurants. They took them to the theatre, the opera, the circus and the ballet. Joy was in the air. They dressed in clothes by Poiret and Worth, wore expensive perfumes and dazzled in their diamonds at the salons of the day; those who could not afford the life of the wealthy, danced to the accordions in myriad outdoor cafés under the stars like the figures in Van Gogh's and Renoir's Paris paintings.

On July 25th 1909 Louis Bleriot flew across the English Channel for the first time. It was a huge achievement. As a journalist wrote:

"For the first time a man driving a canvas bird which vomits fire, a venerable terror-rousing legend, has crossed the ocean and left one continent to take possession of another."

It was a time of celebration, a time of glory; the age of aviation had come. Sarah Bernhardt had arrived, as had Colette, Modigliani, Picasso and, after the Ballets Russes production of *Cléopâtre*, Ida Rubinstein.

Rubinstein was famous, notorious and at home. She could do exactly as she pleased, no matter how outrageous. She had shocked her family and friends by going into the theatre in the first place; now she was horrifying them by appearing nude and simulating the act of sex on stage. Though her own society was totally abashed, much of Parisian society adored her. They were mesmerized and she was soon surrounded by colourful, wild artists and admirers. The moneyed and cultured were certainly in the majority amongst her immediate devotees. Léon Bakst was to remain her votary until his death in 1924; she was his: "beautiful tulip, insolent and dazzling."

Sarah Bernhardt became her friend and mentor, even though their lifestyles were quite different. Although Ida bathed in the notoriety of her stage appearances, off-stage, apart from her intrinsic and eminent eccentricity, she was an exceptionally private person, the discreet, well-mannered, Russian aristocrat in all but title. Conversely, every move in Sarah Bernhardt's life was much publicized and documented. Her scandalous love affairs, menagerie of wild animals and morbidity were legendary. The satin-lined coffin in which she slept; the fact that she would travel miles to witness an execution: to London for a hanging, to Madrid for a garrotting; her necklace of petrified human eyes; all were well known, all added to her image. It was said of her: "If there's anything more remarkable than watching Sarah act, it's watching her live."

It was a strange friendship. Bernhardt's first reaction on seeing Ida was not a good omen for a loving friendship. Perhaps the older actress succumbed to a twinge of jealousy on experiencing the stage presence and charisma which flowed from the young Ida Rubinstein. Perhaps this is why Bernhardt behaved the way she did when she saw Ida's performance in *Schéhérazade*:

"Such enthusiasm persuaded Sarah Bernhardt to see the ballet. Already lame, the great tragedienne had herself carried into the theatre, but scarcely had the curtain gone up than she was seen to become much overwrought. Striking out with her cane she cried: 'Let's get out of here! Quickly... I'm afraid. They are all mutes!'"

Boris Kochno

Bernhardt evidently recovered from this bout of upstaging to become a faithful and loyal friend to Rubinstein. In fact she wished to bequeath her crown as the most famous actress of the age to Ida, going so far as to insist that Rubinstien should take on the mantle after Bernhardt's death, and was privately coaching her with this aim in mind right up to the end.

One of the first people to become Ida's admirer was Count Montesquiou. He soon introduced her to the artistic circle of Ballets Russes fans.

Montesquiou, a homosexual, was aristocratic, a purist and a connoisseur of the arts and fashion. Although both spiteful and a snob who derided those who fell short of his standards in taste, he was an equally loyal and devoted friend. He was well-born and well-off with a genuine flair for spotting talent. He became a powerful arbiter of fashion, developing his "pleasure of astounding without ever being astounded." If anything ever did astound him it was Ida:

"She was young, handsome, strange and somehow mysterious. Robert de Montesquiou immediately fell at her feet and became her devoted admirer. This was not at all the usual romantic affair, but resembled rather the mediaeval, platonic knight kneeling in adoration before the chosen 'Lady of the Heart'. It is said that even now in Ida's house there hangs over the sofa a portrait of Montesquiou. She had not forgotten her 'true and faithful knight'."

Prince Peter Lieven

From his home, the Pavillon des Muses, this "aesthete *extraordinaire*" wrote elaborately symbolist poems. Amongst the Paris dandies Montesquiou was king. He lavished on himself silks of lavender and gold, wore turned-up pink satin cuffs and carried waxed ivory canes. With the coming of the Ballets Russes the style of the dandy had been greatly influenced; it was now the vogue to be seen with a Russian wolfhound in tow. The dandy would be exceedingly well-dressed, wear his hair parted in the middle, write poetry and novels in the eighteenth-century manner, live in a bachelor apartment with Louis XIV furniture upholstered in soft pastel shades and would be at society gatherings with a ballet dancer who had now taken the place of his elderly mistress.

Robert de Montesquiou ruled. In his library there were books bound in Moroccan leather and Japanese silk, a lock of Byron's hair, a portrait of Aubrey Beardsley by Sickert; in his Salon des Roses on the first floor there were oriental and Renaissance *objets d'art* in profusion and blue hydrangeas filled every corner; in his bathroom was a gigantic pink marble urn described by Anna de Noailles as "a rose of joy opening in the tender air." Entertaining from his home he admitted that "at his receptions the guests were the only troublesome part of the decor."

This was where he wrote his poems, entertained celebrities and friends and set his standards of taste among Parisian society. Montesquiou was "what Oscar Wilde would have liked to have been if he had had more money, less talent and no humour."

Montesquiou probably introduced Ida to Sarah Bernhardt. He had been a fan of Bernhardt from the moment he first saw her. He adored her so much that, in one disastrous night of sexual passion, he had his one and only heterosexual experience, which caused him to be "sick for twenty-four hours." Despite this strange, quite uncharacteristic interlude they remained devoted friends.

Bernhardt recognized a great potential in Ida Rubinstein and wrote to Montesquiou with a generous offer:

"I would like to see... your beautiful friend Ida Rubinstein play *La Princesse Lointaine*. Ask her to put her trust in me. I shall make her work and I alone can succeed in making of this admirable artist a complete artist.... It goes without saying that I refuse any payment. I am doing this out of love of beauty and because the young woman loves beauty as I do."

At the moment that Sarah Bernhardt was making aquaintance with Rubinstein, Gabriele d'Annunzio arrived in Paris, where he became Ida's devoted admirer until the day he died. He was a tiny, bald man with a thin nose. Aged forty-seven when he first arrived in Paris, he was twenty-two years older than Ida. His first reputation was that of a ladies' man, romantic and wildly extravagant. He was the most famous living Italian writer.

An unabashedly sensual poet ("sing of biting the fruit of the earth with strong white hungry teeth"), a soldier, statesman, man of letters, patriot, Don Juan and, above all, *bon vivant*. He was a passionate man who, during the course of his life had many scandalous affairs, including a long liaison with Eleanora Duse, the famous, not to say notorious, Italian actress. He had moved to Paris in order to escape his debtors. Robert de Montesquiou fell for d'Annunzio on sight. It is almost certainly he who introduced d'Annunzio to Ida Rubinstein and took a masochistic pleasure in observing their relationship, both professional and private. Montesquiou was certainly in love with d'Annunzio and adored Ida as the androgynous boy/girl with her tall, graceful, animalistic sexual appeal. He adored her as an apparition, a goddess, and took a strange, tragic joy in promoting and encouraging her relationship with Annunzio.

While Diaghilev and the Ballets Russes had thought they had had a success with *Cléopâtre* in 1909, none of them were prepared for the overwhelming triumph of *Schéhérazade*. In May 1910, when the company arrived, Paris was eagerly awaiting their new season.

The Ballets Russes had been promoted from the Châtelet to the Paris Opera House. The Opera House (Salle Garnier) was, and still is, a sumptuous 19th-century edifice which epitomizes the extravagance of an era. The structure is as ornate inside as outside. It was designed for Napoleon III in 1860 by Charles Garnier and took fourteen years to complete. It is such a tourist attraction that tickets are sold simply to view the internal architecture. Even the backstage areas are huge and awesome, not as grandiose and lavishly ornate as the sweeping staircase, magnificent foyers and sumptuous auditorium, but awesome in their very size. There is a gigantic backstage lift which appears suspiciously ancient and fragile; the labyrinth of wide hallways, eventually lead past various offices, dressing rooms, and rehearsal rooms to the largest stage in the world.

In the office of the Conservateur en Chef de la Bibliothèque, amongst the fascinating archives of the Paris Opera House, there hangs an enormous painting, some eight feet long, of Ida Rubinstein. From the myriad stars who have appeared on the stage it is Ida who has pride of place.

When this theatrically historic building was ready to stage *Schéhérazade*, its box office success was assured. The music was by Rimsky-Korsakov, choreography by Fokine, costumes and sets by Bakst and book by Benois.

The production starred Nijinsky as the Golden Slave, Ida Rubinstein as Zobeida, Balakov as the Shah and Enrico Cecchetti as the Chief Eunuch; most important of all, it was being presented by Diaghilev's Ballets Russes.

It is not a pretty ballet. It is wild, demonic and erotic. It tells of an orgy in the harem followed by violent death. Rehearsals were not easy: Fokine was ill-humoured and temperamental; the Oriental style of the new ballet was quite alien to dancers immersed and brought up in the stringently traditional Maryinsky School. The movements required much work and Fokine was a difficult taskmaster.

"During all rehearsals he seemed dissatisfied with everything and everybody, yelling at us, being rude to artistes – and on more than one occasion he stormed off the stage and left the theatre without finishing the rehearsal.

"We could not understand Fokine's mood – everything about *Schéhérazade* augured success. We knew already, from the 1909 season, that Paris admired Fokine as a choreographer and recognized his talents. The artists were wholeheartedly with him and did their best to render each dance and each movement exactly as he wished, to the last detail. But he was difficult to please.

"One possible explanation was his anger stemming from the publication of *Comoedia Illustré* on June 1st in which extensive coverage had been given to the *Saison Russe*. He had been angry because he had seen himself listed last amongst the performers, without mention of his being *premier danseur* or the choreographer. Fokine was very sensitive about publicity, and after that incident had demanded that his name appear in larger letters than anyone else's in the ballet, also that it precede the names of composers, and artists, ahead of Stravinsky, Rimsky-

Korsakov, Benois, Bakst, Golovin, Karsavina, Ida Rubinstein and Nijinsky. Our impresario, Gabriel Astruc, had not complied with Fokine's wishes, having his own ideas about how best to arouse interest and attract the public to the theatre. In the next edition of *Comoedia Illustré*, on June 15th, in a special supplement devoted to the *Saison Russe*, considerable attention was given to the creation of the new ballet *Schéhérazade* but the emphasis was on the artist Bakst and not on the choreographer Fokine."

Bronislava Nijinska

It was not all doom and gloom. Léon Bakst had designed costumes and sets of such vibrant colours and originality that a feeling of excitement and anticipation overcame the difficulties of the choreography. Bakst himself often sat in on rehearsals, helping Fokine find the correct movements and poses for the style of costumes: the tilt of a head here; the position of an arm; the angle of an elbow; the importance of the completely still position. Bakst helped in all, inspiring the company with his infectious enthusiasm. The work was fascinating and challenging; even Fokine began to lose his bad temper as the whole effect began to emerge and the colours, the sensuality and the music took over. The catchy tunes of Rimsky-Korsakov haunted every moment with the whole company humming them long after rehearsals stopped.

"Color is the dominant element in this lavish ballet, color as brilliant and resplendent as the Eastern Sun, color in music and dancing, in lush decor, and in the burning passions that consume the principal characters in the story. Those who are familiar with Rimsky-Korsakov's music, which the ballet uses, know that it is an orchestral suite, program music to a series of stories told by the beautiful Sheherazade to fascinate her husband. The makers of the ballet chose to abandon the composer's musical scheme and to fashion a dance drama that would embody all the mystery, passion and violence that all these tales contained."

George Balanchine

For the opening night of that 1910 Paris season, June 4th, all the tickets were sold out, as they were for most of the season even before the first night. Many of the St Petersburg ballet and theatre critics and many Russian balletomanes attended the gala premiere. The first ballet on the programme was Schumann's *Carnaval* but the highlight of the evening was the second ballet, Rimsky-Korsakov's *Schéhérazade*.

The ballet was a sensation. It shocked, titillated and dazzled. The audience were assaulted, not only by the startling visual effects but again by the sight of the performers sensually caressing and petting as they simulated sexual intercourse. The costumes accentuated the sexual appeal of the dancers. Bakst's original costume designs show bare breasts in some of the women while the design for Nijinsky's costume of baggy gold pants gathered at the waist and ankles has him in a kind of brassiere with the straps on his naked shoulders. Much of his naked upper torso was painted in a bluish colour to add to the sensual effect of his already libidinous performance. Gold bracelets encircled both his arms and ankles; jewels sparkled on his fingers and toes.

All through rehearsals, right up to the first night, Rimsky-Korsakov's widow objected to the use of her husband's music and protested against the cuts being made. The great success of *Schéhérazade* drowned these protests and they were heard no more.

The leading roles were created by Nijinsky, Rubinstein and Bulgakov. These three dancers were magnificent and no matter how many artists later tried to copy their roles of the slave, Zobeida and Sultan Shabyas, no one has approached the artistic perfection so brilliantly exhibited that evening. The critics were unanimous in their unstinting praise.

Bulgakov was majestic in his dramatic talent, with a superb restraint in his pent-up fury when he discovered that his beloved Queen Zobeida was participating in the orgy with his other wives and odalisques.

Rubinstein was exotic. Her unique physical appearance gave her a sensuality and omnipotence that was both wanton and regal. Her tall, slender beauty made her Zobeida striking in every movement and gesture. Fokine himself describes her:

"Her performance was remarkable for giving powerful expressions accomplished by the most economical means. Everything was expressed with one single pose, with one movement, one turn of the head. Nevertheless everything was outlined and drawn clearly. Every single line was carefully thought out and felt. She is displeased by the departure of her husband and expresses her displeasure with a single movement, turning away her head when he comes to kiss her farewell. She stands in front of the door through which her lover is momentarily due to emerge. She waits for him with her entire body. Then (and to me the most dramatic) she sits utterly still while slaughter takes place around her. Death approaches her but not the horror, not the fear of it. She majestically awaits her fate in a pose without emotion. What powerful expression without movement. I consider this one of the most successful accomplishments amongst my ideas of the new ballet."

The ballet opens with the Shah and his brother suspecting that their wives are being unfaithful. The brother is Iago to the Shah's Othello. They pretend to go off on a hunt. Once they leave, the wives and concubines persuade and finally bribe the Chief Eunuch to release the slaves, including Zobeida's favourite, the Golden Slave. At the height of the revels and amidst the erotic orgy the Shah returns. He orders the deaths of all the revellers. Zobeida is the last to be slain and the Shah is tempted to pardon her as he cannot bear the thought of losing his favourite wife, when his brother draws his attention to the body of her lover, the Golden Slave, still in his death throes. The Shah orders his guards to kill Zobeida but, before they can do so, she snatches a dagger from one of the guards and plunges it into herself.

Despite our current familiarity with sex and violence, this ballet can still provide a glimpse of the shock and wonder it aroused at the beginning of the twentieth century. Nijinsky was astonishing for his animalistic savagery, violent in his newly-created dance movement: part snake, part panther. Ida was hailed for her majesty and statuesque beauty, her economy and plasticity of movement. The couplings were emphasized by the sweating, caressing and firm muscles working. The entire production was encapsulated not only by the dancing but also by the frantic, violent lusting.

The moment of Nijinsky's appearance on stage, framed by the door of the gilded cage, caused a sensation. The whiteness of his gleaming teeth was accentuated by his strange bluish-grey make up as his bare torso twisted in the fervour and excitement of his new-found freedom, like a cobra about to strike. Suddenly he sees the seductive Zobeida, reclining on a divan amongst large, soft oriental pillows and brightly coloured scarves. The youth is transformed; with a huge leap he hurls himself from the depth of the stage on to the divan and like a snake winds himself around her slender body.

From the English programme notes for Diaghilev's Ballets Russes, 1921:

"... and the night passes in orgy. Boys bring platters piled high with fruits; odalisques bring wine and incense. There are dances and tambourines, the women and their loves join Zobeida in the dancing. The orgy grows wilder; the whole voluptuous throng becomes a whirl of splendid movement and womens' white arms...

"Rubinstein was strikingly beautiful in her dance; the slender lines of her elongated body, flexible as a reed, oscillated and swayed to the music. The image created by Nijinsky of the negro slave in his half-snake, half-panther movements, winding himself around the dancing Zobeida without ever touching, was breathtaking.

"For the final dramatic scene upon the unexpected return of the Sultan, mad with rage, the whole stage frozen, panic stricken... a moment of paralysis and terror, a vain frantic flight."

[Soldiers armed with huge scimitars mow down the women and

slaves. The Queen's lover is confronted by the Sultan's brother, Shah Zemlan, who with his scimitar inflicts the mortal blow. The dark slave falls, and in his last spasm his legs shoot upwards, he stands on his head and rotates his lifeless body – Nijinsky made a full pirouette standing on his head and rotating his body – before dropping to the ground with a heavy thud.]

"Only the beautiful Zobeida is alive amongst the corpses. The Sultan shudders, vacillating, but his brother points to the Queen's negro lover lying dead. With averted eyes, the Sultan gives a gesture of command to one of the soldiers. Zobeida forestalls him. She seizes a dagger, stabs herself, and dies at his feet."

Alexander Benois described Ida Rubinstein as "absolutely inimitable . . . in her proud, cunning and unrestrained passion" and Nijinsky as "half cat, half snake, fiendishly agile, feminine and yet wholly terrifying."

Any doubts of Ida's charisma after *Schéhérazade* were now dismissed: she was the darling of Paris, the flavour, the taste of all that was erotic and vaguely decadent.

"She caused the same mob hysteria in an audience as that of a crowd at a football match or when panic sets in; the contagious hysteria of fear, hate, or undiluted love, almost of a sexual love; the same hysteria of the revolution."

Bakst's influence and extraordinary colours and designs carried on far beyond the confines of the theatre. The strange combinations of brilliant vibrant colours, blues and greens, oranges, reds, vermillion and gold were to set trends throughout Europe and beyond. Turbans, cushions and materials all bore the stamp of *Schéhérazade*.

"Bakst banished the sweetpea simpering colours so beloved of the Edwardians and replaced them with screaming scarlets, magentas and purples. Orange colour, which until then had scarcely been used, suddenly became the *dernier cri*. Diana Vreeland described it as 'the colour that changed a century,' and it was this orange colour tempered with the jade greens, turquoise and violets that became a virtual signature for the Russian Ballet."

The designs immediately revolutionized fashion. Ladies, descending on their couturiers with a Bakst watercolour in their hands, would emerge as sultanas.

Within a few months Paris and London were gripped with an oriental craze. The whalebone corsets and sinuous S-shapes of the Edwardian hostesses were banished. Harem trousers and peplums were overnight *à la mode*, created by the Parisian designer Paul Poiret, one of the first to recognize and capitalize on and corroborate the fact that exoticism was here to stay.

It was Poiret who had originally conceived Sarah Bernhardt's mode of dress; a scarf knotted at her waist became her trade mark.

Wickedness was hinted with heavily-laden perfumes such as "1001 Nights" and Guerlain's "Mitsouko" (Diaghilev's favourite scent; he even had the theatre sprayed with it prior to performances).

This was the beginning of the Art Deco period. Paul Poiret, undisputed dictator of fashion and design, was directly influenced by Bakst and the Ballets Russes. The explosion of colour and the geometric strength of the designs brought to an end the curves and delicate tendrils of the Art Nouveau period.

Interiors were quick to follow suit. Divans and ottomans boasted draperies in the bold and startling colours. Benois's severe variations on black and white reached epidemic porportions. In lieu of a New Year's card, Jean Cocteau would send Henri Bernstein a black slate with *Bonne Année* scribbled in chalk so as not to violate the playwright's new colour scheme. Before long there was not a middle-class home without its green and orange cushions on a black carpet and women dressed in the loudest colours.

Suddenly the full importance of the Ballets Russes was realized. Here was an extension of art and beauty into everyday life. From the stage *Schéhérazade* emanated sensuality, brilliance and vitality in powerful extravagance. The Russians knew their business. On May 19th, 1910, Russian Bonds dated 1889 rose to $94^1/_2$ compared to a low in 1906 of $77^1/_4$. Bankers and businessmen were delighted as the world of commerce joined in the dance.

6

ARTISTS' MODEL

"It's good manners to join in what everybody is doing."
Stendhal (1783–1842)

Ida further enhanced her reputation with the wild animals she kept as pets. In her apartment she had a black panther and a leopard cub which were far from tame. She was always appearing with great scratches and claw marks which were often difficult to hide in performances. Bakst had seen her injured many times but it never seemed to worry her.

One day, after she had been particularly badly scratched, Diaghilev arrived at her apartment to do something about it. He was wearing his large coat with the astrakhan collar as usual. As soon as the panther cub saw the coat it took an instant dislike to it and started to growl, hiss and tense ready to spring. Diaghilev leapt on to the nearest table with a shriek which startled the young animal even more. It crouched nearby, snarling and yowling, its eyes blazing. Ida, aching with laughter and with tears running down her cheeks, picked up the young cub by the scruff of its neck and put it into the next room. A shaken Diaghilev insisted that it was taken from her saying it was "a danger to human life."

Ida had soon become aware that Paris harboured a smart, fashionable, artistic clique of lesbians. Having built up a reputation as a flamboyant and erotic creature, she allowed herself to be courted by this society. Without a hint of any previous lesbian (or other sexual) tendencies, Ida fell madly in love with the American painter, Romaine Brooks. Ida was, of course, married at the time but the marriage had never been consummated and her husband had virtually disappeared from her life.

Romaine Brooks was born in Rome in 1874 to a rich, unbalanced mother who had been deserted by her husband. Both were expatriate Americans. She was abandoned by her mother at the age of six and taken in by her grandparents who sent her away to schools in New Jersey, Italy, France and Switzerland. In 1896 Romaine went to Rome to study art. After her mother died in 1902 Romaine inherited a fortune, married John Ellingham Brooks, a well-known homosexual, and lived quite openly as a lesbian, first in the homosexual enclaves in Capri, London and then Paris. Her life in France was shared for the most part with her companion of forty years, the American poet Natalie Barney. Romaine Brooks was an exceptional artist who imbued her female models with sinister characteristics. She painted many morbid and eerie nude paintings of Ida and whilst she did so Ida was falling in love. Ida *was* in love; Ida was passionate about Romaine, willing to give up everything, even the stage, to disappear with Romaine to a love nest in the depths of the country.

This did not suit Romaine. She had fled from her mother and settled in Paris and was very much a part of the lesbian community there. In a world where homosexuality amongst men was against the law, people would hardly admit that such a thing as lesbianism even existed. In Paris no one was particularly surprised to see women dressed in men's suits, sitting quite openly in the cafés or dancing in the music halls. Colette had just had an affair with that strange, sexually charged aristocrat, Missy, the Marquise de Morny. Three years earlier not only were they having an affair, they flaunted it on stage together in a piece specially written by Missy herself called *Le Rêve d'Egypte* which received a stormy reception.

Romaine's Whistlerian apartment of black, white and grey luxury on the present Avenue du Président Wilson in Paris established her as a popular interior decorator as well as a portrait painter. Her first one-woman exhibition in 1910 at Durand-Ruel's in Paris consisting, for the most part, of Whistlerian figure studies was very successful. Other artists exhibiting at the gallery that year included Manet, Pissarro and Cézanne.

In subsequent years her portraits recorded, directly or indirectly, her attachments and relationships with the world of French arts and letters, with high society and with the homosexual world of the period. Amongst Romaine's most interesting portraits are those of lesbians. Una, Lady Troubridge (1924), the close friend of the author Radclyffe Hall and a major figure in the latter's scandalous novel of lesbian life, *The Well of Loneliness*, is incisively represented in severe masculine attire with monocle, clipped hair and dachshunds. Romaine was also reputed to have been the model for one of the main characters in the same book.

One of the people she had difficulty painting was Jean Cocteau who, according to Romaine, was "a delicate sitter who had to rest a good deal, and worried about draughts from the window against which I posed him with the view of the Eiffel Tower." However she said he posed beautifully when she blackmailed him with frequent slices of American chocolate cake he could not resist.

One of the most powerful pictures of Ida Romaine painted is called *The Passing*. It depicts a stark naked Ida lying on a suspended white slab shaped like a lily surrounded by dark space. Ida is skeletal, her long black hair falling over the end of the slab, disappearing into the dark of the space. She looks like a sacrifice on some satanic altarpiece without a bit of flesh on her elongated limbs. Her pelvis is turned outwards showing pubic hair so scant she could almost have been shaved. Her eyelids are dark and closed, her flesh a pallid sheet-white, unearthly against the white of the sepulchre on which she is lying. The whole picture, although totally static, throbs with an almost demonic sensuality, something very sinister, almost as if she is waiting to be taken by the devil as his new bride. The sepulchre, the altarpiece, becomes her wedding dress which she has opened completely to reveal her utterly still but acquiescent body.

The Passing was first exhibited in 1925; it was badly received by the critics because of its obvious morbidity, its decadent atmosphere and funereal ambience. The critic Louis de Meurille said of it: "If all the paintings would adopt that style the exhibition halls will have to be made into funeral parlours."

For Romaine Ida personified the ultimate beauty which was originally personified in her painting *Azalée Blanche*. The painting, started in 1911, took a long time. For many years Ida was her main model. Romaine described her:

"...more beautiful when off the stage: like some heraldic bird delicately knitted together by the finest bone structure, giving flexibility to curveless lines. The clothes she wore were beyond fashions for, without effort, everything contributed to making her seem like an apparition. Her face sharply cut with long golden eyes and a delicate bird-like nose: her partly veiled head moving gracefully, from the temples as though the wind were smoothing it back. When she came to Paris she possessed what is now so rarely spoken of – mystery. Hers was a mask whose outer glow emanated from a disturbed inner depth."

Ida was painted and photographed many times. A painting called simply *Portrait of Ida Rubinstein,* by Antonio de La Gandara, again makes her look sexually evil. She stands upright, her hand on her hip, her half-closed, heavily made-up eyes fixing the viewer with a glance that fires the challenges: dare, come, try. She is dressed in a silken gown that falls around her tall, fleshless figure. She is mysterious and threatening but, above all, it is the overt sensuality that envelops you like the embrace of a razor.

Romaine said: "I liked her because she was insatiable! That is why she fascinated me. She was very Russian, very Dostoyevskian, but without the Russian inconsistency. She was Jewish and she was the perfect incarnation of her race. She told me that her mother was a Gypsy and her father Jewish. Her clothes had no set style. She didn't follow fashions of the day. She had her own style and it gave her an air of a ghost. I remember a very cold, snowy morning we went for a walk and Ida was wearing a long ermine coat which was open and revealed her white neck.

Her face was pointed, her long eyes were golden. Her fine nose, aquiline. Her head was partially covered and her black hair was being elegantly blown about her temples."

There is no proof or confirmation of Ida's story of her mother's background. It can be assumed that Ida was trying to make herself appear even more exotic. She was in the business of reinventing herself, adept at making herself "all things to all men," and, particularly in the case of Romaine, all women.

Montesquiou, now fifty, saw in her the embodiment of a youthful androgynous ideal. He paid to have her portrait painted looking like the Queen of Sheba, dressed by Worth and crowned with white feathers. Whether she invented herself or others did it for her matters less than the fact that her very appearance at a luncheon would cause people to stare in open admiration. Words were inadequate for Montesquiou when he tried to impress upon Romaine the particular effect his first meeting with Ida Rubinstein had had upon him. He described her entrance, her gesture, her manner, leading up to the moment of indescribable beauty when she had turned to him and said:

"Monsieur, sit down!"

"To him this was no anti-climax," Romaine wrote. "He was experiencing over again in imagination, just that other quality which gave distinction to everything she said or did."

The pictures together construct a very positive image of the woman. It is worth looking at them to appreciate the feeling and charisma that she emanated. The idea of woman being feline, half-cat, half-human, predatory, waiting to pounce, has been a potent image since the Sphinx. In one of her pin-up pictures Ida is lying on a couch draped in silks, languishing in a Sphinx-like pose, clad in loosely-draped clothes, a huge bejeweled bracelet stretching from her fingers to her elbow, her sandals also bejeweled, a headpiece like a jeweled saucer on the side of her head. Her face, looking upward in complete profile, shows her aquiline aristocratic nose. Her dark eyes are outlined with charcoal, accentuated against the white pallor of her face. At first glance she looks thoughtful, at peace, almost in a trance. It is only as you look longer that the sense of danger creeps in against the background of pagodas and temples on the oriental screen, a danger from which you cannot run away. You are invited; you are challenged, you are bewitched. You can almost feel yourself becoming a slave at her feet.

In 1910 she was painted nude by Serov, glamorously sitting on a cushion looking over her shoulder, her skeletal back very much in view. Jacques-Emile Blanche painted her lying on cushions dressed as Zobeida in *Schéhérazade*. She sat for the fashionable photographer Bert, and Léon

Bakst drew literally hundreds of sketches of her both as herself and for his designs for her various roles.

The nude by Serov caused quite a stir, not because of the painting itself but because Ida posed nude for it in a chapel that was once part of a monastery. During these heady years, even though intensely private, she still seemed to take an inordinate joy in being provocative and shocking.

She was to make the most of whatever she had, physically and mentally, throughout her life. Even today many a young aspiring ballet dancer will unwillingly give up her career because she has grown too tall. Ida took up the challenge of her height and turned it into an advantage. She towered over the corps de ballet, the other leading dancers and particularly her male partners, especially the short, stocky but immensely powerful Nijinsky. It was her height and slender body which drew attention to her and provided her unusual charisma when she first ignited Paris in 1909. She was a giantess whose breasts were level with her partners' heads, towering over them like a great spider. She took Sarah Bernhardt's advice and gave up sweets and coffee, substituting non-caffeinated herbal teas for the everyday China and Indian. She took baths of rosemary and milk, and hyssop and porridge oats. To keep her skin youthful and to discourage wrinkles she coated her face regularly with ground almonds and rosewater.

Perhaps if she had died at the height of her fame and notoriety she may have had a fashionable cult following to this day, just as Marilyn Monroe, whose talent has been both sanctified and derided. Monroe was the star who died in 1962. Ida Rubinstein was the star who died in 1960. One died too early to fulfil her life but sustained her career beyond death. The other died too late and sustained neither her life nor her career. Both had a hunger for life and that child-like longing to be applauded and adored. Both needed the adoration that came from their myriad devotees. Neither knew the love and adoration which most ordinary women get from their offspring. Both lived a life of which most people dream, before the nightmares begin.

7

ST SÉBASTIEN

"The man who can govern a woman can govern a nation."
Honoré de Balzac (1799–1850)

After *Schéhérazade* Ida's fame was complete. Her performance in *Schéhérazade* inspired Gabriele d'Annunzio to write *Le Martyre de St Sébastien* especially for her; her looks were perfect. Ida, the androgynous beauty could play the saint – the effete asexual hero of the piece. He set to work immediately.

"We were in the middle of the Paris season and at the Opera the Ballets Russes was creating a furore. It is possible that he [d'Annunzio] may have been reproached in some ultra Parisian Salon for having not yet seen the famous ballet. Perhaps some woman who interested him at the moment may have asked him to visit the Opera on a definite evening. However it may have been, he asked me one morning ... to go immediately to the Opera and purchase two stalls, for the ballet *Schéhérazade*....

"That evening we found ourselves in the third row of the stalls, five minutes before the curtain rose on the ballet.... As soon as Ida Rubinstein appeared on the stage he ceased to have eyes for anyone else, and from the moment the performance was over till we returned to the hotel at four o'clock in the morning. By one of his usual whims, he insisted on staying up at the bar; he talked to me only of Ida Rubinstein, of the harmony of all her movements, the grace of her attitudes, and above all, the plastic perfection of her legs.

" 'Here,' he exclaimed, 'are the legs of Saint Sebastian – for which I have been searching in vain all these years!'

"To be frank, I could see no connection between the saint and the Russian dancer, and still less why he had been looking for these very legs for years. Ingenuously, I asked him to enlighten me.

"He explained that he had been long nursing the idea of writing a religious mystery for the theatre, according to medieval tradition; that the hero of the drama was to be Saint Sebastian. That he had had to give up because of his inability to find an actor or actress physically adapted to the part, and that only after having seen the incarnation of his dream in the famous Russian actress could he say that he had discovered his ideal interpreter....

" 'I believe she lives at the Hotel Carlton,' he said when at last he left me. 'We will go there tomorrow morning, and discover the best means of entering into communication with her, as we are not personally acquainted. All I know about her is that she is an exceedingly original woman, very difficult to approach and that her life is full of mystery. No one has ever seen her in the company of man or woman. I hear that she only leaves the hotel to go to the theatre, or to go for solitary motor drives in the forest of St Cloud or other isolated spots in the vicinity of Paris, when she leaves her car, and walks for an hour or so by herself, before returning to the hotel. At least, so Montesquiou told me, and since he has the most ruthless tongue in Christendom, we must take him at his word.'

"He wrung my hand and moved towards the lift, but suddenly called me back to whisper a terrible secret in my ear: When she leaves Paris she goes lion hunting in Africa! Then he went up to his room."

Tom Antongini

D'Annunzio sent an 'extremely correct' letter to Ida Rubinstein inviting her to arrange a meeting. A few days later Ida replied.

When they finally met, d'Annunzio "was so enthralled with her that he went down on his knees and literally kissed her feet!"

Many years later Ida wrote of the meeting:

"Gabriele d'Annunzio wrote to me to receive him and it goes without saying that I received the poet, surrounded as he was by a halo of artistic glory, with profound humility and gratitude!"

From that moment they had many meetings and discussions and *Le Martyre de St Sébastien* was conceived. Over the next nine months they were in constant communication. D'Annunzio went on a veritable pillaging campaign of all the Paris shops in search of pictures of every epoch or school relating to the saint, picturing him in every possible and imaginable posture and attitude.

In January 1911 d'Annunzio wrote to Ida:

"My beloved frère,

I have done what I had to do; and I have worked. You will find the first and third acts complete. You will, I am sure, have divined the magnitude of my effort. You will be nailed to the stake, oh, far too beautiful saint! I work every night until the tardy break of dawn. To our speedy meeting. I think of you incessantly, and I love you through the flame of my spirit."

When he made up his mind to make a short trip to Paris in order to consult her and Bakst, he wrote:

"Dear Frère,

All the pierced saints were waiting for the greatest of them, and you did not come! I cannot leave tonight, I do not feel well. The excess and ardour of work are consuming me. You will find me too pale. I will leave for Paris tomorrow evening, but shall only remain there for a few hours. I kiss your two hands with most tender melancholy.

The deluded archer."

At this time d'Annunzio became obsessed with archery, practising shooting arrows every minute of his spare time. When Ida joined him at Arcachon and spent a few days at the Grand Hotel she used to visit him every day at his villa where they "indulged in veritable competitions."

When d'Annunzio had finally completed *St Sébastien* he wrote to Ida: "Work finished. I kiss the wounded knees."

They set to work on the production almost immediately. Gabriel Astruc was brought in as impresario. Ida herself was delighted as she had always considered "the manuscript of one of d'Annunzio's plays as of divine origin." Reading and studying it was, for her, celebrating a rite; interpreting it became a religious experience.

Casting posed a huge problem. All the actresses and many unqualified society women of Paris seemed to want a part in it. D'Annunzio, who had had many a dalliance in his time, had a very difficult task. During these months of the "battle of the ladies" the poet was quietly editing and polishing his work in Arcachon. He was continually implored to return to Paris. He took very good care to do no such thing. He was swamped daily with venomous letters, full of scandal in which actresses tore each other's characters to shreds.

"For the love of heaven, don't give the part to Madame X! She can hardly stand without crutches!"

"I am told that you are going to give the role of 'La fille Malade des Fierres' to Z. But, my dear man, she is not 'La fille Malade des Fierres' – she is 'La Fille du Régiment!' "

D'Annunzio found these letters most entertaining, as when he received frantic appeals from Astruc to hurry back to Paris. Already there were rumblings from Italy about anti-Jewish demonstrations on account of Ida Rubinstein appearing as Saint Sebastian.

Astruc, who was also Jewish, wrote to d'Annunzio:

"I am rather worried because a group of ladies, representing the French aristocracy, has written to me to voice the fear that *St Sébastien*, religiously speaking, may give the impression of profanation. And I do not want to be accused of having crucified the Saviour for the second time."

"My work", replied d'Annunzio, "is a work essentially mystic, and is unassailable from a religious standpoint. Furthermore, my dear Astruc, when Ida Rubinstein makes her appearance – almost naked at the moment of supplication – it will be too late to protest. The public will be conquered by that time."

Slowly and surely the play was cast and rehearsals began, not without troubles. A stream of problems were constantly sent to d'Annunzio.

"You need atmosphere!"

"You must come and hob-nob with the beaux!"

"Madame Simon has thrown up her job!"

"Brady's wild eyes are indispensable."

They looked for, and cast, a virgin chorus. A lady – a colonel's wife – wrote to the poet:

"Monsieur Astruc has dismissed my daughter and I can confirm, illustrious Maître, that she is the only girl, being really a virgin (she has never been out of the house except in my company), who is worthy to fill the role in a work so eminently religious as yours!"

D'Annunzio turned this letter over to Ida Rubinstein who induced the impresario to re-engage the 'authentic virgin'. Ida immersed herself in the rehearsals.

"She is feverish", d'Annunzio said. "She thinks, dreams and only lives for her new creation. She asked me whether I thought she should cancel her engagements in Milan. She had employed a French professor for her diction. She is even losing her looks and that astounds me, for she has two idols: her art and her body."

Like many an artist before and since, Ida was full of self-doubt during rehearsals. She wrote to d'Annunzio:

"Brother, send me a word with fire in it! I could not sleep last night: I had such ghastly apprehensions. It seemed too that I would never be able to do anything again. Tell me that you know everything will be all right, that you believe in your brother, and I will go to work, so that this afternoon you will be contented as you were the other day!"

She need not have worried: d'Annunzio adored her. She was his Saint Sebastian, even though he was not entirely deaf to her flawed pronunciation. He wrote at the time: "I want to create a pantomime for her, if only to return her to her original and divine silence!"

Over the hiccoughs there was a genuine admiration. D'Annunzio raved about her to his friends:

"Lost in the midst of the frivolous actresses of Paris, she stands out like a Russian icon in a novelty shop in the Rue de la Paix."

On watching her in rehearsal: "Before dancing she sat down in silence like a sibyl listening to a god within her... she is motionless in the discovery of herself."

In fact there were only three actresses of whom d'Annunzio spoke hundreds of times without restriction in terms of admiration and gratitude: Eleanora Duse, Sarah Bernhardt and Ida Rubinstein.

Robert de Montesquiou, who had helped d'Annunzio with the script of *Le Martyre* by editing the text and correcting the Italian's unidiomatic French, was another who went through a passionate and emotional involvement during those early stages. He did not miss a single rehearsal or a single performance, even though the overwhelming experience left him limp with fatigue. He regarded the work as a masterpiece and often became so involved that he would personally jump up onto the stage to instruct Fokine on the type of gesture Saint Sebastian would use when he hurled away the arrows which never fell to the earth.

D'Annunzio approached Debussy to write the music with an extravagant letter:

"Mon Cher Maître,

This summer, while I was drafting a *Mystère* that has been haunting me for some time, a lady friend sang to me some of your beautiful songs with the divine intensity they require. My writing, as it took shape, trembled at the sound...

Do you like my poetry?

In Paris a fortnight ago, I wanted to come and knock at your door...

Now I can no longer keep silent. Will you see me and hear me speak about this piece of writing and my dream?

Send me but a word and I shall come at once.

At least I shall have the joy of expressing to you my humble thanks for the beautiful thoughts, that you have so often nurtured in my agitated mind.

Gabriele d'Annunzio"

Debussy began on January 9th, 1911. He had very little time as the work was scheduled to begin rehearsals in May.

"He started the work with feverish haste" and found himself so hard pressed for time that he had to ask André Caplet to help him.

He jotted down the music, and as soon as a sheet of the rough draft was finished, Caplet started carrying out the scoring in accordance with the indication provided. Debussy remained closeted in his room, invisible to all but Caplet, until the day of the first rehearsal.

Meanwhile, people were expressing surprise that so thoroughly pagan a composer should undertake to deal with so definitely religious a subject. Debussy's reply during a press interview was:

"Do you really think that my music is devoid of religious antecedents? Do you wish to put an artist's soul under restraint? Do you find it difficult to conceive that one who sees mystery in everything – in the song of the sea, in the curve of the horizon, in the wind and in the calls of birds – should have been attracted to a religious subject? I have no profession of faith to utter to you: but, whichever my creed may be, no great effort on my part was needed to raise me to the height of d'Annunzio's mysticism. I can assure you that my music was written in exactly the spirit as if it had been commissioned for performance in church.

"Have I succeeded in expressing all that I felt? It is for others to decide. Is the faith which my music expresses orthodox? I do not know; but I can say that it is my own, expressed in all sincerity."

However, just as rehearsals were beginning to go well and music and action were fusing together, the Church dropped its bombshell. On May 8th Cardinal della Volpe decreed that the Papal Index had banned all d'Annunzio's written and dramatic works. The Archbishop of Paris specifically condemned *Le Martyre de St Sébastien* and all French Catholics were forbidden to attend performances on pain of excommunication.

Montesquiou was appalled and organized public tributes to d'Annunzio, giving a brilliant lecture in defence of the wronged poet. D'Annunzio and Debussy protested to the Archbishop that *Le Martyre* was an intensely religious work, but the Archbishop was adamant. Presenting the Martyrdom of a Christian saint as a theatrical entertainment was sacrilege enough: having him played by a woman was tantamount to profanation. Perhaps one reason for the Archbishop's uncompromising attitude was d'Annunzio himself.

"D'Annunzio had slightly irritated the Archbishop by making himself too much at home in Notre Dame. On the pretext of an artistic need, he used to have the organist play for him alone, threw the vestry into turmoil and with his friends climbed the private staircase leading to the organ loft. He even gave a garden party in the small garden that is hemmed in between the masonry and the river."

Elisabeth de Gramont

The more the controversy raged about the banned work the more interested the public became. It was brilliant publicity. Even though a few eminent Catholic families in Paris cancelled their boxes, the less conspicuous boxes in the theatre appeared to be extraordinarily full.

Le Martyre de St Sébastien opened in the Châtelet Theatre in May 1911. The *Comoedia Illustré* said of it:

"*Le Martyre de St Sébastien* shows us the sensuality of a belief which is among the most violent and most delicate.

"Once again Gabriele d'Annunzio, painter of voluptuousness, is above all demonstrably an artist. Praised as 'a work of decadence', the play managed to combine divine love with the bound and tortured image of the handsome young saint, L'Athlète du Christ, in Cocteau's well-chosen phrase."

Bakst also received praise:

"In an Orient which is never vulgar, it is full of love for brilliant materials, a feast for the eyes. Bakst's excessiveness can be seen in strange accessories. Rubinstein's entrance in a box twice as big as herself; a giant tray is carried in by dwarfs; enormous headdresses; a white horseman on a white charger against a violently coloured set: all brilliant *coups de théâtre.*"

Henri Gheon called the work: "Barbarity all the more dangerous as it wears the Mediterranean mask of beauty!"

Marcel Proust attended the first night: "Everything that is foreign in d'Annunzio took refuge in the accent of Madame Rubinstein…. She's a cross between Clomesnil and Maurice de Rothschild and her legs are sublime."

"I can still hear Rubinstein's hoarse voice. In her scarab-like armour, she was truly the sexless stripling that one sees in triptychs by Italian masters of the Renaissance."

Elisabeth de Gramont

On the whole the play had very mixed reviews, although the band of Ida's most ardent admirers were rapturous about her performance. D'Annunzio was delighted to see his dream of the androgynous saint come to fruition. Ida, for him, was perfection, the girl/boy, the tragic, beautiful saint.

Jean Cocteau saw it many times, but whether because of the play or because of Montesquiou is open to question. Cocteau fell madly in love with Montesquiou at the time, changing his style of dress to that of Montesquiou, down to the smallest detail, to the satin cuffs and the ivory-topped cane. Montesquiou seemed totally unaffected and treated him with his usual disdain and cruelty.

Cocteau was clearly being loyal to Rubinstein when he cleverly underplayed her failings:

"She strikes the ear as a primitive picture strikes the eye. There is the same noble awkwardness, the same precise breadth of treatment, the same shy charm…. She is some saint from a stained glass window who, suddenly called to life and still troubled by the thought of his translucent immobility, has not yet grown accustomed to the newly-bestowed gifts of speech and gesture."

Debussy's score was a triumph. "The music makes you believe in heaven since it takes you there."

Elisabeth de Gramont

It was Ida's first professional appearance where she was both producer and actress. Whatever its limitations or failings she had brought together on the same playbill Debussy, Bakst, d'Annunzio, and Fokine, four of the greatest talents of the day, not to mention contributions from Cocteau and Montesquiou.

Between the overwhelming success of *Schéhérazade* and the premiere of *Le Martyre de St Sébastien* Ida Rubinstein first met Walter Guinness, the first Lord Moyne, one of the richest men in England. Apart from her husband and Romaine Brooks, the only person with whom Ida had been romantically linked was a millionaire Greek nobleman, Antoine Mavrocordato, an elderly admirer who gave Diaghilev large sums of money to back his projects. Other members of the Ballets Russes's inner circle regarded him with suspicion; Astruc called him 'The Sombre Mavrocordato', and Montesquiou dismissed him as a 'cold jellied crow.' With the arrival of Walter Guinness he disappeared into history.

Guinness was so struck with Ida's beauty, charm and art that he put his fortune at her feet. It was with this man that she shared a deeply caring love and friendship which continued until his tragic death in 1944. It was an extraordinary affair.

Guinness was married. In 1903 he had wed Lady Evelyn Hilda Stuart Erskine, daughter of the fourteenth Earl of Buchan, a talented lady of great beauty and unusual sensibility. Moyne was a gifted and spirited man. At Eton he rowed for three years and in due course became Captain of the Boats. In the South African War (1899–1902) he was wounded, mentioned in dispatches and awarded the Queen's Medal. In 1907 he entered the House of Commons, representing Bury St Edmunds until 1931. During the 1914/18 war he was promoted to Lieutenant-Colonel, again mentioned three times in despatches and awarded the Distinguished Service Order in 1917, and bar in 1918.

"Guinness's high public spirit and wide interests led him to pursue an extremely full life in which politics, scientific travel, and a share of his father's benefactions in England and Ireland, as well as the Guinness Breweries, were intertwined."

Guinness was always able to combine his public service with an eagerness for travel that he so enjoyed. As early as 1902 he had gone on the first of many big game hunting expeditions but, a great man before his time in many ways, he soon gave up shooting his prey to photograph them instead, killing only as necessary for food. His service as a statesman took him from Under Secretary of State for War in 1922, to Financial Secretary to the Treasury in 1923. He became a member of the Privy Council in 1924 and entered the Cabinet in November 1925 as Minister of Agriculture. With the defeat of the Conservatives in 1929 he retired from office and in 1932 he was raised to the peerage as Baron Moyne of Bury St Edmunds.

Ida, who also had a penchant for travelling, immediately warmed to this man. She had travelled to many strange and exotic places that had rarely been visited by anyone, let alone by a woman, certainly not by a woman alone. She travelled all over the world with Guinness, both on his photographic safaris and his explorations. After one of these expeditions she brought back a panther as a pet, echoing the times of Sarah Bernhardt.

Guinness bought her a beautiful townhouse in the Place des Etats-Unis which became her magnificent home, and gave her all the luxury she wanted until the end of his life. It was not a necessity, as Ida herself was immensely rich. To be close to Ida he kept his own house at 12, Rue de Portiers in the exclusive Faubourg Saint-Germain. When Ida formed her own company his bottomless coffers were a continual infuriation to Diaghilev who was plagued with financial difficulties throughout his career.

Ida never used her married name. After some time her husband, Vladimir Horwitz, realized he was chasing an impossible dream. Not only was he not seeing his wife, her relationships with both Guinness and Romaine Brooks had now become known to him. In desperation and jealous rage he asked for a divorce. Ida refused to see or, curiously, divorce him. Divorce then required a witness to adultery or some other marital crime. Vladimir had her followed by a private detective. Although her liaisons with Guinness and Brooks were well known within her inner circle, Ida was completely discreet, so he was never able to obtain a divorce and seemed to fade out of her life.

After being raised to the peerage Moyne became Financial Commissioner to Kenya in 1932, Chairman of the West Indian Royal Commission in 1938 and, in 1939, placed his yacht *Rosaura* at the disposal of the members for both residence and transport. He had used the yacht for many of his travels. During the thirties he travelled to the island of Komodo, near New Guinea, and brought back living specimens of Komodo Dragons for the London Zoological Society.

The following year, 1935, he travelled to New Guinea again, which he described in his book *Walkabout*, and in 1937 he journeyed to Greenland and the little-known Bay Islands off the coast of Honduras. These he wrote about in his book *Atlantic Circle*. It was his yacht, *Rosaura*, that he lent to the Prince of Wales for that cruise which first alerted the public to his relationship with Wallis Simpson. The yacht would not have impressed Ida whose own yacht, *Istar*, with its interiors designed, of course, by Bakst, and a permanent crew of ten men, was larger than the royal yacht itself.

In 1939 Moyne insisted that Ida, being Jewish, flee France and come to England. This she did. Moyne set her up in the Ritz Hotel where he looked after her until his death in 1944. During this time her house in the Place des Etats-Unis was razed to the ground and all her antiques and treasures were confiscated, looted and stolen. Her magnificent library of first editions, her rooms of fine clothes were all gone. Moyne took complete financial responsibility for her during this time in England until she could safely return to her adopted France.

On the outbreak of war Moyne became Chairman of the Polish Relief Fund and lent part of his London home at 10 and 11 Grosvenor Place for its offices. Although he had served as Minister of Agriculture, he agreed to serve as Joint Parliamentary Secretary to the Minister on the formation of Churchill's Government in 1940. The following year he succeeded Lord Lloyd as Secretary for the Colonies and Leader of the House of Lords. In January 1944 he became Minister Resident in the Middle East, but on November 6th he was assassinated in Cairo by terrorists of the Stern Gang.

Today it would be impossible for this relationship to be common knowledge for so many years and never mentioned in the press, as the Prince of Wales' relationship with Mrs Simpson was never mentioned until Parliament entered the picture. Even later, in the early 1960s the President of the United States was quite safe from the press in his many adulteries. Today the tabloid press would have a field day.

On the news of his death, his cousin by marriage, Sir Henry 'Chips' Channon, wrote an intimate description of Moyne:

"Walter Moyne was an extraordinary man, colossally rich, well-meaning, intelligent, scrupulous, yet a *viveur*, and the only modern Guinness to play a social or political role, being far less detached than most of his family. He collected yachts, fish, monkeys and women. He had a passion for these, and for long expeditions to remote places. He had a curious frenzy for the very early Gothic, and all his houses were in that style, and hideous…. He was careful of his huge fortune, though he probably had about three millions."

Having started her career as a star, Ida Rubinstein was determined to remain one. She settled in Paris to pursue this ideal. Apart from her extraordinary beauty and her strange liquid movements, Ida's talents appeared to be limited. She had a charisma, an undeniable stage presence and enormous courage to appear naked on the stage at that time. This was her persona, her magic, but beyond that there were doubts. She had never been trained as a dancer in the conventional way. Because she had not been a pupil at the Maryinsky School and had never taken classes with other students or with other dancers, she would never feel comfortable with a rehearsing ensemble. Apart from the two Diaghilev productions in which she appeared she was always the impresario. Consequently she was always able to arrange for her rehearsals to be private, while the rest of the company rehearsed together without her. She would join the company for the dress rehearsals. The usual tensions and nerves which build up in a company before a first night were much heightened when the day that Rubinstein was to join them drew near.

Would she have taken Paris by storm in the same way if she hadn't been in Diaghilev's productions? In a mediocre production with indifferent costumes and nondescript sets, insignificant music and a dancer other than Nijinsky to play opposite, she obviously would never have had the same impact. No one under those circumstances would shine, but would whatever talent she had rise, like cream, to the top? It is doubtful. Ida needed the superlative art of others to dignify and decorate her own artistic endeavours.

She needed the Baksts, Fokines, Stravinskys, Rimsky-Korsakovs and others to define and clarify her art. She also needed and used her strangely exotic angular body. Nudity and notoriety played a vital part in her career. As Benois remarked:

"She is game for anything as long as she can take off her clothes – if she can take off her clothes she is happy."

In this idea Ida is much like Madonna today. Not only was she to take every opportunity to disrobe in public, she would do many things in the course of her 'art' which shocked many people. Both women are exceptionally shrewd in business matters and are their own best publicists.

To illustrate the courage Ida needed to embark on any sort of theatrical career, let alone appear nude on stage, one has only to realize that her younger and charming cousin Madame Renée de Monbreson had never met Ida because:

"We were not allowed to have anything to do with her because she was in the theatre. My mother would not let me meet her because of this."

Apart from *Salomé*, *Cléopâtre* and *Schéhérazade* she appeared nude under her tunic in *St Sébastien*, and in the death scene under rose petals in *La Pisanelle*. She was painted nude by Romaine Brooks and Serov and she was photographed by the fashionable photographer, Bert. Indeed, nudity, sex and even violence were clearly evident in all Ida's early career.

Violence and passion were much to the fore in *St Sébastien*. Her androgyny was a prerequisite to her role where it was vital that she should not appear to be a woman.

Whilst rehearsing for *St Sébastien* Ida was due to appear for Diaghilev in *Schéhérazade* and *Cléopâtre* in Monte Carlo. She let him down badly by reneging at the last minute. This was at the dress rehearsal, barely leaving time to find a replacement, and to have a costume fitting. However, she did turn up on April 23rd for two performances each of *Cléopâtre* and *Schéhérazade*, thus saving Diaghilev from being sued for breach of contract for not having all the named performers as contracted. She stayed four days during which time Fokine invented for her the dance she would perform in *St Sébastien*. This was her last performance for Diaghilev.

"Misunderstandings occurred which caused the definite break between her and Diaghilev.

"Apparently Ida Rubinstein became tired of being given only miming roles. She became bored by plastic movements, caresses, embraces and stabbing herself. She wanted to dance. Diaghilev, who knew perfectly well that she was no good as a dancer, gave her a decisive rebuff. She realized that a dancing career with Diaghilev was closed to her for ever. Relations between them were severed and she never forgave Diaghilev for turning her down. In the following year she began to mount productions of her own. *St Sébastien* was one of these. In spite of the collaboration of such great powers as d'Annunzio, Debussy, and Bakst, nothing but a cold academic success was achieved."

Prince Pieter Lieven

Diaghilev was most perturbed by the fact that Ida had started her own company in Paris. He only thought and talked of Ida (now that she was no longer involved in his company) as a rich amateur who had only danced roles which required a certain acting ability and good looks rather than the ability to be a good dancer.

He wrote to Astruc:

"Bakst claims that we lack confidence in his work, but I must say that I have never seen so astounding a betrayal of every artistic and aesthetic principle as he has shown in his dealings with us. When Bakst took on the production of *St Sébastien*, he swore to me that it would in no way interfere with our work, which he held much dearer. Now I declare that we have now been completely sacrificed to the work of Rubinstein and d'Annunzio."

Pieter Lieven wrote:

"Diaghilev had many feminine traits of character: he was capricious, jealous, and easily offended. Jealousy had a great influence on his work, an influence which had by no means a negative effect. He was extremely jealous of any manifestation of rivalry or competition to his work. It was the cause of many of his quarrels with his friends, especially with Benois and Bakst. If Bakst collaborated with Rubinstein, or perhaps Benois with somebody else, Diaghilev would always be moved to recriminations and abuse. 'Unfaithfulness' was something which he could not forgive.

"At the time Diaghilev was jealous of Benois's collaboration with Ida Rubinstein, and made scenes about it. 'Why do you do it?' he would ask. 'Come now, do *Philémon et Baucis*, and show that you can do better for me than for Ida.' "

But in May 1911, a month later, Ida opened *Le Martyre de St Sébastien* in Paris.

8

THE PRODUCER

"Pleasure may come of illusion, but happiness can come only of reality."

Nicholas Chamfort (1741–1794)

During her life as a producer Ida employed a galaxy of talent. In addition to those previously mentioned she used choreographers Bronislava Nijinska, Léonide Massine and Kurt Jooss; she commissioned original scores by Maurice Ravel, Igor Stravinsky, Henri Sauguet and Arthur Honegger; librettos by Paul Valéry and André Gide; designs nearly always by the ever-faithful Alexandre Benois and Léon Bakst. New ballets presented included *La Valse* (1929), *La Bien-Aimée*, *Boléro* (1928), and the melodrama *Perséphone*. Although Ravel wrote his *Boléro* for her, amongst some of the most famous and memorable music ever written, Ida herself is hardly remembered.

"Unfortunately she had always insisted on dancing herself, in a manner that even in her youth was unfamiliar to her. She had been famous as a mime, but here she was showing us an extensive repertoire that only a Karsavina could have carried, from the cold classicism of *Princesse Cygne* to the warmth of Spanish dancing in Ravel's *Boléro*. So many near-masterpieces were presented that season one lamented the fact that their inspirer was not content to play the role of the super-impresario."

Arnold Haskell

Had Ida been content to be a super-impresario, her place in the pantheon of the dance might never have been in question, much less obscured. However, despite all his harsh comments about Ida's talent, Diaghilev and Nijinsky invited her to play the head nymph in *L'Après-Midi d'un Faune* to music by Debussy. At first Ida agreed. Nijinsky was to choreograph the production and star in it as the Faun.

Diaghilev needed another success and, as always, needed more backing. In June the previous year, 1911, the Ballets Russes went to London. Diaghilev's main sponsor was a Lady Ripon, one of the few English ladies who really belonged in Paris society. At a party in London Nijinsky made an appalling faux pas which nearly cost Diaghilev his sponsorship. Lady Ripon had introduced a game into the party in which everyone decided what sort of animal each person most resembled. She had started the ball rolling by saying that Diaghilev looked like a bulldog and Stravinsky like a fox. She then turned to Nijinsky and asked him what he thought she looked like. Nijinsky looked at her and told her the awful truth: "Vous, Madame – chameau." ("You, Madame – a camel.") It was the last thing Lady Ripon had expected, for chameau also means 'bitch,' and her reputation in Paris was many-coloured. Despite her laughing and repeating "A camel? How priceless. How amusing. A camel? Really?" she was embarrassed and deeply perturbed

Bronislava Nijinska told of the rehearsals for *L'Après-Midi d'un Faune*, 1912:

"The participants in *Faune*, as we called the ballet for short, were the Faun, the Nymph, and the six nymphs of her entourage. Ida Rubinstein had agreed with Vaslav and Diaghilev to perform the role of the Nymph, and Vaslav had mounted his ballet with her in mind, the tallest amongst her nymphs and, more important, taller than he as the Faun. He demonstrated all the steps and poses with great ease, assuring us it was all very simple and easy; he could not understand why the dancers looked so awkward. The artists were actually applying themselves, were trying their best. In fact as long as they were standing still, holding the pose as shown them by Vaslav, the group was very effective and approached visually what Vaslav wanted. But as soon as the nymphs had to change their poses and move to form a new group or simply resume walking, they were not able to preserve the bas-relief form, to align their bodies so as to keep their feet, arms, hips, shoulders, and heads in the same choreographic form inspired by archaic Greece.

"The dancers complained to me that they would never be able to make their bodies assume such unusual positions, no matter how long they worked. When Vaslav talked to me he also sounded discouraged: 'Look how they are distorting my choreography.' I tried to encourage him, saying: Perhaps for these preliminary rehearsals it would be enough for the dancers to learn the steps, and then in time they will acquire a feeling of freedom for the performance of the new postures.

"Ida Rubinstein came one day and attended only one rehearsal. She was indignant about Nijinsky's choreography and, after that first rehearsal, announced that she would not perform in *Faune*. Possibly she found the part of the Nymph too difficult for her, but probably she did not want to spoil her friendship with Fokine. She was loyal and devoted to Fokine, who had been her teacher from the earliest days when she had followed him on holiday to Switzerland. He had been overlooked by Diaghilev for both the role of the Faun and for the choreography of the piece. Instead Diaghilev had given both the role and the choreography to his young lover, Nijinsky. Fokine felt upset and slighted. Rubinstein could easily have harmed her working relationship with him by appearing in the production. For the role of the Nymph, Lydia Nelidova was engaged.

"Many years later when I was working with Ida Rubinstein, in 1928, I asked her why she had refused to perform such a wonderful role as the Nymph in the *Faune*. She told me about that rehearsal, the only one she had with Nijinsky: 'In my part there was not a single natural movement, not one single comfortable step on stage. Everything was topsy-turvy; if the head and feet were turned towards the right, then the body was turned towards the left. Nijinsky wanted the impossible. If I had submitted to his direction I would have distorted my body and would have been transformed into a maimed marionette.' "

If all the dancers in the Company were having difficulties with Nijinsky's choreography, it must have been infinitely harder for Rubinstein who was neither as highly trained nor as gifted a dancer.

As Bronislava suggests, perhaps the part was too difficult for her. Perhaps her intuition told her Nijinsky would command all the attention and accolades in this production. If so, she was correct. Not only did he take all the plaudits, he made certain he became the major talking point when he shocked all of Paris and the ballet world by apparently masturbating on stage at the end of the ballet. Finally, Ida was already very busy preparing for her own productions.

Over the next few years Ida worked hard to establish herself as a producer. Having had a considerable personal success with *St Sébastien*, she was constantly looking for vehicles to showcase her talents.

At her house in the Place des Etats-Unis she set up her headquarters. For a public figure she emerges, incongruously, as an extremely shy creature, always in the background. A 'front man' protected her and did all her business; she rarely met anyone face to face. Her house became her citadel from which she wove her dreams. When she was working on a new production with her company she would not appear until the dress rehearsal, and even then would very often just plot the moves, declining to say her lines with the minimal excuse that this way they would be much fresher at the opening. This inevitably led to a very nervous company and nerve-wracking first nights. Even in these early days Ida appeared to be wracked with the most debilitating stagefright, but she was committed body and soul.

This wealthy heiress, used to any luxury which took her fancy, would visit the smallest village halls and provincial theatres to perform for country folk who could barely understand a word. She would be terrified and yet paid for the privilege by financing these shows herself.

She fully appreciated the artistic importance of Diaghilev's reforms and succeeded more than once in provoking Diaghilev's jealousy in the productions she staged.

Ida immersed herself in the pursuit of her star and the search for new ideas. Once she had an idea, virtually nothing would stop her going to almost any lengths to set it in motion. When she was planning her 1934 season in Paris she had set her heart on a ballet entitled *Oriane la Sans-Égale*, a medieval love story. She decided to ask an old friend, Florent Schmitt, to write the music. However, when she actually came to tell him she found he was far away in his country retreat at Artiguemy in Hautes-Pyrénées. Schmitt remembered:

"It was a beautiful summer afternoon, I was in Artiguemy, lying under the apple trees facing an incomparable southern peak untouched by snow, completely at peace, thinking no evil thoughts, when a sound like an earthquake shattered the quiet. A motor car, foolishly tackling the goat-path, had smashed itself around the great oak and hurled its two lady passengers onto the ground.

"The oak tree had only a few scratches. As for Madame Ida Rubinstein, everyone knows that she is above such calamities: tracing the line of the oak tree, as erect, as high and still smiling, she scarcely realized that she escaped the most picturesque of deaths. By her side, no less unscathed was Madame Fauchier-Magnan, a friend of Ida's. They came – eight hundred and seventy-three miles – to offer me this ballet *Oriane la Sans-Égale*."

Apart from these occasional eccentricities, she was organized. She employed a secretary as day-to-day manager to deal with the endless queue of visitors, writers, actors, journalists, fine arts officials and all kinds of favour-seekers. The secretary, or "The Shadow" as she became known, was Ida's protector, guard and way of dealing with the imprecations of the real world.

The Shadow's diplomacy and intuition were unbeatable, her patience equal to all tests and her courtesy exquisite, whilst her natural goodness and indulgence enabled her to listen, understand and resolve everything. Her little office acted as a screening point and filter before the large office, like the hub of a great wheel in perpetual motion. Everyone came via this little slip of a woman; all were passed on by her, good or bad; but always she took great care never to offend. The Shadow became the keeper of the citadel.

Ida's collaboration with d'Annunzio and Bakst on *St Sébastien* had caused a furore from Diaghilev. He was livid. He accused Bakst of being unfaithful, which was both unfair and hurtful to Bakst who, even though he was designing for Ida, was continuing his work for Diaghilev and was totally loyal. If he could manage working for both he would do so.

Cyril Beaumont described Bakst in his *Favourite Ballet Stories*:

"A brisk blue-eyed dapper little man – what a fine Pantaloon he would have made – who walked with that elastic poise which comes from daily fencing exercise. His hair was auburn, his complexion fresh coloured, and he sported a fine moustache. He wore a rimless pince-nez. In the lapel of his coat he wore the red ribbon of the Légion d'Honneur. When he had taken his seat he would rest his head on his chin and gaze at the proceedings with a cold and critical gaze which missed nothing."

He was born in the chief provincial town of Grodno in Russia around 1866. He was Jewish and moved to St Petersburg as a child. At twenty he entered the Academy of Fine Arts in St Petersburg from which he was expelled for painting a picture which depicted a weeping group with the Madonna as Jewish peasants.

Poverty stricken for some time, he eventually became a portrait painter and the Grand Duke Vladimir became his sponsor. It was through Bakst that the Ballets Russes was eventually sponsored by Vladimir. Bakst built up an impressive reputation in St Petersburg, not only for his portraits but also his book illustrations and interior decoration. He was introduced to a wider circle of the art world by his friend, the painter Alexandre Benois, thereby meeting Serge Diaghilev.

The mime ballet *Le Coeur de la Marquise* was his first theatre design in a private production, followed by his first professional work *La Fête des Poupées* for the Maryinsky Theatre. When eventually he came to Paris he designed for the great fashion houses, Papain and Worth. He was not a happy person, even though his work seemed to mirror a great joy of life and colour; he died, alone, in 1924.

Much of the success of *Cléopâtre* and *Schéhérazade* had been due to Bakst as, in its lesser way, had *St Sébastien*. Ida was, not surprisingly, very keen to have him work on any new venture. Bakst, a devoted admirer of Ida, did his utmost to oblige. So, when d'Annunzio finally finished his script of *La Pisanelle* for Ida, Bakst was the first to be called.

D'Annunzio, who had been inspired by Ida's remarkable physique to let her impersonate an unforgettable Saint Sebastian, had been delighted in the production of his piece.

"D'Annunzio is sympathetic, quick and lively of thought, a charming narrator. A little 'scented' and affected and at the same time sometimes shy and abashed. He informed us about his newest piece which he wrote especially for Mlle. Rubinstein, and because of this there is so much mime and so many dances, that it requires as much music as a pantomime.

"Whilst he talked he unfolded such an array of rich pictures and colours that one became quite enchanted, although in the end one had to confess that he had only put together a series of designs, costumes and ceremonies. He intimated that he would have liked me to write the music…. But Villmoeller said to me afterwards that it would have been an unsuccessful labour. He does not believe in d'Annunzio as a playwright. D'Annunzio and I separated warmly, with many germinating plans, and this meeting has pleased me much."

Ferruccio Busoni

D'Annunzio, once again, wrote *La Pisanelle* specially for Ida, Bakst again created the designs and Ildebrando Pizzetti wrote the score. It was choreographed by Fokine but unfortunately fell under the ban of the Church, not only because it was written by d'Annunzio but also because of the highly sensual scene in which Ida was smothered to death under a pile of roses.

La Pisanelle ran for eleven days, from 11th to 21st June. The premiere was an extravagant society occasion despite the ban; everyone who was anyone in Paris was there in his or her glittering finery. It was an evening not to be missed.

Ferruccio Busoni managed to see it and wrote to his wife:

"Now I am going to the Châtelet, to *Pisanelle* or *La Mort Parfumée*. I shall see Mlle. Rubinstein, of whom it is said by one that she cannot speak but can dance, by another that she has a beautiful body but cannot dance, by a third that her body is not womanly, therefore not beautiful. She is just like St. Sebastian, pierced with arrows by all."

In his next letter:

"Yesterday evening, Théâtre du Châtelet, full house, mostly women. Big orchestra, dilettantish music, music making which was suitable for everything and for nothing. Curtains, with large patterns *à la* Reinhardt. Behind the curtains, yet another curtain, the first scene is a hall from the Kremlin. How did it get to Cyprus? It was painted by Gospodin Bakst (of the Russian Ballet). Fräulein Rubinstein is also Russian. Half the audience, I noticed, consisted of Russians.

"The first act is tedious and produces no effect…. The second act is a harbour. It is all red: red walls, red ground, red ships, and some blue water in between. A slave (Rubinstein) has lost her way; a young king arrives and gives her his white mantle and his white horse and Fräulein Rubinstein rides off in triumph. She has neither danced, nor spoken, only stood on stage, tightly swathed in some sort of stuff, with a square pattern.

"Third act an unintelligible scene. A number of nuns come in, and so it is obvious that one is in a convent. I was so tired and irritated that I went out in the rain, there was nobody in the streets, although it was 10.30 p.m. I knew *Pisanelle* will be smothered by roses in the last act. Hence the name *La Mort Parfumée*….

"The whole play seemed old-fashioned, declamatory, pathetic, and mostly full of excitable gestures, long tirades, inexplicable blabbings, deaths and screams. Melancholy and without humour. It is like an aesthetically Wildenbuch play. On the other hand, it may be a master-piece, and I may be admitting myself to be unappreciative. It is possible. The succession of artistic emotions has been too rapid during the last few days and I am partly confused and partly blunted by them."

Even though *La Pisanelle* was poorly received it did not lessen Ida's resolve. If anything she became more determined. She was working incredibly hard. Before the production had been mounted she was preparing for the next. She was learning fast the necessities of a producer. For *La Pisanelle* alone over 200 people had been employed. Surveys had been carried out on all the principal players of the day, especially for the young and romantic parts, always notoriously difficult to cast and made even more so by the fact that Ida was so tall. All artistic and financial matters had to be finally decided by her: there was no detail in which she wasn't personally involved. There is an interesting correspondence between Bakst and Stravinsky which demonstrates Ida's commitment.

Bakst to Stravinsky:

"Dear Igor,

I do not know whether you are aware that Ida Rubinstein and I are doing a production of Shakespeare's *Antony and Cleopatra*, which is to say I am designing the costumes and sets. She has asked André Gide to provide a literal translation of the text (the first in French), and now she wants to ask you to write the music, specifically the introduction and incidental pieces – as you see fit and feel inspired to compose them, much in the way that Debussy wrote for her in *St Sébastien*. You would be entirely free as far as the music is concerned but, if possible, do not use voices. She had asked me to get a decision from you one way or another and to tell you that she would need the music in six months, if that is possible. So, dear Igor, write to me giving your decision and intention, as well as your terms. Personally, I believe that the production will be extraordinary: she is thinking of engaging Firnin Garnier as the director. I began preparing for it a long time ago, but the plans were stalled. Keep this to yourself, though the secret is hers, not mine. I await your prompt reply. I kiss you affectionately,

Lev Bakst.

My regards to your wife!"

Telegram from Stravinsky to Bakst:
"Would like to compose music for you but can decide nothing before seeing you and cannot come to Paris."

Bakst to Stravinsky:

"Dear Igor,

I have your telegram and am very glad that you gave your in-principle agreement. Unfortunately, I cannot leave Paris now, not until I finish the hundred-odd things I have to do… in other words, not for another month. When I read your telegram to Ida Rubinstein, she said that she has always communicated by letter concerning the finer details. On the basis of her experience with the productions of *Sébastien* and *Salomé* (for which she commissioned Glazunov to write the music) she thinks you ought to take into account the lack of resonance offstage.

Debussy had miscalculated this and the part that was offstage was messy and ineffective. He was eventually obliged to move the orchestra into the pit.

All of this assumes, of course, that you decide to set any portion of the various scenes to music. She would very much like to have parallel music during Cleopatra's death scene. You know the scene, which is one of the greatest works of human inspiration. But she leaves everything up to you… the length of the music, its importance and its distribution….

Write to me with all your questions and I will answer immediately, also any doubts you might have. And send me your estimates concerning time and money, and your choice of conductor.

I think that the production will open in the Paris Opera, but this is a secret. Let me know also about the dates for the instalments and other related conditions. The more garrrulous you are, the better. I kiss you affectionately.

Lev Bakst.

Regards to your wife!"

The letters went back and forth with many arguments and discussions, Bakst strongly defending anything that might compromise Ida!

"That even if I believed this interpretation of Shakespeare's tragedy to be a good and valid one, I would not try and defend your point of view, because I am morally responsible for making this an opportunity for Rubinstein to display her rare talent: my sets and costumes would therefore be completely inconsistent with her work, as well as with Gide's and Shakespeare's. But if you cannot accept my view, the problem is still easily resolved.

"Madame Rubinstein has left the composition and distribution of the music to you. She thinks (and so do I) that it would be good to have an overture to each act, then music for the appearance of the Roman camps, on the ramparts and in the private chambers, and, finally for the 'death of Cleopatra'. All of this would be evoked in the pit, not on the stage, for reasons about which I have already written to you….

"It would be best if you yourself made up a draft contract. Depending on whether changes are to be made, Madame Rubinstein will sign it through her business representatives. If you start immediately the contract can be signed in three or four weeks."

This was the way Ida operated. She controlled every aspect of the production without appearing in person. Here we have Bakst undoubtedly writing on behalf of Ida and any contracts that were to be signed were to be done through business representatives.

A letter from André Gide to Stravinsky takes up the tale of *Cleopatra*:

"… Finally, I wanted to tell you that my translation of *Cleopatra* is finished, and to ask you to write a score to illustrate the text?

As you know my deepest wish, now and always, is for you to do the music. I questioned Madame Rubinstein on the subject, but she claims not to have heard from you in ages. I was convinced that she, too, desires your collaboration.

So I told her that I would write to you again and enquire about your intentions. The question cannot be put off any longer, and I thought that perhaps you would write more candidly to me than her, if you have reservations or objections."

Stravinsky replied to Gide's letter:

"My dear Gide,

Thank you so much for your kind letter. Someday I will send an equally substantial communication to you, but at the moment, with deep regret, I can only tell you I have to dismiss the idea of our proposed collaboration on *Antony and Cleopatra*.

After quite a few letters and telegrams, and many financial concessions on my part, Madame Rubinstein, through Charles Paquin, her agent, has said that she will not go above her last offer, which was far from satisfactory for me.

I was surprised therefore to learn from you that she still expects me to be in communication regarding the project, unless her agent does not keep her informed, but acts on his own. But even if Rubinstein were to accept my terms I could no longer do the work, having started another one, *Histoire du Soldat*, which is fascinating and has me captivated."

9

WAR AND REVOLUTION

"Life may often seem like a long shipwreck, of which the debris are friendship, glory, and love; the shores of our existence are strewn with them."

Madame de Staël (1766–1817)

On 28th July, 1914, at the outbreak of World War One, Ida was in Switzerland with Romaine Brooks. For Romaine it was an irritating interruption to their trip: "These mass suicides are inevitable since mankind will not practice birth control: the war is an infernal nuisance and it interferes with my work." They packed immediately and returned to Paris.

By 28th August Paris was in danger. She was a different city: streets were deserted, theatres closed, cafés and restaurants all shut before dusk and, as darkness fell, searchlights probed the sky for Zeppelins.

On 29th August guns were heard in the far distance. The Germans were only twenty-five miles away. Amiens, Rheims and Senlis had all been overrun by the enemy.

By 2nd September the government had fled Paris for Bordeaux. Tens of thousands of people, women and children, the sick and the terrified, the old and the panic-stricken, fled from what appeared to be a city in peril of being overrun. Many of Ida's Paris socialite peers decided to take no chances and retired to their houses and estates as far away from the fighting as was possible.

Ida remained. For her it was the opening of another veil; it revealed a deeper, more compassionate side of her character. She threw herself into the war effort, raising money through recitals, starting her own hospital for the wounded (with uniforms designed, of course, by Bakst) and almost totally dropping at a stroke all her plans and designs for new theatrical productions.

It was almost as if she had found herself. The war engaged her with as much energy and passion as she had devoted to the theatre. If she had made herself a legend on the stage then she made herself a saint to those she helped during the hostilities. This was no wealthy socialite paying chequebook service to the war effort; this woman personally nursed the wounded, tended the dying, changed the bandages on putrefying flesh and spent every working moment devoting all her energies to the ghastly mutilations brought into her hospital day after day.

Her devotion to the wounded and the victims of the war lasted throughout the hostilities and for years afterwards. She became actively involved with the Association Générale des Combattants et Mutilés, giving both her time and money, and personally raising funds by giving regular charity performances.

Ida stayed in Paris throughout the war, even when Paris was being bombed. Montesquiou wrote hugely patriotic and emotive war poems under the title of *Offrandes Blessées* which Ida took to countless recitals throughout the city to raise money for the war effort. This proved to be very popular as she gave them not in her jewels and finery and furs of the great dame of the theatre but as a woman at war, dressed in the nurse's uniform designed by Bakst. Bakst also designed the sets and costumes for the fourth act of Racine's *Phèdre* which she mounted at the Opera in the summer of 1917 for a charity to benefit impoverished Russians. It was a huge success. The costumes were splendid and not wasted; she wore them at recitations of Montesquiou's second volume of war poems *Sabliers et Lacrymatoires*, raising more money for the war effort, even though many engagements had to be cancelled or postponed because of the German bombardment of Paris. At the end of the war she was awarded the Légion d'Honneur for her services.

Another who found great motivation during the war was Gabriele d'Annunzio. He added another dimension to his personality by turning from a womanizing, priapic poet into a soldier and patriot. By 1914, watching the events of Europe unfold from his home in Paris, d'Annunzio became convinced that the only future for Italy lay in joining the Allies. He returned home to Italy, touring the country making impassioned speeches in this cause. Italy finally declared war against Germany, one of the major reasons being d'Annunzio's efforts. He immediately joined the forces, fighting with the cavalry, infantry, navy, and finally air service, directing bombing raids and formulating strategies. "War was for d'Annunzio," it was said, "what a lake is to a swan: the setting for his nobility and his beauty."

He wrote several books on the technique of aerial combat, a type of warfare being used for the first time. He was wounded many times, the most severe resulting in the loss of his left eye. He was awarded the Gold Medal for Valour, four silver and two bronze medals and was awarded the status of officer of the Military Order of Bravery.

The most extraordinary part of d'Annunzio's career occurred immediately after the war. The Allies, who had made a secret promise that Italy would be awarded Fiume and Dalmatia as a reward for entering the war, refused to grant Italy the port of Fiume. This infuriated d'Annunzio who would not let it rest there. His fury drove him to an act of out-and-out piracy. In an inspired fit of heroic madness he put himself at the head of a band of volunteer troops which attacked and occupied the city of Fiume. Once there he defied the whole world. He proclaimed a new state with himself as governor. He was to rule for fifteen months until the government of Italy, bound by the Treaty of Rapallo, had to attack the new 'state' by force and drive him out.

D'Annunzio was not punished but retired to his home by Lake Garda as a national hero. His grand gesture had fired the Italian imagination and he was named Prince of Montenevoso in 1924. His reunion with Ida after the war would be a story in itself.

Walter Guinness was also engaged in the forefront of the war. He served as a major with the Suffolk Yeomanry in Gallipoli and Egypt, in constant danger, causing a great deal of anxiety for those he left at home. He later served with the 10th Battalion of the London Regiment, retiring in 1918 as Lieutenant Colonel.

Jean Cocteau threw himself into the war effort in his inimitable way. He joined an ambulance unit, spending much time close to the front lines, in constant danger from shellfire, dressed in an exquisite uniform designed by Poiret. He was adopted as a mascot by a company of Marines in Flanders. Despite appearing a light, dandyish figure, Cocteau showed no fear. He was a brave man and was recommended for the Croix de Guerre. He said simply, for one of the only times in his life: "Either you do your share for your country or you commit suicide. I love life, and prefer to die for her if necessary."

Claude Debussy echoed the despair of war when he asked: "When will we cease to entrust the destiny of nations to men who consider mankind as a stepping stone to success?" By the end of November, after the Battle of the Marne, France had lost five hundred thousand men.

Romaine Brooks painted two of her most famous paintings during this period. Even though the war itself was merely an irritation, an interruption to the flow of art, this waste of time and talent, the obscene slaughter, the tragic carnage had made their mark. The paintings were to become her masterpieces.

She wrote to d'Annunzio:

"During this time of tension there is no doubt that a barbarian world would tear us apart from our familiar surroundings and the aesthetic expressions that were the apex of it. I tried to express that in the painting, who better than Ida Rubinstein with her fragile androgynous beauty could suggest this appearance of familiar Gods?"

"To Romaine, Ida's elusive personality, commanding presence and outrageous style was less seductive than what she personified. She had a kind of ethereal sensuality, as it were, purified of the instinctual, animal and female. She was more or less a woman, as Montesquiou believed, and as d'Annunzio recognised when he cast her in the role of a boy saint. She was the third sex, a creature who had fused the attributes of both sexes into a superbly androgynous whole, and it was as the androgyne that Romaine painted Ida. Ida became Romaine's ideal nude."

Meryle Secrest

The painting of *The Cross* showed Ida as a Red Cross nurse, as the allegorical figure of France against a war-torn landscape. It was published in a newspaper accompanied by a poem by d'Annunzio.

Romaine said: "Ida went to war to recite poems to the soldiers at the front. This painting is a celebration for all the young women who sacrificed their careers, art and time for the battlefield."

Romaine took many photographs of Ida during this period, both naked and in her clothes, because she always had great difficulty in getting Ida to pose for any length of time.

"I wonder if she would have posed more for me if my studio was somewhere else? Ida once told me it was the ideal setting for a suicide. Ida started the sitting in an elated state and then sank into despair. Maybe it was the influence of my studio. Perhaps that is why she didn't like to pose."

The studio was black, white, grey and crystal, with a long terrace covered with white flowers. Perhaps Ida simply couldn't justify the time it took posing.

The Weeping Venus (1916–1917) was Romaine's other masterpiece of the period. She wrote to d'Annunzio:

"I have started a reclining nude with the sky above. This has made me ill because the person who posed let me down after five sittings and I had to continue with several other models. This is a very good painting and I'm sure you will love it. I tried to paint a beautiful woman this time instead of the unhappy beings I normally paint."

In another letter: "I have almost finished the said Venus. I call it the *Sad Dream* and she cries large tears. As soon as it is finished I will photograph it and send you the photograph."

In 1918 it was finished. Romaine was very happy with it: "This is the best thing I have ever done." However, in her autobiography she is not so satisfied and admits to some weaknesses in the painting, particularly in the legs.

"Ida wanted to pose at the beginning but afterwards she became so capricious that I decided to use others. However the face is hers. Each trait is fixed in the spirit and each colour must follow this inner direction. I don't like it too much because the left leg was not finished by the time war broke out. I have never seen legs of such delicacy and magnificence. I finished the legs after the war and when I looked at it I said 'No! No! This is not quite right.' "

Romaine explains the fascination Ida exerted on her during the years of the war. She said Ida embodied the end of the century spirit but: "Ida was very vain: a vanity that never surpassed her beauty. If I remember rightly in these years that we have been friends she has never posed for anyone else except Bakst, who adores her."

In fact Ida posed for artists Antonio de La Gandara, Serov and Jacques-Emile Blanche and for photographers, one of whom was Bert, a fashionably popular photographer at the time. In many of these pictures, equivalent to later pin-ups, Ida adopted sphinx-like poses, enhancing her reputation as a femme fatale.

The Weeping Venus is an exceptional witness to the decadent imagination and was the first sign of symbolism. The black and white colour scheme was Romaine's signature. Natalie Barney wrote a poem of the painting:

> Laid out as dead in the moonlight shroud,
> Beneath a derelict of cloud,
> A double wreckage safe from flight
> High-caged as grief, in prisoned night –
> Unseeing eyes, whose clustering tears
> Tell the pure crystal of her years –
> No crown of thorns, no wounded side,
> Yet as the God-man crucified.
> Her body expiates the sin
> That love and life with her begin.

There is a less flattering description of both the poem and the painting in George Wickes's biography of Natalie Barney, *The Amazon of Letters*:

"Those years might be dated by several works in which Romaine Brooks and Natalie Barney paid tribute to each other. The first is a poem called *The Weeping Venus* which takes its title from a cadaverous nude of Ida Rubinstein which Romaine painted in 1915; to her 'that fragile and androgynous beauty' represented the death of the old gods and the mutilations of the war. Natalie's poem gives the painting another interpretation ending with a characteristic feminist twist."

Montesquiou commissioned Léon Bakst to paint a portrait of Ida during the war years to hang on the walls with the rest of his art collection in his Palais Rose.

Ida wrote to Montesquiou in May 1917:

"The portrait is finished. I think it beautiful. I hope it will please you.

Bakst himself is satisfied with it and told me how happy he is to think it will be in your house. For myself, I have had the joy of posing for you!"

Montesquiou was so delighted he immediately wrote a poem about the painting and sent it to Bakst who replied:

"Dear Master and friend,

I am so happy and proud to receive your remarkable verses inspired by the portrait of Madame Rubinstein! Your friendship and kindly lance broken on my behalf touches me still and I am so pleased to think that my portrait is among your fine collection of art."

While Bakst and Romaine were painting, d'Annunzio fighting and Ida nursing in her hospital, events in Russia would cut off Ida from her childhood and upbringing forever. By 1917 conditions for the Russian people had become unbearable. Hunger had driven them to strikes and riots. They had watched their country being controlled by a weak and ineffective Tsar dominated by his German wife, the Empress Alexandra. She in turn had been extraordinarily influenced by an uneducated and scheming monk, Rasputin, who, to all intents and purposes, controlled Russia and wielded the real power until he was murdered in 1916. Finally, in March 1917, the soldiers in the capital turned against the Tsar and the Cossacks gave their allegiance to the plight of the people.

By 15th March, the Tsar, no longer upheld by his army and the rule of the sword, was forced to renounce his throne. He signed the abdication of his throne in favour of his brother, the Grand Duke Mikhail who, a few days later, also abdicated.

The Tsar and all his family were interned in one of the family palaces which resembled a palace from a fairy tale, in Tsarskoe Selo, a few miles south of Petersburg. While they were there two political exiles returned home to St Petersburg. In an East End church hall in London, fourteen years before, Lenin and Trotsky had split apart the Revolutionary movement. Now they were working together, ensconced in Kschessinskaya's magnificent home.

There sprang up "soviets," groups of workmen and soldiers who were politically much more radical than before. They became the Bolshevik party which grew in power at such a rate that on 7th November they were able to seize government. The "Council of People's Commissars" was established and, at a stroke, Lenin became the most powerful man in Russia. His cabinet included Trotsky and Stalin.

In these early days the government abolished any sort of class privilege and seized the large estates of the nobles for distribution amongst the workers. They separated the Church from the State, seized Church property and took over all transportation, commerce and industry, stating that in the future it belonged to the state and not individuals.

Whilst the revolution spread the Imperial family were moved first two thousand miles away to Tabolsk in Siberia. Eight uncomfortable months later, after increasing pressure from left-wing extremists in the prison guard and much talk about escape plots, the family was suddenly transferred again, to Ekaterinburg in the Ural mountains.

On 30 April 1918, as the closely-guarded train pulled into the station, the Emperor murmured: "I would have gone anywhere but to the Urals. Judging from the local papers the workers there are bitterly hostile to me."

At Ekaterinburg the Romanov family disappeared.

"In Ekaterinburg, the Tsarina marked the date of arrival on the wall by the window of her new room; above the date she pencilled a swastika, which in 1918 was still a symbol of good luck."

There, on the night of July 16th to 17th, the whole family were executed: at a stroke the Romanovs were eliminated.

Poignantly, three days later, on the 20th July, a communist poster appeared.

"The family of Romanov has been taken to another and safer place."

Even though Ida had moved most of her vast wealth and fortune out of Russia before the Revolution, all that remained was lost and she could never safely return.

Although exiled, Ida showed neither the slightest hint of homesickness nor any concern for any of her family who might have remained there. It was as if they never were.

Even the ambition-dictated Diaghilev was very nostalgic for Russia and, as late as 1921, would cross-examine anyone who had just come from there about the revolution.

There is a story about Ida's aunt Lou-Lou, told by Lou-Lou's niece, the delightful Renée de Monbreson. Lou-Lou approached Ida for help after World War II. Lou-Lou was a refugee in France during the Russian Revolution but was taken by the Germans to Auschwitz, because she was Jewish, during World War II. She managed to escape (it is not known how) but lost everything. She was very concerned about the plight of the rest of her family in Russia and wished to send them supplies and food parcels through the Red Cross; having lost everything of her own she decided to approach Ida.

Lou-Lou paid her a visit and was shown into the salon of Ida's sumptuous home by Ida's English butler. Ida arrived after a few minutes and was, as usual, most courteous and charming, though perhaps a little distant, offering her afternoon tea which Lou-Lou declined.

"I am too upset to eat or sleep at the moment," she declared.

Ida looked suitably concerned: "My dear, why? What is the matter? You look most disturbed."

"It is the family in Russia!"

"What family?"

Lou-Lou was shocked. "Why, our family, Ida, of course."

Ida's dark, almond-shaped eyes seemed to glaze over as if a veil had been lowered over them: "My dear Lou-Lou, I hardly know any of them."

Lou-Lou was desperate: her worst doubts were being fulfilled:

"But Ida, I have received news from several of our family who are still there, news which has exposed the terrible condition not only materially but in all manner of ways!"

Although it was very expensive, it would have been possible through many organisations to send parcels of clothing, food and medicines which had to be paid for in dollars or sterling. To Ida the expense would be neither here nor there, but her reaction was total indifference: it was a great shock.

"My poor Aunt Lou-Lou came back indignant and in despair," said Renée de Monbreson.

It seems strange that Ida, the philanthropist who pumped fortunes into helping the poor, the needy and the wounded during both wars, had no interest in helping her relatives. She appears to have been one of those strangely caring people who feel for the plight of the world in general but not for her kith and kin.... Perhaps the treatment she recieved from her sister and her husband on her first visit to Paris, and the way her peers were appalled when she first wanted to appear on stage in Russia, made her deny that side of her life completely.

A footnote to the revolution in Russia is a rather touching postscript to the tale of Matilda Kschessinskaya, the principal ballerina of the Maryinsky Theatre. She was first the Tsar's mistress, then the mistress of the Grand Duke Vladimir and thus one of the most powerful women in Imperial Russia.

Anatole Bourman:

"Favourite of the Tsar, friend of artists and nobles and idol of her audiences, Madame Kschessinskaya remained democratic and unaffected to everyone who knew her, despite the published accounts of her autocratic wielding of heartless power. To be sure, her whims were laws irreversible, and her word, once pronounced, carried little prospect of appeal, which may account adequately for those who failed to penetrate to the selflessness of her character and, in consequence, felt only her tremendous superiority in Kschessinskaya's presence.

"I knew her well, better than most who have written about her, yet I never saw her use her power meanly. On the contrary, I have seen her exert it on more than one occasion to assist unrecognized artists towards success that could hold no personal interest for the grand Kschessinskaya. Talent was bound to call for her generous patronage.

"The only thing I ever heard against her that I credited was a report that she was responsible for the resignation of Prince Volkonsky as a director of the Imperial Russian Theatres. The story goes that Kschessinskaya was told to wear one costume but preferred another which she wore. Her name was posted on the official bulletin the following day, together with the amount of the fine imposed upon her; and on the day following Prince Volkonsky resigned. Rumour had it that Kschessinskaya's influence had reached far and above the head of Prince Volkonsky despite his position as one of Russia's foremost powers, and that he paid for insulting the mighty ballerina before the entire company. Whether or not he, Volkonsky, had proffered his post suddenly, without pressure is one of the mysteries forever buried in the history of Imperial Russia, but it is generally admitted that Kschessinskaya, if she chose, could readily have forced his actions.

"Gold and jewels poured into the Prima Ballerina's overflowing coffers until she was the wealthiest woman in the empire, with gorgeous palaces dotting the countryside: at Streina, in the Crimea, in the Caucasian vastness, to furnish her with sequestered retirement when the vivacity of the capital and life in her white palace on the city's most enviable site finally bored her. Villas in France and Italy were awaiting the mood that sent her dashing across Europe in a private car as often as in a public conveyance. This in the very early 1900s when owning one's own private car was almost as much of a luxury as a private plane is today.

"Her Villa Alan at Cap d'Arle was a centre of gaiety when Monte Carlo offered a setting for her opulence. A few of us were permitted to call her Mala and, occasionally, the most intimate, the diminutive, Mititchka. When Kschessinskaya entertained, roubles were spent by the thousand, and when she gambled she threw her money around like a profligate queen. Monte Carlo acclaimed her as 'Madame Dix-Sept' for seventeen was her number and she played it with splendid abandon.

"Her son Vona was only a few years old when I knew her best and I watched her run to fulfil his slightest wish. He was one of the handsomest boys I have ever seen, the refinement of his features betraying the dominating Russian blood that he might boast. Little lakes were laid out on his mother's estate so that he might ride in swan boats. A miniature railway was constructed in order that he might drive a tiny locomotive…. Rehearsals were abruptly halted by his childish voice commanding 'Mamma! Vona wants a kiss!' Not another step did Kschessinskaya dance until Vona had been kissed!

"In *The Daughters of Pharaoh* she caused a sensation when the tomb of the mummy was opened and revealed the still living daughter of Pharaoh, a daughter ablaze with diamonds from the crown of her exotic

Egyptian headdress to the toes of her dainty sandals, illuminated when her enormous emeralds and rubies sent shafts of colour arching through her scintillating costume.

"That opulent character always astounded her audience, unwilling to credit their eyes, yet unable to doubt that the gems clothing Kschessinskaya were authentic stones, since no paste jewellery could glitter with such power, even under the artful glow of the foot and spotlights. Pearls strung in tiny globes on a metal wire, wrapped her exquisite body in yards of rich lustre....

"In 1922, I met her unexpectedly in Monte Carlo; she burst out: 'Do you know I own nothing more than the clothes on my back. It has made me laugh so often! I was dancing at the Maryinsky, just practising, and all I had with me was my practice suit and my ballet slippers in a little bag. You know how it was during the Revolution... there were no carriages as before. When I finished practising I strolled back to my palace and I couldn't get in for the crowds around it. I spoke to a woman in the crowd, asking: 'What's going on here?'

"The woman looked at me without recognition, for she was poor and I was dressed simply enough. 'Oh, madam, it is nothing exciting,' she said. 'Lenin and Trotsky are holding a meeting in a palace that has just been taken over by the government, and we are waiting to see them: they are such great men.'

"'Such great men!' Kschessinskaya laughed. 'And all my jewels in the safe for Lenin and his Bolsheviks.'

"I opened my lips to sympathise, but her face was wreathed in smiles. 'It was so funny. Imagine losing everything but your ballet slippers and tights. And now? I am a ballet mistress if you please!'

"That woman, once a veritable goddess with unlimited prestige and wealth, devoted to her son and his imperious demands, was the same who stood there stripped of all her wealth. She was a great star and is glorious still."

10

CRACKS IN THE MASK

"We get so much in the habit of wearing disguises before others that we finally appear disguised before our-selves."

François, Duc de La Rochefoucauld (1613–1680)

Immediately after the war Ida began working on her next theatrical production: *Antoine et Cléopâtre*. It was fraught with difficulties and took nearly two years of argument and temperament before it opened on 14th June, 1920.

A few weeks before this most important first night Ida appeared for the last time as Zobeida in *Schéhérazade* with Diaghilev's company at the Opera in a gala in aid of Russian refugees in France. Sadly, Nijinsky was no longer her lover, the Golden Slave, his part being taken by Massine.

The opening night of *Antoine et Cléopâtre* was a spectacular and lengthy affair. It went on and on and it wasn't until nearly two a.m. that Cleopatra at last decided to die. Apart from the length, the play and Ida received good reviews.

"Ida Rubinstein has already gained so many victories for herself and here again she triumphed…. We are indebted to her for an evening of art of the most meritorious kind; she justly deserves a major share of the applause which throughout the evening greeted this very difficult and complex reconstruction of *Antoine et Cléopâtre*."

Le Gaulois

The critics had often complained of the length of productions in the past. Seldom had they sat through anything as long as this. For Ida the whole thing had been quite long enough. It was two years before she staged another major production. She spent much of this period travelling, sometimes with Walter Guinness, more often than not alone except for her retinue of native bearers; always to strange and inaccessible places but with an extravagant wardrobe. "Pyjamas of gold lamé, boleros covered with precious stones, turbans with plumes like those of a sultana, magnificent hunting attire, dainty lingerie."

Marguerite Long

Michel Georges-Michel told how she was travelling alone with her entourage in South Abyssinia when she was seen by the richest planter of the area:

"...Astride the traditional mule and dressed completely in brown buffalo hide, her legs encased in saffron-red boots and her fine fingers twirling above her head a parasol in white Veronese kid. The planter approached and paid his respects. He offered her the hospitality of his house and table. But Madame Rubinstein was faintly amused because she had with her ... on her pack-mules her tents that made into bathrooms, kitchens and reception rooms. She countered by inviting him to dinner.... That evening he was literally stunned when the huntress received him wearing on her head a turban, upon which a diamond brooch sparkled, a low-cut silver lamé gown, on her feet little gold slippers, and dripping with brilliants and precious stones from head to toe."

She visited Djibouti in French Somaliland, Hjin, the Blue Nile, writing letters to Montesquiou from various oases and deserts, describing her adventures and keeping him up to date with her future plans.

She was first to dance in a new ballet at the Opera, *Artémis Troublée*, with Bakst as not only designer, but also librettist. Again Ida herself received very favourable reviews: "An aristocratic goddess, a great lady in disguise... she assumes a series of poses of a precious beauty, rich in pictorial and literary erudition."

"An incomparable mime whose most profoundly original qualities were developing still."

Le Journal

"Her interpretation of the role of Artemis is interesting; one is conscious of all her intelligence in it and applauds her talent."

Charles Bert

"With angular grace, at times of an almost pure sculptural beauty, recalling an Egyptian or neo-Greek fresco."

Jane Catulle-Mendes

Romaine Brooks was probably one of the first to recognize Ida's limitations behind the panoply of her stardom. Although Ida had had successes beyond any dream, they had been in highly stylized performances which required an expert degree of mime and someone strangely beautiful with a charismatic, mesmeric presence; these Ida had in abundance. When Romaine met Ida during the height of the Ballets Russes success, Ida was at her most exquisite. She was ravishing in her extraordinary way. Romaine was as bewitched by her as everyone else had been.

"Ida looked like an heraldic bird, delicately knit together by the finest bone structure. Romaine remembers one white, snowy morning when they walked together around the Longchamps race course. Ida was wearing a long ermine coat which was open to reveal the bare, fragile chest and slender neck rising out of a feather white garment. Her precisely modelled face with its delicate, birdlike nose, its languid oriental eyes and cadaverous skin, her black hair partly veiled. Ida presented a study in black and white, whose overtones of the outspread wing took immediate hold of Romaine's imagination. She was even more beautiful off stage. She was an apparition."

Meryle Secrest

This was Ida's strength, the essence that swept Paris off her feet. But behind the glorious image there were limitations. Even though she had been privately coached by Fokine for specific roles and dances, she had never been trained as a ballerina and, within the broader outlines of the dance, her talents were restricted.

"She had a superb gift as a mime, yet what she really wanted to be was a ballerina. Romaine, full of misgivings, would watch with a frown as this divine creature, inches taller than any other girl in the class, would jump and pirouette while the dancing teacher, not impressed, would talk about the 'plus petite' pupil who was so much more talented."

Meryle Secrest

During the war, Ida had seen much of Sarah Bernhardt, who had encouraged her to star in *La Dame aux Camélias*, one of Bernhardt's greatest triumphs. She had even coached Ida in the part, schooling and directing her and encouraging her, planning to pass on her mantle as Queen of the French Theatre. If Sarah had seen this sort of dramatic talent in Ida, it was lost on Romaine Brooks.

"She would make Romaine listen, listen for hours while she read, with a strong Russian accent, speeches as Sarah might have read them, and then make Romaine choose the pitch; Romaine chose the lower only to be informed by Ida that Sarah preferred the higher."

She had had many comments about her vocal talents during the run of *Le Martyre de St Sébastien*, when Marcel Proust had said of Ida that "everything that is foreign in d'Annunzio took refuge in the accent of Madame Rubinstein." Even one of her greatest admirers, Jean Cocteau, had been forced to admit that "she strikes the ear as a primitive picture strikes the eye."

Indeed, it was Ida's blindness to these limitations that blighted her own performances and jeopardized her productions. Diaghilev, who knew her throughout her working life until his death in 1928, said:

"Ida Rubinstein has lived in Paris almost as long as I have, and she is Russian by birth; these two facts are almost all we have in common. She calls herself an actress and a dancer! I call her merely a beautiful woman, of almost super-intelligence, who has always had a great deal of money with which to indulge her many caprices. The world of art proclaims her a great personality; I do not – she is generous, kind-hearted, when her desires are not interfered with; she is a good friend when one knows how to approach her; otherwise she is cold and calculating. Of her artistic sense there is no question, for while she spends fortunes on a play or ballet, the production is so perfect from an artistic point of view that a certain public put up with her performance – thus her claim to fame is in her theatrical productions which are the most beautiful individual ones in Europe today."

Considering how Diaghilev had been infuriated and exasperated by virtually every move Ida made from the moment she broke away from the Ballets Russes to form her own company, apart from the occasional piece of bile which distorts a true picture of her personality, even he had to admit, albeit grudgingly, praise for her productions, through the lavish amounts spent on them.

Colette felt that Ida's strength lay in her mimed roles and tried to persuade her to concentrate on this side of her talent:

"A mime inhabits your stunning body…. Mime is your empire. Survey it with the calm passion of impassive voluptuousness."

However, from many different sources over the next decade came disturbing reports of how Ida's performance let down her own productions.

Keith Lester described her to the writer in his last interview:

"She was a great patroness of the arts, elegant, charming and distinguished; but as a dancer she was less than effective. Tall, with a lion's tawny mane, aquiline features and faultless taste in clothes, she drew herself up when talking to women but relaxed when talking to men. She wore black on white; black with white pearls and white with black pearls, as the saying went. The port and air of a goddess and, enchantingly, the laugh of a child. The goddess aspect was formidable; all that money to back all that culture. She spoke several languages, as well as the private tongue of commerce. I liked her."

But even liking her, indeed even admiring her as a person, when it came to Ida as a professional dancer he is in no doubt:

"If art is what one makes in God's image, then creating a ballet for Rubinstein must have been a choreographer's purgatory. Certainly she could move, but the principle of ballet is the dancer. In everyday life Rubinstein moved graciously and with some distinction: but in the theatre her presence seemed to regret its intrusion into the unlikely world of movement. On the stage her role was evoked by the poet, her image by a composer and these evocations never integrated into a living personality; there was no individual manifestation.

"It is difficult to fault Rubinstein for being less than what Gide, Valéry and d'Annunzio imagined. Her failure to understand her kind of production, her kind of talent and her own kind of personality led to ballet masters being commissioned to distort her presence publicly. The result was nonsense. The masque, which has so illustrious a history in England, could have served her well, but the word 'ballet' has misled even accomplished choreographers to involve themselves, to their detriment, in the production of displays alien to their talent."

When asked about what he considered makes a dancer, Lester was emphatic. Although Rubinstein was a dancer in that she was trained, she was not what he would term what a dancer is truly to be. In his most determined view, a dancer was one who was born to be a dancer. One who just had to dance, no matter what, and had behaved in this way since childhood. He explained his own case, when as a child he had been called "Mr Arms and Legs" because he wouldn't keep still and was always jumping about. This, he emphasized, is a dancer, "and Ida Rubinstein was not!"

"In her youth she must have had a natural grace of movement that time and tide had eroded; she was a highly educated and intelligent woman but choreographically inept. This can only mean that she was not a dancer, and never had that unbiddable passion to move that is the true cross and paradise of dancers.

"She was brave if deluded, grand if regrettable; and the laugh of a child can make up for many a regret. To face the French public and the critics must have been agony enough; but think of her friends, those ladies who sat in the best seats and sharpened their tongues on the steel of polite dismemberment. Ida's next soirée could have been in the nature of a post-mortem, with the corpse intervening. I liked Rubinstein."

During the writing and preparation of *Le Martyre de St Sébastien* Ida fell in love with Romaine Brooks. This was not what Romaine had in mind at all. Ida wanted to give her life to Romaine completely. She was willing to sacrifice everything on the altar of Romaine's love: her career, her fortune, her house, her past, her future, all to disappear to some little farm deep in the heart of nowhere, so she could spend every breathing minute with Romaine. She would consecrate her life to her, and when Ida decided to consecrate her life, it was virtually impossible to prevent her. When Ida had first decided to go on the stage nothing, not even incarceration in a mental institution, could stop her. Her dedication to her goal was absolute. When both world wars came she again abandoned everything for nursing and helping the wounded, and finally, after the Second World War, after all the loves of her life had gone, she turned all her energies to God, preparing herself for a sort of stardom in the afterlife, training and equipping herself as wholeheartedly as only Ida knew how. She worked as hard preparing herself for sainthood as she had done for her career. She evolved from being a narcissistic zealot to a religious one. To Romaine this passion was daunting. It was this strength of commitment which Romaine found too overbearing: "I can't be loved like that."

Also, Romaine was embarking at this time on her one and only heterosexual love. Romaine, completely out of character, fell in love with Gabriele d'Annunzio. It was an extraordinary triangle. For it was exactly at this time that d'Annunzio was falling for Ida's plastique in the role of St Sebastian. Watching her rehearse as the boy saint "with such a poetic sense of the part's pathos that her admirers were prepared to deify her on the spot." The part of St Sebastian had a great symbolic significance for d'Annunzio, which helped fan the flames of his infatuation. But Ida was besotted with Romaine and, as far as Romaine was concerned, Ida was merely a pawn in the game of love she was playing with d'Annunzio. Poor Romaine was obsessed – her writings at the time are written in blood:

"I think of you all the time, as often as I breathe," Romaine wrote from Italy. "Because I tell myself you have breathed this air and I embrace you in taking it…"

"Dear Gabi, my sadness is endless…. Since one can never be sure of you and doubt makes me hesitate…"

She desired him, head, heart, and body, from the might of his mind to the point of his priapus!

"Gabrielino, I must be in love with you to write to you without reason – I am doing it for the pleasure of giving you the palpable proof of my constant thought. I have lost a pile of money… at the moment; but it does not matter, if I could have you at this moment just to myself, for one night – you say the word – I am mad about you – about your adorable body. I see you in raw detail – completely naked on a bed in the painter's studio. So you realize how much I was in ecstasy before your nudity. I am exalted by you. I am insane about you tonight. Never has a woman appreciated you as much as I. I run from you because I am sincere – because I could not live another minute…"

It was extraordinary that this white-skinned, fleshy, short, balding, almost gnome-like figure could enchant and seduce women almost at will. He had a fascinating and charming mind which he used like a razor to cut through any barriers to his advances. Many of the most desirable women in Europe fell into his bed; once ensnared the majority became his sexual devotees for ever. One who was neither, Liane de Pougy, was one of the most famous and beautiful courtesans of the day. In her memoirs she remembered meeting him:

"I met him in Florence when I was dancing there. It was 1902. Yesterday I came across a book which he gave me then: his *Francesca da Rimini*, bound in parchment tied with green ribbon, and copiously inscribed. I remember, he praised me for my "corporeal grace" – his expression – and invited me to visit his capponcina. I accepted. He sent his carriage for me. It was filled with red roses. It was May 1st, which is the date of the rose festival in Florence. On my arrival I was greeted by workmen and young boys making a hedge between the gate and the front door of the house, all holding handfuls of roses which they threw at my feet. Inside, a poetic decor, rather rubbishy and designed to impress. His conversation was marvellous. But there before me was a frightful gnome with red-rimmed eyes and no eye lashes, no hair, greenish teeth, bad breath, the manners of a mountebank – and a reputation, nevertheless, for being a ladies' man, and a man who was, to say the least, ungrateful to the ladies. I used every possible trick to resist him, and escaped by promising to return. Two days later he sent the same carriage for me. I substituted my maid for myself with a note – a long note – saying: 'Stellio (the name of one of his heroes), that which has not been is still to do… one cannot get used to such happiness all at once.' – Agreeable and uncompromising clichés. He had flown to the door to greet me and recoiled in furious dismay at the sight of my sniffy old Adele. He pulled himself together and showed her the dinner which had been prepared, the table, the lit candles, the path I would have trodden spread with embroidered cherubles and scattered rose petals (from the roses of two days earlier, no doubt). He gave her a folded paper for me containing these words: 'You light candles from afar, as well as nearby. Take care. Stelli….' "

Liane de Pougy was one of the great loves of Natalie Barney, who was the lifelong love of Romaine Brooks, who fell hopelessly in love with d'Annunzio, who was infatuated with Ida, who wanted to give her life to Romaine Brooks, who lived with Natalie Barney, who had a love affair with Liane de Pougy who turned down d'Annunzio, who…. And on and on.

The relationship between Romaine Brooks and d'Annunzio was to be short-lived. It had always been one-sided, Romaine being very much the pursuer. D'Annunzio covered his walls with photographs of women he both loved and admired, with one notable exception: Romaine. "You are not a woman", he jokingly said as his reason. Romaine was deeply hurt.

"If I don't see you before I leave, I believe, dear Gaby, that I shall carry away souvenirs of certain moments of our friendship which will always be sacred to me as precious, sparkling red jewels which I will wrap up in a tiny grass bed like a souvenir that is tinged by a sad perspective of the past.

"Adieu … Adieu? … Do I wake or sleep?"

Romaine returned to her studio and buried herself in her painting. She began a picture called *The Masked Archer*, depicting Ida as St Sebastian, naked, tied to a post, about to be shot by an arrow aimed by d'Annunzio as the masked archer. Perhaps it was a way of venting her feelings, dealing with the pain she had been through, but it was a most effective revenge. In her anger and her hurt she painted the masked archer as a small dwarf in a tasteless, indecorous bizarre costume, standing on a table. Thus she caricatures d'Annunzio, castigating his short body by turning him into a dwarf, mocking his love of clothes by dressing him in an absurdly graceless costume, with his overwhelming passion for glory pilloried.

However, after the hurt died, and the love affair had finally ended, Romaine painted a portrait of d'Annunzio that hangs in the Luxembourg. "His powerfully modelled bare skull and his greenish face like an antique found in the ruins of some ancient city buried by Etna." Despite this portrait they would remain the best of friends until the day he died.

1 Ida Rubinstein as Cleopatra, by Léon Bakst.
By kind permission of Mr and Mrs N. D. Lobanov-Rostovsky

2   Ida Rubinstein as the Blue Sultana in *Schéhérazade*, by Léon Bakst.
By kind permission of Mr and Mrs N. D. Lobanov-Rostovsky

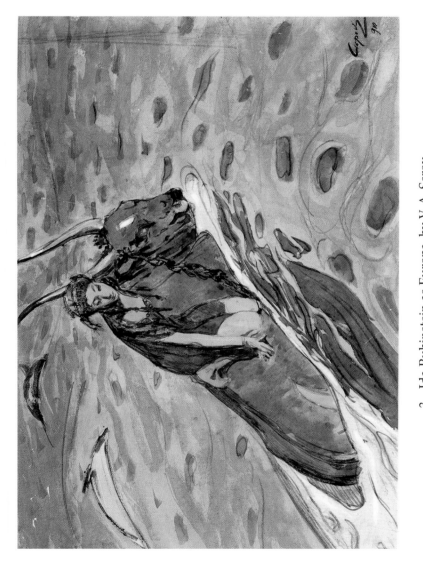

3 Ida Rubinstein as Europa, by V. A. Serov.
By kind permission of Mr and Mrs N. D. Lobanov-Rostovsky

JACQUES-EMILE BLANCHE IDA RUBINSTEIN AS ZOBEIDA IN SCHÉHÉRAZADE, C.1910.

4 Ida Rubinstein in the role of Zobeida in *Schéhérazade*, Paris 1910, sketch in oils by Jacques-Emile Blanche.

By kind permission of Mr and Mrs N. D. Lobanov-Rostovsky

11

MILAN

"Whoever makes two blades of grass to grow where only one grew before renders service to the state."

Voltaire (1694–1778)

Ida did not meet Gabriele d'Annunzio again for many years, even though they kept in constant contact by letter. When they finally met it was a momentous occasion. Ida was going to revive *Le Martyre de St Sébastien* and bring it back to La Scala, Milan, as part of a short tour of Italy in March 1926. Gabriele d'Annunzio was going to emerge from exile on his country estate and appear at the first night. It was marvellous publicity and the public were enthralled.

There is an excellent eyewitness account of the momentous production from one of the dancers in the show. The account also shows the escalating worries about Ida's capabilities. She was beginning to get the most terrible stagefright, far worse than in the past. It is an extraordinary description:

"How the six or eight weeks which preceded the 'little tour' of Italy (Milan and Rome) raced by, I know very little, because I was living in a turmoil, an unbroken series of meetings, practices, rehearsals, sometimes at the Place des Etats-Unis for intimate scenes, sometimes on the stage of the Vieux-Colombier Theatre for the bigger scenes....

"Moreover, I was thrown amongst about twenty actors and actresses of different ages who were rather slow to accept me. Firstly I did not know them, and secondly they looked upon me as Madame Rubinstein's favourite and so they handled me with care and before me, above all, they held their tongues. I had great difficulty in making them believe that I was one of them, not receiving any special privileges, and was less the 'gentleman' than a down-to-earth person the same as themselves.

"I thought, all the same, the last rehearsals allowed them to judge how little intimacy there was between Madame Rubinstein and I. It was not until this last Parisian show was about to depart that she came to mingle with the company. Her reserve and her timidity had not left her. How much her pride added to it, I do not know and was never able to discover. But I am convinced that, at home, day and night, she worked on the scripts unremittingly.

"Milan. La Scala. In three days the 'Premiere' of *Le Martyre de St Sébastien*. It would be a sensational premiere. Gabriele d'Annunzio, the celebrated author of this Christian mystery play, who, brought back after several years of voluntary exile on his estate on Lake Garda, after his stormy postwar Nationalistic political activities, would be reappearing in public that evening, for the first time.

"Everywhere, in all classes of society, there was intense curiosity. The piece, in fact, had been written some fifteen years before, by this celebrated Italian for the beautiful Russian... and the legend made into a love story. They wanted to meet face to face, she on the stage, he in his official box. The theatre had been fully booked for quite some time, everyone wanted very much to witness this meeting, certainly more than the martyrdom of poor Sebastian.

"Those three days of final preparation are forever engraved on my soul because if everyone in the city was just waiting for d'Annunzio, we already had with us the no less celebrated and formidable Toscanini, who directed the airy and heartrending music which Debussy had composed to accompany and surround this tragedy of the Faith.

"In this show...I had the luck to witness the extraordinary work of an absolutely captivating conductor, managing at one time the orchestra, the actors, and even the electricians and stagehands, let alone the director and Madame Rubinstein! There, with no refusal permitted, he directed her unceasingly, obliging her to place herself in the required positions, to speak more loudly, to play her part properly, and she accepted it all! She, the eyes and ears of everything, adapted to his style, lost her temper, then burst out laughing. Then he, with a little joke, eased the tension, because he loved her style. For her, all this made no difference and nothing caused her to hold a grudge against his kicks and gibes.

"In the spare moments I, myself, went to look – and to admire – everything, the auditorium, a marvellous masterpiece of the 18th century, with its numerous boxes of gilded wood, but of an elegant simplicity. Then, on the stage, the display of scenery by Bakst, which I examined closely in order to study the style, at the same time strange yet classical, and thoroughly with the drama. Were it not for what followed – and what I feared – some days later (at the Manzoni Theatre, where we were waiting for *La Dame aux Camélias* and *L'Idiot*) I would have wallowed in happiness.

"And then, the work began again, more intense every day, and Ida Rubinstein spared herself no less effort than the rest of us, in spite of all the costs which were down to her. But her 'real' Martyrdom however awaited her later on – but not much later – tomorrow at the Premiere!

"On that first night at the exact time, we were ready, in costume (I played Sebastian's Captain of Archers) on the stage of La Scala, listening to the distant murmur from the auditorium through the thick stage curtain. Bringing up the rear Madame Rubinstein appeared as Sebastian and went to take up her position two paces from a group of archers, just in front of me.

"This was the climax for all of us. Everyone alike, teeth gritted in concentration for her, bowing before the absolute beauty of this apparition. Ida Rubinstein was evidently born for this role which d'Annunzio had so cleverly foreseen. She appeared to have descended from a primitive fresco, her tall silhouette, her slender hips, her broad shoulders and her clearly defined clean-cut features, which, for the French in particular, served her, here, marvellously … and her armour, designed by Bakst, with its black and gold damascening, the lofty visored helmet on her pageboy hairstyle, did not make her a travesty as a female playing a male role, but truly one of those adolescents, a little ethereal, destined for the life of an archangel.

"The bright signal shone, the steady lightning flashed, we knew that this was the time, as each of us took our exact place around the red hot embers of the big brazier. Beyond the curtains we were aware of distant murmurings in the auditorium and also the last checks of the instrumentalists. Solemnly, three strokes of the gong resounded. Toscanini struck up the first harmony of Debussy. Sweetly, the incantations rose, and I listened, moved by the marvellous music, so splendidly conducted, my eyes staring firmly into the distance, into the emptiness. But all at once, in the emptiness, I saw something tremble, yes, and this something was the point of Sebastian's bow! The bow itself trembled, the hand which held it, and all that radiantly beautiful silhouette trembled. How I pitied her! This woman, whose name the newspapers had printed a thousand times in all sizes of print, this name which was spread over everything since Paris, on our railway carriage, on our luggage, and here on every wall in the city. This woman that fifteen hundred people were feverishly anticipating on the other side of the curtain, this poor woman, so extravagantly rich, was afraid … extravagantly afraid.

"Did she feel, at that moment, my sympathy? I have no reason to doubt it because without relinquishing the priestly pose, she slowly turned her young warrior's profile towards me, and said to me quietly and intensely 'But … why am I an actress?' Startled at first I hastened to give her some sort of reply. 'Be brave … this is so beautiful!' Hoping to inspire her. Hoping to inspire in her the love of beautiful things which she certainly had. (Hadn't she, on the only poster for this evening, been able to gather together the names of d'Annunzio, Debussy, Bakst and Toscanini?)

"Next, slowly, very bravely, the heavy curtain was opened. The auditorium was in a dim light, high and low from floor to ceiling it seemed scattered with stars. I have never, in my life, seen or dreamt of such a blaze of stars.

"All La Scala's splendid boxes sparkled with thousands of diamonds which, for this evening, had been taken out of their strongboxes and jewel-cases, in honour of 'Ida and Gabriele.' Ostentatious luxury, very childish, I said to myself. But next, little by little were all carried away by the divine music. I hoped, with all my heart, that Ida Rubinstein would find comfort and spirit in it.

"The show – very much on time – went on as far as the last interval – with great success. But something was missing: d'Annunzio. The evening waited for him. He was there, we knew that, but where? Was he waiting for some grand effect – some cue from the Almighty?

"In reality he was calculating things in a masterly style. Concealed until then, it was during this last interval that he suddenly appeared in his official stage box, just at the last call when the chandeliers in the auditorium were about to be dimmed. It had all the splendour of truly great evenings. The applause was unprecedented, interminable. This last interval was his very own, his show, his triumph!

"When we got back on stage from behind the curtain we could hear the voice of Gabriele d'Annunzio, an actor's voice, of extraordinary skill and richness which he could use to cheer any heart. For so many months, years even, he had renounced the pleasure of public speaking, denying himself this intoxication, which he put over without any trouble like a great actor, as this high-class audience recognized. What did he say? We know nothing of him, we the French in the show, but the reactions of the unseen audience and the stage technicians were sufficiently moving that the temperature rose. They were electrified! He lost himself in an endless discourse, where his poetic flights of fancy were mixed with direct political declarations.

"Now, at the same time as the rest of us, 'Sebastian' (Ida Rubinstein) had arrived on stage for her approaching death, not on her feet, like us, but carried on an ordinary cane-bottom chair. Why? A celebrated, and very beautiful drawing by Bakst explained it: here one sees Sebastian tightly bound hand and foot, wrapped in a thousand bonds, flattened against the twisted trunk of an old olive tree, with his body transfixed by a large number of arrows. To bring this about, Sebastian was wrapped up in advance, in the dressing room, arms, hands and legs tightly confined, and carried on stage, where, with one or two twists of cord, she is quickly and rapidly tied to the tree.

"It is then in this way that we see her enter, bound and carried on her chair in the middle of the political discourse of her dear poet! Surrounded by her little court, dressmaker, hair-dresser, make-up artist, secretary, Ida the beautiful began to smile at the tempestuous spirit of the improvised speech, and the no less passionate reactions of some of his public. Everybody seemed to have totally forgotten Sebastian and his imminent pathetic end, just as much as his interpreter.

"Poor thing. D'Annunzio talked on and on. Visibly everyone was suffering with her, but she mostly with her physical discomfort. She looked like a chrysalis bent in three … and the speech continued … she was very dignified, yet she said nothing, but her features were twitching. Her close associates leant over her, supporting her to the right and left to allow her to avoid the hard bars of her chair. The Shadow, looking everywhere, held a glass of fresh water to her lips. The duty physician, a few steps away, did not take his eyes off her. The director of the Scala, nervous but restrained, asked her what to do, looking for advice in her expression. But Ida's eyes were tight shut. She did not have the capability, first in her bonds, to shrug her shoulders, much less to wring her hands!

"It was then that, in a diabolical fury, Toscanini burst abruptly into the scene, baton in hand, hair bristling. 'That's enough, that's enough! Silence! Is it forgotten that this is La Scala and not the Chamber of Deputies. We have nothing to do with these political hobby horses. Silence! Mr Director, clear the room and I will begin. Otherwise, I warn you, it is I myself that will go!' With that he stormed out and was gone. The director hesitated, looked at Rubinstein again, but from her no reaction at all. She had her eyes closed in disbelief. The director made up his mind – he lowered the house lights.

"At a stroke, dead silence. We realized that the auditorium had been abruptly plunged into darkness. Amazement everywhere … then we heard: 'Lights! lights! lights!' from all sides. But the director was determined. D'Annunzio as well: as if nothing had happened, in the total darkness … the indomitable and humorous orator took up his speech where he had left off and once again got into his rhythm, and did not let go until he was good and ready, in a dazzling finale and a 'delirium' of applause. When, little by little, the exuberance was calmed, one heard the voice of the poet ring out pleasantly: 'Lights, if you please.'

"But all of us, who could see nothing behind the great curtain, were asking ourselves: 'And Toscanini … has he gone?' No! May the God of Sebastian be praised, we heard the first harmonies of the prelude, and quickly, everyone resumed his place. Poor Ida on her chair was raised, totally immobilized and already half dead. But the first bars of Debussy seemed to revive her. She was swiftly carried to the foot of the old olive tree, set up against the trunk, and lassoed with a cord tightly to it. Abandoned to her martyr's fate just a few seconds before the curtain was to rise.

"So she went to her death, tranquil under our arrows, whilst the tunes of the musical grand finale rang out before the golden gates of Paradise. As clouds of incense wreathed Sebastian as he was laid beneath his shroud, surrounded by the squad of archers, waiting for his blessed resurrection. Kneeling on the ground we surrounded him, all listening to the pageboys' 'Hallelujahs' in which the orchestra joined with the massed choirs, invisible, at the back of the stage. I sensed, under the impassive mask of death, the final peace recovered by that terrified woman who had not been able to hold back the cry 'Why am I an actress?'

"As the applause mounted at the final curtain and cries of 'Encore' rang through the theatre on a stage bestrewn with flowers perhaps she had her answer. Ida Rubinstein stepped forward looked up at the box where d'Annunzio was standing applauding and their eyes met. Their faces wreathed in smiles of joy as the applause seemed to go on forever."

Ida's evening was crowned when a note arrived from d'Annunzio; "Little sister, this evening you have again surpassed yourself. You were more beautiful than ever, more melodious, more ardent. I am going, with my heart beating in time with yours, to the great Toscanini's house. Rest peacefully, sleep soundly in the arms of poetry."

It was one of the few moments of triumph, echoes of Cleopatra and Zobeida, that Ida enjoyed during those intervening years. Time had taken its toll. Ida was now forty-one, "the beautiful tulip, insolent and dazzling" was no longer the fabulous flower that Léon Bakst described. Bakst had died: her most loyal and fervent admirer, her "cavaliere servente" and designer of genius had passed away. He died alone, in a clinic at Rueil-Malmaison, a few miles outside Paris, of what was medically described as kidney failure inducing pneumonia.

He had been a sick man for quite some time. Not only physically, but morally and mentally, he had been very low. The strain of overwork and nervous tension had taken an alarming toll. One day after climbing up to the property rooms at the top of the Opera he had a breakdown.

"He suddenly lashed himself into a state of great excitement, without any justification, and, bursting into wild and abrasive shrieks, he ran out of the theatre… from that day none of his friends saw him again."

Prince Peter Lieven

He was taken to the clinic at Rueil-Malmaison where he died on 27th December 1924. Ida was abroad on one of her travels; Benois was back in Leningrad; Bakst's former wife was in Italy; Nijinsky was deteriorating into the darkness of his schizophrenia; Diaghilev was in London with his Ballets Russes season at the Coliseum.

When rehearsals were interrupted and he was informed of his friend's death, Diaghilev rushed from the theatre in uncontrollable tears. Even though in his final years Bakst had had long periods of depression and isolation, between these periods he still had a considerable charm.

"Everyone who saw Bakst will agree with me that he was a man with great charm, but the Bakst of 'those early days' was quite exceptionally delightful. Later, when he was at the height of fame, it was difficult to imagine how modest and shy he had been as a young fellow. His near-sighted eyes and very fair lashes, his sibilant voice and slight lisp, imparted something half comical and touching to his personality...."

Alexandre Benois

As Diaghilev said: "He infused the theatre and our lives with new spirit."

He was not the only one of Ida's immediate circle of admirers who had died. Another of her 'cavalieri serventi', Robert de Montesquiou, made his last public appearance in December 1920 at the baptism of his great-niece Consande. "Are you the father of the child?" asked the verger. "Certainly not!" cried the Count indignantly, muttering "What a jazz-band baptism!"

Montesquiou retired to Dr Couchaud's clinic at St Cloud with nephritis. He emerged for his last amiable correspondence with Proust and then, as summer ended, paced the Palais Rose taking his own blood pressure and reading in it his death warrant. "Shall I send for Dr Robin?" asked the faithful Henri Pinard. "What do you suppose Robin could do for me now?" replied the Count. "No, send for nobody, I'll die alone." He fled to the mimosas of Menton where Henri brought him *Élus et Appelés* fresh from the printer saying: "Look, here is your newly born!" He died on 11 December 1921. A few loyal friends – Dr Couchaud who made a speech; Mme Delarue-Mardrus who recited a poem; Ida Rubinstein who dissolved in tears; Mlle Breslau the painter; Elisabeth de Gramont and Coco de Madrago – attended his funeral on the 21st.

He was buried in the Cimetière des Gonards at Versailles beneath the statue of the Angel of Silence whose finger is ever on its lips. His volume of essays, *Élus et Appelés*, was dedicated to Ida Rubinstein.

Losing friends from within her close circle left Ida devastated. An intrinsically private woman, her true friends were very few. She took her grief into herself and either disappeared for months at a time on her travels or threw herself into more and more lavish theatrical productions.

During this time, in March 1923, Sarah Bernhardt died. During the last years of her life she had taken Ida under her wing, spending hours training her in the dramatic roles in which she had excelled. She was preparing Ida to take over her mantle as first lady of the theatre. It was a strange friendship because they were so different, Bernhardt the extravagant extrovert and Rubinstein the reserved introvert, but friends they became, and Bernhardt obviously saw in Ida some divine spark to keep the candle of her legacy to the theatre alight.

Sarah decided, at the age of seventy, to have her leg amputated after years of pain. Towards the end she could not even stand without leaning on something to take the weight. On 22nd February 1915 she had the operation. Ida paid all her clinical and surgical expenses and visited her often during her convalescence. Soon they were planning Sarah's return to the theatre. She was already thinking of playing *La Princesse Lointaine* with Ida Rubinstein as Geoffrey Rudel.

When her wound was healed Sarah flatly refused to wear an artificial leg. She would not be seen with a terrible limp. She would appear with her one leg, leaning on furniture, actors and pieces of scenery: hadn't she had to learn to lean for years before the leg was amputated? She soon became a familiar figure being carried in her special chair made of white wood and cane, which was narrow enough to slide into a car or lift.

By October she was preparing matinées for charity for the troops. In the spring of 1916 she was carried round the front performing for the army theatre. Sarah Bernhardt was back. As she said: "I often think about death, but only to assure myself that I shall not die until I am ready." She was not ready yet.

Under Sarah's tutelage Ida became most competent in the role of Marguerite Gautier in *La Dame aux Camélias*. It was very different from Sarah's rendering but most effective in Ida's individual style. Over a period of two years, Ida gave over fifty performances in the role.

Sarah worked unstintingly to the end, travelling to America, London and extensively in Europe. It was an exhausting schedule. Much of the last months of her life were spent in her villa at Andemos, in the valley of Arachan, only half an hour away from the villa where Gabriele d'Annunzio was living. He would visit her sometimes. One day, on his return from one of those touching visits, he said: "She is truly wonderful. Think of that woman, old, ill, finished, having but one leg on which to stand, paying the debts of her family; that incomparable artiste, still acting, leaning on chairs, tables and other actors, with one desperate desire (she has confessed to me): that of dying some night on stage in the course of a final triumph. What a St Sebastian she would have created when she was twenty-four" (Tom Antongini).

She almost had her wish, collapsing on the set while playing the fortune teller during the filming of *Le Voyage* on 15th March 1923. By 20th March doctors declared there was no hope. The press and photographers began to congregate outside her home, waiting night and day. But she hung on. On 24th March she said to her son: "How slow death is coming. It is springtime, I would like to have a wealth of flowers."

On 25th March she spoke her last words with a smile. She had asked if there were any journalists outside. When given the answer she said: "The press has tormented me enough all my life. I can certainly plague it a little by making it kick its heels now."

She shut her eyes and went into a coma. At half past three on the afternoon of 26th March she received extreme unction and at half past eight she died.

She had her wealth of flowers. Her pillow and bed were surrounded and covered by roses and white and purple lilacs, forget-me-nots and parma violets.

The thousands of people who came to see her walked through a house packed with garlands of flowers. She was dressed in white satin, on her breast the insignia of the Légion d'Honneur, round her neck a gold locket with a picture of her son and a lock of his hair and in her hands a crucifix of ebony and gold. She was buried on Maundy Thursday 1923, with the whole of Paris out on the streets to mourn her passing.

12

LA DAME AUX CAMÉLIAS

> "There is no trade in the world so toilsome as that of pursuing fame. Life is over before the main part of your work has begun."
>
> *La Bruyère* (1645–1696)

Ida Rubinstein, plunged in grief, isolated herself in her home at the Place des Etats-Unis. There she hid, distancing herself from the outside world, mourning yet another friend who had believed and trusted in her talents. It was an aching void which she could only fill with work. She worked out every day in the studio she had especially designed in her house, complete with a raked floor in the traditional manner of the theatre. It was a large, high-ceilinged room which occupied the whole of the ground level, decorated in white and blue with a whitewood floor.

Here she rehearsed classical dances for two or three hours every morning to keep herself fit and prepared. Her isolation, with all its pain, was cocooned in luxury: to Ida mere normality, to average mortals extraordinary.

Léon Bakst had designed her house for her. Its sumptuous and lavish furnishings were straight from a Tolstoy romance. The library was full of the rarest books, first editions, bound in silk and leather. Priceless paintings hung on walls draped with Genoan velvet upon which violet-coloured foliage stood out from a fine golden lattice. Russian-style sofas covered in the same fabric, exotic rugs, and large palm trees rising to the ceiling: it was a place for a Cleopatra to meditate.

When Keith Lester rehearsed privately in her house he was given a room in which to change:

"Around the walls, at the middle and upper levels were shelves in which were drawn up a legion of shiny cardboard boxes of oval shape. After a few days I could resist the temptation no longer: I mounted a chair and had a look into one of them. It contained a pair of shoes, a hat and a pair of gloves all to match. I peered in expectant amazement at several others, their contents were the same. I was astounded and slightly repulsed. It seemed too much; it set her apart from dancers and dance.

"The gossips of society said that, like Josephine de Beauharnais, she never wore the same lingerie twice, even though it was exquisitely designed for her and hand-embroidered in an Italian convent. The convent was employed constantly to maintain a supply of these marvels. Rumour had it that in *Cléopâtre* at the Opera she wore, for a few minutes, a royal mantle of Egyptian design which had taken a year to make and cost over a million francs. Even if these rumours were exaggerated the truth was even more high-flown.

"The dream-built garden was also designed by Bakst, the flower beds designed so that the flowers could be changed to complement the clothes she decided to wear.

"The vast greenhouses were filled with flowers of many different hues to match the myriad dresses she would wear to her summer evening garden parties. These dresses, again designed by Bakst, caused many problems for the gardeners, for each time more lavish gowns were added to her collection, so the choice of coloured flowers had to be more varied in the greenhouses."

Fernand Nozière described the scene:

"The paths of the little garden are of blue mosaic. There is a fountain. There is a pergola. Suddenly, there are only mauve hyacinths, then red azaleas, then the uniform whiteness of lilies. Rapid transformations, total, magical! Ida Rubinstein, whose dresses harmonize with these efflorescences, passes by, mysterious – and smiles."

Here she continued to work on *La Dame aux Camélias*, building on the tuition given to her by Sarah Bernhardt, remembering the hours she had spent in Sarah's flat, which was "a kind of Victorian translation of *One Thousand and One Nights*; velour hangings, deep ottomans, gazelle horns, Persian carpets, canopies and innumerable cushions."

Determined to fulfil Sarah's legacy and present *La Dame aux Camélias* to the public once again, she gave her first performance at a gala at the Théâtre Sarah Bernhardt on 27th November 1923. Paris society came in droves and the proceeds all went to the war-wounded. The crowds of fashionably dressed people who attended the gala made it a huge social occasion, like a gala dinner at a casino on the Riviera or the elegance of a party in Biarritz.

With reservations, it was a success. It was magnificent to look at, the staging, decor and Benois's designs were sumptuous and luxurious in the grand manner; gilt furniture and marble, ormolu and alabaster, velvets and embroidered hangings gave the impression of some ancient grandeur, a stately flourish of "Second Empire" charm.

Into the sets Ida sailed like a queen. The four or five costumes which she wore as Marguerite Gautier during the course of the play emblazoned each entrance. Each one harmonized with colours of the sets in each act. The crinoline and silver lace costume she wore for her first entrance belonged to the Empress Eugénie. Then there were the incredible jewels that accompanied the costumes, a regal necklace of huge diamonds and rubies with bracelets to match, not theatrical paste, but real diamonds, real rubies, dazzling and dancing in the light.

The problem was that the play itself had dated; the overt sentimentality of the love story could no longer be taken with the same seriousness as when it was first performed. The picture of Marguerite Gautier, the melancholic tubercular child with the beautiful face framed with brown curls with her look of such sweet sadness, melted everyone's heart who set eyes on her. It was everyone's dream of great love. She embodied what Balzac described as the "Splendeurs et Misères des Courtisanes."

Originally the play had been considered a masterpiece, now it was not even considered to be Alexandre Dumas' best work. Bakst was delighted to see that Ida "does not die like a little slut; she dies like a princess."

It also required a twenty year old to play the part with a huge emotional range of passion and ardour. It would take an exceedingly accomplished actress to weave the magic: to play a beautiful young girl of twenty when she was almost twice that age. Sarah Bernhardt had done it but she was the supreme actress of her generation; Bernhardt had been able to play Hamlet when she was over sixty and with only one leg. At the age of sixty-five, Sarah did not hesitate to take the part of Joan of Arc. The climax of the play did not come when Joan was condemned to death and burned at the stake, but when she was taken before her judges and asked: "What is your name?"

"Joan."

"What is your age?"

"Nineteen."

The audience gasped, not from disbelief but sheer wonder and admiration. Then a moment's silence and spontaneous loud applause. However well Ida had been schooled she was not, by any stretch of the imagination, Sarah Bernhardt.

Ida gave a modulated, controlled performance. Her splendid voice, which Keith Lester described as "full, stereophonic, tinged with Victoria plums", was tempered carefully and when she was required to show any emotion it was equally modified and tempered in its passion. She had dignity and a sense of period and moved beautifully. It was successful enough for her to give another fifty performances over the the next two years. The definitive success of Sarah Bernhardt in the part invited inevitable comparisons. Ida emerged relatively unscathed.

One person who saw her in *La Dame aux Camélias* was Romaine Brooks, who had been driven to distraction years earlier listening to Ida going through her lines after her lessons with Bernhardt. Romaine must have known the play by heart, and the last thing she could have wanted was to hear Ida "with her strong Russian accent" go through the part again, but she remained a close friend.

Ida spent much of her time with Romaine and Natalie Barney and was often at their soirées. She was probably closer to them than to any other single person. The soirées at their house had become more and more famous, or infamous, over the years. They attracted a large crowd of artists, intellectuals and talented women, united mainly through lesbianism.

Years earlier Colette had been invited to perform at one of Natalie's garden fêtes in Neuilly: "Willy (Colette's husband) was kind enough to lend me Colette who was to recite Pierre Louÿs's *Dialogue au Soleil*. At the end the audience's attention was distracted by a spectacular apparition: a naked lady riding a white horse with a turquoise harness appeared through the shrubbery. It was Mata Hari."

A later party, Natalie continued, "was planned for a more restricted gathering… when I arrived at their house to invite Colette to this little fête I was giving at my property in Neuilly, a rather hastily organised one at which Mata Hari had promised to give an encore performance of her Javanese dances in the all-together before a limited audience of women only, Willy took umbrage at being excluded and refused to give his consent without setting certain scabrous conditions. On the way Colette confided in me: 'I'm ashamed you were given such a close look at my chains.' "

Colette's relationship with her husband was eccentric to say the least. As far back as 1907, she was not only having an affair with Missy, the Marquise de Morny, but was flaunting it on stage, appearing in a piece specially written by Missy, called *Le Rêve d'Egypte*. Michèle Sarde describes the first night in her biography of Colette:

"The first performance was scheduled for January 3rd…. Willy planned to be there in a stage box alongside his new companion, Meg Villars. The performance began. At the moment when Colette and Missy were to exchange a long rapturous kiss on stage – a kiss that was obviously not simulated – the audience … began to shout protests and to boo. Willy then stood up in his stage box and began to applaud ostentatiously. The public fury was thereupon diverted to the complacent husband who was forced to depart in a roar of booing."

"It is almost impossible to describe to respectable readers," Felisien wrote in *L'Éclair de Montpellier* on 7 January 1907, "the revolting scandal created by the comportment of Mme La Marquise de Morny dressed as a man, and Mme Colette Willy, in her husband's presence, a scene so

repugnant that the audience was forced to intervene and demand order...
M. Willy, the husband, was so amused and complacent at a spectacle that
could just as well have been a production of scenes from the private life
of the three persons involved and it presented a spectacle of such
audacious immodesty that the entire audience rose up against them!"

Colette wrote about these later gatherings at Natalie's as these
"cultural interminglings"; "terminatriums devoted to curaçao over ice,
café cognac, multi-volume novels and the drama, beneath which lay
another much more subterranean, much more literary kinship".

The kinship however was hardly subterranean; it was entirely free and
open. Natalie Barney, "the wild girl from Cincinatti", with "her feminine
figure, golden hair, pastel coloured skin", was a writer and a poet. The
courtesan Liane de Pougy, for a long time Natalie's lover, wrote with
carefree abandon a whole series of novels about Sapphism and her affair
with Natalie. When Liane de Pougy went to confession it was said she
finished by saying: "Father, except for murder and robbery I've done
everything."

The soirées were famous throughout Paris. They attracted a freedom-
loving and passionate group of women of all kinds, along with many
men. In his secret journal Montesquiou noted a remark made by one of
the inner circle: "People call it unnatural; all I can say is, it's always come
naturally to me!"

Journalists were always trying to interview Natalie about her life and
her soirées, but Natalie had a delightful way of turning them down by
saying simply: "You must forgive me if I refuse to disappoint you."

Natalie and Romaine had many separate affairs but had worked out a
lifestyle together which suited them both. In Natalie's pavilion at Neuilly
they had a self-contained apartment with a separate entrance. Her
philosophy was that to sustain a living-together relationship she had to
maintain a physical distance. They had a common meeting room and
loggia spanning separate quarters and individual front doors.

"For me to live alone as my own master is essential, not for egotistical
reasons or lack of love, but in order that I can bathe in passionate intimacy
on a daily basis whenever I wish, whereas living together in the same
house, and often the same bedroom, with the loved one has always
seemed to me the most certain way to lose somebody."

Natalie wasn't the proudest of housekeepers. When someone pointed
out that her house was dusty, she replied: "But the dust is pretty; it's
furniture's face powder!"

The arrangement obviously worked well for both; they remained
together for over forty years.

The list of the famous who visited Natalie and Romaine is endless.

Amongst them were: Dolly Wilde (Oscar Wilde's sister); Gertrude Stein; Alice B. Toklas; the Duchesse de Clermont-Tonnerre; Radclyffe Hall and Comtesse Anna de Noailles.

Amongst the many with whom Natalie had affairs were: Liane de Pougy, who remained a great friend for the rest of her life; Dorothy Strachey (Lytton Strachey's sister); Isadora Duncan; Una, Lady Troubridge; Edith Sitwell; Djuna Barnes; Emma Calve; Renée Vivien, the poet who died an anorexic alcoholic in her twenties; and Vita Sackville-West, the English writer and one-time lover of Virginia Woolf.

The men who visited them during these years included Ezra Pound, Ernest Hemingway, Thornton Wilder, Truman Capote, Ford Madox Ford, Paul Valéry, George Antheil, James Joyce, Somerset Maugham and Marcel Proust, who only visited once at midnight and bored his hostess.

Natalie continued her Friday salon, which had lasted throughout the 1920s and 1930s, after the Second World War. She held her last salon in May 1968 when student riots were turning Paris into chaos. She was ninety-one. Jean Chalon, a young writer who was there, remembers "the corks popped, keeping time with explosions in the streets."

Ezra Pound, in *The Egoist*, classed Natalie as one of those people who get a great deal out of life, "perhaps more than was in it!"

13

NIJINSKY

"The evening of life comes bearing its own lamp!"
Joseph Fourbert (1754–1824)

There were two men, Diaghilev and Nijinsky, who, alongside Ida during the height of her fame, enjoyed the same heady triumphs of those first two Ballets Russes seasons, becoming as famous as she during those years before the First World War. They, however, sustained their fame to become legends in the history of the ballet, while Ida virtually disappeared.

Yet Nijinsky and Ida both spent the latter part of their lives in obscurity. Ida's career lasted longer than Nijinsky's which, in its own way, did her more lasting harm.

Death relieved each of them of their solitary and sad existence. Nijinsky had been sentenced to the solitary confinement prescribed for advanced and chronic schizophrenia, unable to respond to or appreciate the love and loyalty of his wife and friends.

Rubinstein, in spite of her substantial wealth and the long-standing friendships and loyalties which she seemed to inspire in people, was sentenced to a reclusive and barren existence of anorexic guilt and fanatic religiosity.

Vaslav Nijinsky was the most famous dancer of his (or any other) generation and his legend is still the yardstick against which other dancers are measured. Through him, sensuality and dance became entwined.

He was born in Kiev in 1889, growing to only 5ft. 4ins. Both his parents were dancers. He was the middle child of three with a younger sister, Bronislava, also a famous dancer and choreographer, and an older brother who had been put into a mental hospital.

As a child he entered the St Petersburg Ballet school in 1898. (The Maryinsky Theatre School was the Imperial Ballet School, affiliated to the Maryinsky Theatre.) There he trained until he was eighteen, graduating with great honours, having been hailed from the beginning of his time there as a child prodigy. He was not an academic, was rather remote and, as a child at the school, had very few friends.

Nijinsky was very much Diaghilev's personal property when first brought to Paris with the Ballets Russes. The company attracted homosexuals of all types and with Diaghilev as leader, backstage became a hotbed of affairs and gossip. Nijinsky, as Stravinsky said, was a weak man, as weak as his muscles were strong, and he became Trilby to Diaghilev's Svengali.

When Nijinsky created his sensation at the climax of *L'Après-Midi d'un Faune*, Stravinsky said "Of course he made love only to the nymph's scarf; what more would Diaghilev have allowed?"

Diaghilev's misogyny was notorious and his jealous passions legendary. He was powerful, plump, thirty-seven and obsessive over the lithe, muscular nineteen-year-old Nijinsky. Many of the other males in the company found the young Nijinsky unbearably attractive, amongst them Jean Cocteau:

"And now: Vaslav Nijinsky. In him is reincarnated the mysterious child Septentrian who died dancing on the shore at Antibes. Young, erect, supple, he walks only on the ball of his foot, taking rapid, firm little steps, compact as a clenched fist, his neck long and massive as a Donatello, his slender torso contrasting with his overdeveloped thighs, he is like some young Florentine, vigorous beyond anything human, and feline to a disquieting degree. He upsets all the the laws of equilibrium and seems constantly to be a figure painted on the ceiling; he reclines nonchalantly in mid-air, defies heaven in a thousand different ways, and his dancing is like some lovely poem written in capitals."

Diaghilev was well aware of the dangers of Nijinsky's attraction to the rest of the company and was determined to make sure none of them got too close to play with his personal panther.

Cocteau particularly was a danger as he was most attractive, had great charm, devastating wit and considerable good looks. "He walked with the pride of a wild bird that had dropped into a poultry yard."

He was also a most entertaining conversationalist. Diaghilev called him 'Jeanchik,' allowing him to mix with the company, well aware of his great publicity value. At the same time he kept a keen eye on him, allowing him to help dress Ida in her role of Cleopatra but making sure Jeanchik kept as as far away as possible from the showers, massages and rubdowns which Nijinsky required after a performance.

Bronislava Nijinska wrote of Cocteau: "The young man was very thin, with hollow, rouged cheeks and had thick black curly hair over a high forehead: his eyes were big and dark. He was always fashionably and elegantly dressed and, in addition to rouge, wore lipstick."

When Bronislava asked Nijinsky why Cocteau wore make-up, Vaslav laughed: "This is Paris…. He advises me to do the same, to put some make-up on my cheeks and lips… this is the poet, Jean Cocteau."

When Nijinsky failed to return Cocteau's ardour and admiration, he ceased to be Cocteau's "lovely poem written in capitals" and became "a sort of middle-class Mercury, an acrobatic cat stuffed full of candid lechery!"

It was all part of the exotic troupe which Diaghilev called his family, with himself as the figurehead. He was jealous, vindictive, sarcastic, and used his power for disgraceful favouritism, although Nijinsky had his little ways of getting round him.

"I can still see Nijinsky ready to go on in his role of the black slave in *Schéhérazade*, saying to Diaghilev, 'I won't go on unless you promise to go back to the pawnshop tomorrow and get my Kodak!' Diaghilev flared back: 'Certainly not!' But he knew that Nijinsky meant what he had said, that he really would not go on, and so he gave in."

Jean Cocteau

Blackmailing Diaghilev aside, Nijinsky was a professional through and through. He totally immersed himself in every part he played. He was perpetually preoccupied with his work.

During rehearsals of *L'Après-Midi d'un Faune*, when he went out for supper in the evening with Diaghilev and Bakst, he worried them for several evenings by moving his head as if he had a stiff neck. When they asked him if he was all right he would not reply. It was only later that they learned he was preparing his movements for when he was wearing the horns of the faun.

Bronislava Nijinska describes him during *Schéhérazade*:

"As soon as he put on his costume Vaslav assumed the character he was to portray. There was something animal, ape-like even, in the expression on his face as he drew back his lips to bare his gleaming white teeth.

"As I came on stage I saw Vaslav already in the wings. Behind him stood several dancers engaged in conversation. But Vaslav was not speaking to anyone; as usual he was limbering up.

"I watched fascinated by his absorption as he worked on the flexibility of his hands. His hands performed their own dance, brightly coloured gems in his rings twinkled and scintillated in the air around his body. His agile fingers moved as lightly and swiftly as a spider and his fingers twisted with the power and elasticity of an octopus.

"Physically Nijinsky was all but a demigod. Every muscle in his body was so perfectly developed that the doctors in St Petersburg had often brought him before them in order to study the action of the living tissues rippling beneath his satin skin."

In 1913, whilst touring in South America, Nijinsky fell in love and married Romola, a dancer in the company.

When the news reached Diaghilev, he was in Switzerland with Stravinsky. Stravinsky says he watched Diaghilev "turn into a madman who begged me and my wife not to leave him alone." In his jealousy Diaghilev not only sacked him but severed all contact.

Nijinsky tried to go it alone, but failed miserably. A tour of America had been a disaster. When the company finally arrived in New York he would not appear for any interviews or publicity. He disappeared into his own shell, much to the despair of the sponsors and of the company. His reluctance to show himself at all led to a jingle:

"Oh Mr. Nijinsky
Where have you binsky?
And if you are here
Why don't you appear
And save the ballet from ruinsky?"

Nijinsky danced for the last time in 1917 when he was twenty-eight. He appeared to be becoming mentally unstable and slowly the unhappy realization dawned that Vaslav's mental state was degenerating at a frightening pace into irredeemable schizophrenia.

Perhaps his illness was precipitated by the loss of his position with the Ballets Russes. Although he was doomed to be felled by this hateful disease it is possible that its advance was accelerated by the trauma of Diaghilev's vindictiveness and the predicament in which Vaslav found himself. Up to this point Nijinsky had had no responsibilities other than his work as an artist. Diaghilev had taken on all the responsibilities of everyday life and made all his decisions for him. Nijinsky had never even bought a railway ticket for himself. Now he had not only the responsibility of a wife, and soon a child as well, he had the heavy responsibilities of an impresario to boot.

Immediately following his dimissal from the Ballets Russes he had taken on the difficult task of mounting a production and running a company. The strain of this undertaking for the uneducated, unworldy scion of a family prone to mental disorder, where he was answerable for everything, was too much for him. Not only did he fail, and fail miserably, but it broke him. He who had the strongest of bodies, had the most fragile, delicate and sensitive mind. It was an unequal struggle and it was his mind which gave out.

In his diaries written around 1919, many of his thoughts and guilts emerge. They are written with a child-like openness, a strange innocence.

"I loved music. One day I met a Russian Prince who introduced me to a Polish Count. I have forgotten his name because I wanted to. I do not want to hurt his whole family. This count bought me a piano. I did not love him. I loved the Prince not the Count.

"Ivor introduced me to Diaghilev who asked me to come to the Hotel Europe where he lived. I disliked him for his too self-assured voice, but went to seek my luck. I found my luck. At once I allowed him to make love to me. I trembled like a leaf. I hated him, but pretended because I knew that my mother and I would die of hunger otherwise.

"I understood Diaghilev from the first moment and pretended to agree with him at once. One had to live, and therefore it was all the same to me what sort of sacrifice I had to make. I worked hard at my dancing and was always tired. But I pretended not to be tired at all in order that he should not be bored with me. I knew what he felt; he loved boys and therefore could understand me. I do not want to think that Diaghilev was a villain and that he should be imprisoned, I would cry if people were to harm him. Oscar Wilde's trial and imprisonment was still much in people's minds. I do not want to cause pain to anyone. Everyone will be shocked reading these lines, but I want to publish them in my lifetime, knowing their effect."

As Nijinsky meanders in his memories, many resentments come to the surface about Diaghilev:

"Diaghilev has both logic and feelings, but his feelings are bad. I have good feelings. Diaghilev's head is bigger than others. But there is bad feeling in his head.

"I know the tricks of impresarios. Diaghilev is also an impresario. He has a troupe. Diaghilev has learned to cheat other impresarios. He does not like to be called an impresario, as all impresarios are supposed to be thieves.

"Diaghilev wants to be called a 'Patron of Art,' he wants to get into history. Diaghilev cheats people and thinks that no-one sees through him.

"He dyes his hair in order to look young. Diaghilev's hair is white. He buys black dyes and rubs them in. I have seen this dye on Diaghilev's cushions; his pillow case is blackened by it. I hate dirty linen and therefore was disgusted by this sight. Diaghilev has two false front teeth. When he is nervous he passes his tongue over them. Diaghilev reminds me of an angry old woman when he moves his two false teeth. His front lock is dyed white. He wants to be noticed. Lately this lock has grown yellow, because he has bought bad dye. In Russia it looked better, I noticed this much later as I did not like paying attention to other people's hair.

"Diaghilev liked to be talked about and therefore wore a monocle. I asked him why he wore it, for I had noticed that he could see very well without it. Diaghilev said that he could not see well with one of his eyes. I understand that he had lied to me and felt deeply hurt that Diaghilev was cheating me. No longer did I trust him in anything, and began to develop independently, pretending to be still his pupil."

After he was married, he wrote:

"I have now been married for over five years. I lived with Diaghilev also for five years. I cannot count. I am now about twenty-nine. I know also that I was nineteen years old when I met Diaghilev. I admired him sincerely and when he told me that love for women is a terrible thing I believed him. If I had not believed him, I could not have done the things I have done."

In the early part of the twentieth century there was even less known about schizophrenia than today. The drugs which now often keep the more unbearable aspects of the disease at bay were largely unknown. Nijinsky's wife, Romola, stood by him for thirty years to the end. She tried everything. She took him to consult C. G. Jung in Switzerland, Sigmund Freud in Vienna and other prominent doctors. Freud told her that psychoanalysis was hopeless in schizophrenia, yet she never gave up.

Both Romola and Nijinsky died in Britain, Nijinsky in 1950, aged 62, thirty-three years after he had given his last performance. They left two daughters, Kyra and Tamara.

14

THE 1928 SEASON

"The length of our passions is no more within our control
than is the length of our lives."
François, Duc de La Rochefoucauld (1613–1680)

In 1927 Ida was in Paris preparing for her 1928 season. Had she been
content just to commission and inspire she would have had far greater
success. Sadly, she still commissioned and mounted these productions
purely as vehicles for herself. Now in her middle years she was beginning
to risk her dignity by aspiring to difficult dancing roles beyond the
capabilities of many dancers.

As always, her company contained some excellent dancers, rehearsed
and tuned to perfection. But the productions were all built around
Rubinstein herself. After the splendid company build up to her entrance,
the forty-three-year-old Ida would come on, "hauling herself up on
point," and the whole effect would decline.

Bronislava Nijinska was artistic director and choreographer for the
company, using both classical and contemporary music for her ballets.
"She collaborated on the selection of music with the composers Honegger,
Tcherepnin and Milhaud who orchestrated works of Bach, Borodin,
Schubert and Lizst for her. She also worked with Stravinsky and Ravel. For
the performances of his *Boléro* and *La Valse* Ravel conducted the orchestra,
as did Stravinsky for the premiere of his new ballet *Le Baiser de la Fée*."

Léonide Massine agreed to interrupt his work in New York to join Ida's
company to choreograph two ballets, *David and Goliath* and *Alcine*. The
sight of the Châtelet and the Opera, with Copeau's statue of *La Danse*
outside, brought back a host of memories for him: "One of the ballets she
had engaged me to do was based on the story of David and Goliath; the
libretto was by Dodoret, and the music by Sauguet. It was not a success.
Rubinstein, who was really more of an actress than a dancer, was
beautiful and statuesque, but though she had a striking presence it was
difficult to get her to move gracefully. As she was dancing the part of
David, and the whole ballet centred on her, I had very little opportunity
for original choreography."

Months of rehearsals were allowed for only a few performances.
Among the new, young dancers to benefit from rehearsing so long and

painstakingly with Massine and Nijinska were Anna Ludmilla, Alexis Dolinoff, Frederick Ashton, David Lichine and William Chappell. The young dancers were required to practise and rehearse from 9 a.m. to 11 p.m. It was an exhausting schedule but Nijinska assured them they would soon get hardened to the regime, and after four months they were like steel. The dancers used to refer to themselves as "La Compagnie des Répétitions de Madame Ida Rubinstein" as they rehearsed for so long, without ever performing. It was an object lesson in the art and discipline of rehearsal and choreography for which Ashton was always indebted.

William Chappell remembered Ida as the most polite, thoughtful and kindly of ladies. When asked what he felt about being made to wear a clean shirt and Eau de Cologne which she supplied on the rare occasions she actually rehearsed with them, he replied:

"But we loved to be given clean shirts. We sweated so much as Nijinska worked us so hard that it was a delight to be given cologne. We had little money for such things. Boys got three shillings a performance, girls got two and sixpence. Boys were harder to come by so they got the extra sixpence. She was such a lady in every sense of the word, and so very grand. My memories of her are of an extremely tall, elegant woman swathed in furs. Not that she was wearing a fur coat, but everything was edged in furs, swirls of it. Wonderful! And she was so kind, such a lady, extremely grand and aristocratic. You know she spoke eight languages fluently, and whenever she spoke to any of the company – we were all different nationalities, you know – Poles, Romanians, Italians, Spaniards, Americans, Fred and me, she would pay the person she was speaking to the kindness of speaking to them in their own language. What a lady! You know, when I visited her backstage at Covent Garden in 1931, she said nobody had visited her after the performances. I was amazed. You would have thought that she would have had a lot of grand friends in London, wouldn't you? You know, Walter Guinness and all that. But she didn't. She seemed a very lonely person."

Many times she is described as 'remote and majestical' which perhaps to William Chappell was simply 'lonely':

"She liked being a public figure. I think she must have done because it must have been torment being a ballerina, having never been trained as a ballerina. It must have been agony. She was an original stage-struck lady and wasn't going to be stopped doing it, regardless. I think she was naturally slender. [This is contrary to what is known about her in her later life.] She really had a marvellous figure, particularly as a nude, because she looked absolutely like the ideal perfect twenties lady. No extra bits; she had a neat little bosom and that was it, you know, tiny hips."

Frederick Ashton, who had introduced William Chappell to Ida, enabling him to join the company in 1928, was very popular with the other dancers because of his ability to do wicked impersonations.

"He entertained them with imitations of Queen Victoria, Pavlova and Rubinstein taking an arabesque and dropping her false teeth."

Ashton wrote of Ida:

"She was an enigmatic personality of compelling appearance. Though we were all remote from her in her company we were constantly reminded that Mme Rubinstein was *très distinguée*. She did all her rehearsals privately, for she must have been aware of her technical limitations and feared the cold scrutiny of her hard-working company. She would walk through her parts, white-gloved and richly clad in furs, while her mystified company looked on. At performances she died of nerves, and I used to wonder why she had established this lavish company to torment herself. We had the feeling of being a company run by an Electress of some Palatinate for her own amusement. Only the very best collaborators would do to produce her concept of beauty – Valéry, Gide, Debussy, Ravel, Honegger, Stravinsky, to name a few of the great men from whom she commissioned work. Being highly cultivated, she surrounded herself with the first-rate – her talents never allowing her to reach their heights. Nevertheless she created her lonely legend and she is a true Grande Dame of the theatre. I owe her a great debt of gratitude."

The productions of the Ida Rubinstein company for the 1928 season were:

La Valse	– Ravel
Boléro	– Ravel
David and Goliath	– Sauguet
Alcine	– Auric
La Bien-Aimée	– Schubert and Liszt
Le Baiser de la Fée	– Stravinsky
Psyché et L'Amour	– Bach
La Princesse Cygne	– Rimsky-Korsakov
Nocturne	– Borodin.

All had their premieres at the Paris Opera and were included in the 1929 seasons at the Théâtre de Monte Carlo, La Scala, Milan, and the Opera House, Vienna. They were performed at Covent Garden, London, in 1931.

Also in November 1928 Diaghilev's important English season began. The company was in Manchester from November 12th to 17th, then touring Birmingham, Glasgow and Edinburgh, when Diaghilev left for Paris to see Ida Rubinstein's season there. Diaghilev was obsessively jealous of her, firstly, because she employed many of the artistes who had first worked for him and, secondly, because financing productions for Ida was absolutely no problem. He never minded Pavlova having her own company and touring the world, as Diaghilev always felt she was a disciple and had a great need to take ballet to the people. But Ida made him almost apoplectic in his jealousy. He said of her:

"I ask myself only one question, What's the use of all that? [Her company.] No, we need somebody, a Napoleon or the Bolsheviks, to come and blow up the shamstress, with her public and her tarts who fancy themselves artistes, and do away with the millions they spend buying musicians!"

Diaghilev wrote to Serge Lifar on November 25, 1928:

"My dear,

Paris is an awful town, impossible to find five minutes for a couple of words even! Everyone seems to have collected here, it's the most awful muddle. Let me begin with Ida. The house was full, but there was a good deal of paper about, mostly her friends. Not one of us, though, were given seats, neither myself, nor Boris, Noive, Sert or Picasso … we only just managed to get in. ALL OUR PEOPLE were there, Misia, Juliette, Beaumont, Polignac, Stravinsky and other musicians, not to mention Marakovsky, etc., etc."

Misia Sert was known as "the queen of the Russian Ballet" and recognized by all as the power behind Diaghilev's throne. She was a wealthy woman, married three times, who spent most of her money helping artists. When he first arrived in Paris she had promised Diaghilev to help him all she could, canvassing her rich and influential friends to give their support, and buying up any empty seats in the theatre. Her approach to art was every bit as extravagant as Diaghilev's. She commissioned Pierre Bonnard to paint a frieze for her apartment, but finding the long straight edges of his canvas rather tedious she cut them into a scalloped pattern. The purists amongst her friends were horrified at her lack of respect. Misia unhesitatingly replied, "I don't respect art; I love it." She was Diaghilev's intimate to whom he poured out all the problems of the ballet. "You are my sister, the only woman I love." This dyed in the wool woman-hater remained close friends with her until his death.

Princesse Edmond de Polignac was an incredibly rich American. Born Winaretta Singer, daughter of the inventor of the sewing machine, she became the greatest patroness of Diaghilev and the Ballets Russes. Many of Diaghilev's ballets were dedicated to her. Her ambition was to have her bust next to Richelieu's in the Louvre.

Diaghilev continued:

"The whole thing was astonishingly provincial, boring and long drawn out, even the Ravel which took fourteen minutes. But worst of all was Ida. Strangely enough she was dressed the worst and when she appeared…

nobody, not even I, could recognize her. She was bent, with red hair dishevelled, wearing ballet shoes – this is to make her less tall.... Her dancing was quite impossible: she goes on her points, with bent knees, and Vilzak leads her forward the whole time, with legs apart.... It's a big company but totally lacking in experience. They were making fault after fault and seemed not to have the slightest notion of ensemble."

Diaghilev went on to tear the show apart and to say it had no success and that the press was lukewarm about the whole thing.

"Stravinsky," Diaghilev fumed, "was seen in Ida's dressing-room, where it appears he said, 'Delightful: I say it from my heart, charming.' Argutinsky himself told me the story. But the morning after the show Stravinsky rang up to say how disappointed he had been, how indignant the whole thing made him.

"All this you can read during supper to the principal dancers. I have exaggerated nothing. Tomorrow we have the second performance."

Diaghilev concluded the letter with a typical Bakst ending:

"It is very useful to look at rubbish: it makes one think."

On November 28, Diaghilev wrote another letter headed: "Second Ida Evening."

"I'm just back from the theatre with a fearful headache as a result of the horrible things I've been seeing.... What went on on stage is impossible to describe. Bronia Nijinska showed not the least gleam of invention, not one single movement was decently thought out....

"The theatre was full, but as for success – it was like a drawing room in which someone had suddenly made a bad smell, no one pretended to notice. Stravinsky was twice called to the curtain. The whole thing was stillborn."

He went on to describe the evening in detail and pull it apart piece by piece, each ballet, each pas de deux, using adjectives such as "tiresome, lachrymose and ill-chosen". The music sounded "drab and that it lacked vitality."

"Tomorrow two more of Bronia's ballets are going to be done. But we've got to prove to the bourgeois crowd how immeasurably superior we are, in spite of the fact that our costumes aren't quite so fresh. All the time I'm on the boil about next season's productions...."

Diaghilev in his jealousy was blind to any good that might have come out of these productions. He cruelly dismembers anyone who had ever worked for him whom he now considered a traitorous rival: Stravinsky, Sauguet, Benois, Massine, Nijinska, Vilzak, Schollar and, of course, Ida Rubinstein. He, more than anyone, had raised her to fame.

However, when the curtain came down on the 1928 season at the Opera, Ida had the gratification of knowing she had succeeded in mounting more original works in one season than any independent impresario in living memory.

A gypsy once prophesied that Diaghilev would die on water. It was the reason he never sailed and never went to South America on the tour during which Nijinsky met and married Romola. In a way his fears were justified, and in a way the gypsy's prophecy came true. He died in Venice, unexpectedly, after a few days illness. He died in a hotel on the Lido whose windows overlooked the Adriatic. It was 5.45 a.m. and amongst those present were Misia Sert, Boris Kochno and Serge Lifar. Misia Sert described the scene:

"An essentially Russian manifestation, such as you meet in Dostoievsky's characters, took place in the little hotel room, where the greatest magician in the world of art had come to die. Serge's death must have been the spark that caused the explosion of the mutual, pent-up hatred between the two boys, Kochno and Lifar, who had lived so close to him. A kind of roar struck the silence with authentic drama. Kochno hurled himself on Lifar, who was kneeling at the other side of the bed. They rolled on the floor tearing at each other, biting one another like savage beasts. They were in the grip of real fury. Two mad dogs were fighting over the body of their master."

Diaghilev was buried in Venice. An independent impresario on the grand scale, he accomplished his dream: to reveal Russia to itself and to the world, and reveal the world, the new world, to itself.

He was not a creative artist at all. If anything he was probably lacking in creative imagination. His genius was as a propagandist for art and as a businessman. As Benois said, he had one characteristic, one ability which none of them had and which made of him what he became: he knew how to "will" a thing into practice.

He did not write any music or design any sets or paint any pictures. As Fokine said: "I cannot remember one single choreographic idea of his. Cocteau, Vaudoyer, Benois all gave ideas but never Diaghilev. I have created sixty-five ballets and the majority have been either before or after my association with Diaghilev. Without him my work would not have been universally known, but it exists just the same."

He alone was able to crystallise and fuse the talent with which he surrounded himself. He once compared himself to a bartender: he had all the ingredients and he alone knew how to make the perfect cocktail.

His vision of ballet replaced interminable five-acters with short pieces in a single setting. Realistic scenery was replaced with poetic settings which conveyed the feeling of the piece. He re-introduced the leading male dancer and drew the corps de ballet into the action.

Stravinsky wrote of him:

"He seemed to be descended from a line of Russian lords who did not know the meaning of economy and nonchalantly buried themselves in debt for the sheer pleasure of satisfying their least whim. Diaghilev upheld his ancestral traditions. He loved to produce his life in the grandest manner. He lived through the Ballets Russes, spending huge sums on every production, while having to dismiss his own valet when at one point he lacked money to pay his wages. In proportion, as Bakst's stage costumes grew more lavish, his opossum coat grew increasingly threadbare. He had the make-up of a passionate monk, but, unwilling to deny his appetite for splendid decor and for young men, he placed his apostolic energies at the service of art."

With Diaghilev's death the Ballets Russes died too. The company was disbanded overnight; dancers were left unpaid, stranded in Monte Carlo, and he left enormous bills from his sumptuous productions.

He died on August 19th and was buried two days later. His remains were ferried across the lagoon to the cemetery of Saint Michael in a funerary gondola, draped in black and gold, mounted at the bow and stern with winged angels.

His permanent legacy, his lasting memorial, is that he, more than anyone, turned ballet into a popular and accepted art form. He fused ballet with painting and music, making it capable of showing the huge range of human experience and emotion, in a formula that encompassed the world, unshackled by the barrier of language. He said: "Beauty in art is feeling – told in images." That feeling was best achieved by one mind, that of Diaghilev.

15

COVENT GARDEN 1931

"Who can feel sure he has ever been understood?
We all die unknown."

Honoré de Balzac (1799–1850)

MOST ROMANTIC WOMAN IN EUROPE
ARRIVAL IN LONDON WITH 70 TONS OF LUGGAGE
DANCING GENIUS
LOVELY RUSSIAN'S THRILL
AT HER COVENT GARDEN DEBUT
By a special correspondent

"Europe's most romantic woman has come to London.

"She is Mme. Ida Rubinstein, the famous Russian actress and dancer whose beautiful and magnetic personality has won her homage in every European capital.

"Her first season in London opens at Covent Garden on Monday. It is probable that Gabriele d'Annunzio, the Italian soldier-poet, who is a great admirer of her art, will dash from Italy to see her.

"Mme. Rubinstein flew to London yesterday from Paris, and she was followed by her cast of 100 artists and seventy tons of luggage.

"What is the mystery of Mme. Rubinstein's genius and beauty? This is a question which has been discussed by artists all over Europe. Among the greatest successes in her repertoire is *The Martyrdom of St Sebastian* which d'Annunzio wrote especially for her, and *La Dame aux Camélias*.

"Tall and stately, Mme. Rubinstein sat in her London hotel last evening and told me of the thrill that her coming Covent Garden debut was giving her...."

So wrote the *Daily Mirror* on Saturday, July 4 , 1931. Covent Garden was to house a full repertoire both of plays and ballet. *The Times* had announced the two-week season on Thursday, April 16:

"Mme. Ida Rubinstein, who is to appear in London for the first time, has now completed arrangements for her two-week season on July 6th at the Covent Garden Opera House. Her programme, which will consist of two French plays and ten ballets, will open with *Le Martyre de Saint Sébastien*, in which she will be supported by a chorus of 85 performers.

"Originally visiting Paris with the Russian Ballet, Mme. Rubinstein quickly left the ballet to remain in Paris as her own producer. Having seen her dance as Cleopatra, Gabriele d'Annunzio offered to write specially for her in French verse *Le Martyre de Saint Sébastien*, and as this was her first Paris production, she is acting and dancing the leading part. For this production the music was composed by Debussy, and the scenery and costumes were designed by Bakst. Since the war Mme. Rubinstein has done much to make younger French composers better known, her programmes in Paris usually consisting of trios of new ballets, for which the scores and scenarios have all, with two exceptions, been written by Frenchmen. On the second night at Covent Garden she will present three of these ballets – *David*, of which the music is by Henri Sauguet; *Boléro*, a glorification of the Spanish dance by M. Maurice Ravel, who will himself conduct the performance in London; and *La Princesse Cygne*, taken from one of Rimsky-Korsakov's operas.

"Other ballets which will be given on later nights, are *La Valse*, also by M. Ravel, *Les Enchantements d'Alcine*, of which the music is by M. Georges Auric, with scenario taken from Ariosto by M. Lois Lalory; *Les Noces de Psyché et de l'Amour* and *La Bien-Aimée*, the author of the scenarios of both being Alexandre Benois. The music of the former is Bach's, orchestrated by the composer of *Le Roi David*, M. Arthur Honegger. The music of the latter by M. Darius Milhaud; others are *Nocturne*, of which the music is Borodin's and Stravinsky's *Le Baiser de la Fée*, inspired, as the composer says, by Tchaikovsky's muse."

Sadly, Ida, at the age of 46, was to fly to London on the wing of her past successes. She was no longer the femme fatale, the glorious, imponderable, irresistible seductress of twenty years before and the season proved to be a success only in its lavish staging and its sumptuousness. Ida received the worst of the criticism. The critics were united in their disapproval and sometimes extremely cruel. Ida's stage fright was getting worse and worse. She was seen time and time again in paroxysms of fear. Why did she torture herself? It would have been only too easy for her to choose some other way of life. Could she deceive herself so totally as to believe she remained the mesmeric star of her youth? Did she really believe her androgynous beauty, her extraordinary presence of 1909 and 1910, still invested her abilities and talents as both actress and dancer? Perhaps she did. Sarah Bernhardt herself had bestowed the mantle of 'Grande Dame' of the theatre upon her.

She was, without question, irresistibly drawn by the love of the theatre; so this shy, frightened woman continued to seek fame and glory. She devoted her time and fortune to pursue her art. She took delight in being a great patroness, fulfilling the role with honour and great competence, bringing together some of the greatest artists of the day. Yet, at the same time, when it came to performing, there was this paralysing fear to overcome. She was immensely vulnerable, bringing herself actually to approach the roles only when she was forced to by the presence of an audience, waiting for last minute 'inspiration.' Her fellow actors and dancers must have felt desperately under-rehearsed, even though months were spent on the productions for very few performances.

The sadness of the season, for Ida, can simply be shown in the notices.

"In each of the ballets Mme. Rubinstein was the central figure and it cannot be said that she was very successful in filling that responsible position. For, while the movements of her arms are graceful and her poses well conceived, she seems to be a mime rather than a dancer. However Mme. Rubinstein is supported by a competent and well disciplined company, and it is long since London audiences have been presented with such beautiful stage pictures. For Mme. Rubinstein is nothing if not lavish in scenery and costumes...."

"The beautiful Mme. Ida Rubinstein gave a sumptuous evening of three new ballets, including Maurice Ravel's already famous *Boléro* (conducted by the composer), last night at Covent Garden.

"We were left with the impression of two of the most beautiful stage pictures ever seen, namely, Benois's Botticellian setting for Sauguet's *David* and then his brown-and-yellow Spanish inn yard after Goya, when the slowly rising crescendo of the *Boléro* was enacted....

"What of the art of the generous giver of these costly shows, the famous beauty, the elegant Mme. Rubinstein? She posed with consummate grace; as a dancer she used her arms and hands to an effect of poetry. But her performance somehow did not kindle – fire was lacking in her even at the climax of the *Boléro* when the scream of the music was giving one goose-flesh...."

Richard Capell

The *Sunday Times* of July 12th, 1931 was scathing:

"Mme. Rubinstein's ballets have been mainly notable for the beauty and sumptuousness of their settings. If Mme. Rubinstein herself has no great qualities as an actress, she is even less remarkable as a dancer: indeed, her work this week has consisted for the most part of a few of the more elementary tricks of the trade repeated ad infinitum in ballets of the most diverse kinds, with a great deal of graceful arm movement.

"She is the same in everything she undertakes, partly because her technique is limited, partly because of a general failure in mental animation. Her limitations were severely exposed, perhaps, in Ravel's *Boléro*. The whole point of this ... is that a dancer on a table in a Spanish inn so works up the company by her dancing that bit by bit the infection spreads … till in the end the room is in a general frenzy. But Mme. Rubinstein's movements were so lacking in any suggestion of sensuous vitality that it was simply impossible to understand a Spanish crowd getting worked up by them, and the result was that the ballet fell woefully flat…."

"*La Princesse Cygne* is the worst ballet in Mme. Rubinstein's repertoire, in spite of the fact that it has the benefit of some of Rimsky-Korsakov's most delightful music…. Mme. Rubinstein's costumes were executed by a certain well known Paris House of dressmakers but no amount of draw-string could turn the first scene of the ballet into anything but a mannequin show of bathing costumes…."

Her acting in *La Dame aux Camélias* was received little better although the staging of the show was universally praised:

"This brilliantly staged production may seldom have touched the heart, but it feasted the eye abundantly…."

The *Telegraph*:

"In this production its 1848 settings are exquisite. They have been worked out to the last detail with the most loving care and they will live in my memory when every other feature of last night's performance has vanished into limbo."

But, again, Ida herself received strong criticism:

"Her Marguerite seemed less a woman in distress than a queen in a pageant.

"Madame Rubinstein is not a great tragic actress, by any manner of means. She is a decorative but intensely artificial actress. Her appeal to the eye is tremendous, to the ear not so great, to the emotions non-existent. Not once did the sorrows of this cold and statuesque Marguerite touch me or excite my concern."

Finally there is the *Sunday Times* review by James Agate, most revealing in its detail:

"This revival … might be characterized as Mme. Rubinstein's war. First in a series of engagements of which all but one were successful was the 'space-time' victory. It is no mean feat to get any spoken play across that yawning gulf which is the well of the Covent Garden orchestra when nobody is in it, and it must always be a considerable achievement even for the splurgiest of virtuoso actresses to galvanize the old 'drama' into any semblance of life. How much greater the achievement, then, when one considers that Mme. Rubinstein is essentially not an actress but a dancer! It is only proper to say that I have not seen Mme. Rubinstein dance, and that I make my little statement without prejudice to the converse opinion. But the twofold victory was pulled off. The credit going in the first place to the extraordinarily handsome, elaborate and faithful scenery of M. Alexandre Benois.... The stage at Covent Garden is immense, too big even for a production designed to be carried round the opera houses of the world, and so it came about that each of the five marvellous sets, designed incidentally by an artist and not by a mere furniture dealer, was framed in crimson billows and scarlet eddies....

"Then the dresses! ... The painter does not, or ought not to, live who could resist Mme. Rubinstein in any one of her gowns, particularly the black one in the fourth act from whose imprisonment the actress's dazzling shoulders escaped to battle in the rivers of diamonds which it would be impertinent to call French. And then that ultimate bed chamber, that mother-of-pearl sea with its swansdown wavelets into which this Venus must now decline! No man may describe such an apartment without hyperbole, and permit myself to say that for its decoration Africa appeared to have been denuded of its ostriches, and the Arctic and Antarctic of its bears....

"Then again, the cast! Mme. Rubinstein deserves our thanks for assembling, perhaps, an admirable company. These are French actors, from whom no secrets of the Dumasian Theatre are hidden....

"And now, I suppose, the time has come to talk of Mme. Rubinstein, though one would rather not, since to fail to find her performance good is rather like objecting that a hostess who has entertained one royally is unworthy. Mme. Rubinstein imposes by her appearance: she is as tall as the men in her company, but looks taller, and moves through this play's troubled waters like some majestic liner indifferent to crest or trough. She has nothing that I should like to call facial expression, and even when she has contrived some approximation to emotion it is, within the next second, as though nothing has happened. So a mountain after a passing cloud. Her most successful moments are those when she most faithfully reproduces Bernhardt's cadences and intonations: when she is not doing this she is doing nothing of her own...."

How did these criticisms affect Ida? Her company and entourage protected her. They covered her with praise and made sure that the newspapers and the truth were hidden from her. They could not have succeeded totally. Many references have been made to 'her brave smile,' her 'dignity' and her loveliness. She was surely too artistic to be totally blinded by any sycophantic flattery from within her own entourage. She might have been soothed, but fooled? Surely not. The theatre was her magnet and the uncontrollable alluring pull became her torment, when her most sincere efforts and her commitment became prey to its caprices. All we have is the infinitely sad and lonely picture that William Chappell painted when he visited her backstage during that 1931 season. When she

– who had been the toast of society – told him how pleased she was to see him, as no one else had come backstage after her performances.

" 'We have had such small audiences,' she said. 'Why do you think that is?'

"How could I tell her that it was because of her, because she was now passé?"

16

THE PARIS OPERA 1934

"Man's passions make him live.
His wisdom merely makes him last."
Nicholas Chamfort (1741–1794)

Ida packed her seventy tons of luggage and returned to Paris. There in the Place des Etats-Unis, safe in her 'ivory tower' and protected by 'The Shadow,' bruised but undaunted, she began to dream of her next season. The scars of time were beginning to show, the buffets and billows of a life in the limelight were taking their toll. Her travels and the long voyages on her yacht were no longer a panacea; her work followed her. Telegrams and letters were sent all over Europe: organising, setting up meetings, booking dates for her next venture, all written from the yacht.

Not only had her art suffered, physically she was affected too. As far back as 1930 Bettina Bergery had been to one of Natalie Barney's 'Fridays':

"Natalie Barney seemed an elegant version of the Wizard of Oz and Romaine Brooks looked like Tweedledum or Tweedledee. I remember lunching with Natalie and Romaine and a long-eyed skeleton in an old dress made by Léon Bakst, a scarecrow left over from the Ballets Russes who turned out to be Ida Rubinstein. All three congratulating themselves and each other on having reached the summits of their chosen careers.

"Natalie, Romaine and the Duchesse de Clermont-Tonnerre were not grotesque like Gertrude Stein and Alice B. Toklas or, in a lesser way, like Colette, who was a squat, neckless woman with toes like bunches of muddy carrots and a forehead like a Greek temple, concealed by a shrubbery of frizzed hair, though the old cat's eyes were piercing."

This is one of the few overt attacks on Ida's looks. On the whole she was described as 'elegant,' 'refined' or 'graceful' and cut a well-known figure dressed in long fitting coats, ornamented with fur, with matching fur hats, low fronted shoes and the usual impeccable white gloves. It seemed an appearance ideally suited for the actress-impresario, the well-groomed Russian of noble station.

One of the people who joined Ida's company in 1934 was Keith Lester, an English choreographer and teacher who had studied with Serefina Astafieva and Nicholas Legat. He made his stage debut in Basil Dean's

1923 production of Flecker's *Hassan*, which had choreography by Fokine. He later danced with Tamara Karsavina on her European tours and with Olga Spessivtseva, notably in a season at the Teatro Colon, Buenos Aires, when Fokine revived several works for this illustrious ballerina.

The description of the 1934 season is from his unpublished memoirs:

"The first person of the Rubinstein entourage that I met was a most efficient little lady, a private secretary; neat, trim, French, respectable, she arranged everything. She had, for me, an air of anonymity, of non-commitment. When she went she ceased to exist....

"Rubinstein's company was in every respect heterogeneous. Different nationalities, different schools of dance, and very different outlooks. The British and the Americans tended to move together because of a common understanding; the French were at home anyway, so had little need of cliques to preserve their identities. In 'Dance', Russians could be divided at that time into two distinct categories. The greatest and the best of them, and indeed how great, were devoted to 'Dance' for its own sake, albeit they were its high priests; they accepted any dancer of standing, whereso-ever he or she may have come from. The rest felt they had prior claim to ballet and interlopers were treated with coldness and recriminations; they had no right to poach on the preserves of Russians. Their lesser dancers were émigrés, the children of émigrés and, far from absorbing the many virtues of France, had rather contracted her shortcomings. They were referred to as 'Gaspoda'.

"Kurt Jooss was the Maître de Ballet for the first 1934 production which was Gide's *Perséphone*.

"Then Fokine arrived.... I was on the platform to welcome him. The Gaspoda were upstream and cast rather baleful glances towards me; I was clearly an interloper. Fokine stepped out of the train almost opposite them: cries of "Mikhail Mikhailovitch" and a sweep of 'reverences slaves' filled the platform. Fokine accepted all in good part with the simple grand manner of a true American ... and the Gaspoda escorted him to his hotel. He looked apart amongst them, he was no longer socially a Russian....

"He started rehearsals on *Diane de Poitiers*; Ibert, Benois and the inspiration of Arbeau's *Orchésographie*. The steps grew from Arbeau to Opera House, the social dance expanded into ballet. The choreography was Fokine's finest – like *Spectre*, happy, delightful and a pleasure to dance; Vilzac's saraband with Ida Rubinstein stately, befitting Henri Deux and a drama by Goryon. Then was a pas de quatre, two boys, two girls, on which Fokine actually consulted me. 'You have done acrobatic lifts in America, show me some.' So, overwhelmed at the command to help, I collected one of the girls and worked out lifts and spins for him. He took what he wanted and the pas de quatre of acrobats was made. Sometimes

I sat beside him at rehearsals when he would explain his ideas about ballet-making: 'Each ballet has its own style; when you have found that, you can do just what you like; it's all of one conception.'"

Arnold Haskell recalled in his book *Balletomania*:

"Fokine was hard at work preparing four new ballets for Ida Rubinstein. I watched some of the early stages. Fokine entered armed with a large portfolio of musical scores and notes. First he sorted his dancers into groups, explaining carefully the setting of the scene, and what each one represented. He told them also the chief characteristics of the period. Then he went ahead of each group, dancing, letting them follow, dancing again. He made them try a few steps a number of times, rejecting and building up again, but always as if he were perfecting a work already in existence. There was nothing tense in the atmosphere, no trace of impatience. The company was good, and he had plenty of time to laugh and joke, while carefully indicating every shade of intention, explaining by example, skilful parody and over-emphasis the meaning underlying every movement, splitting it up, analysing it in a manner I have never seen done before, but always allowing a certain individual latitude of expression. He also related the movements of ballet to the natural movements of everyday life. He did not impose himself at all, but worked up a genuine mass enthusiasm."

At this time Fokine was very nearly bald, narcoleptic in appearance, more striking even than in the early days. He still danced with great fire and the most perfect control. He was to choreograph *Sémiramis* by Paul Valéry, music by Honegger, designed by Yakovlev. Apart from Ida, the ballet had only one principal dance role which was danced by Keith Lester:

"Fokine talked about the ballet. I sat entranced: a splendid three-act ballet to be created at the Paris Opera, and the principal role for me. I did, of course, realize that Rubinstein would be in it somewhere, but envisaged her as a sonant rather than a mobile attraction....

"Of Fokine's personal feelings with regard to Ida Rubinstein I knew nothing, he vouchsafed nothing. Only twice did humanity intervene: once when he told me that I had a hole in my tights and it might be embarrassing at a private rehearsal with Madame; and one other time when, weary with teaching Rubinstein how to stand without the traditional hand on hip of the danseuse, he said to me: 'She likes you, try to stop her doing that terrible position.'

"By now we were occasionally on the stage of the Opera with scenery. 'Come in this afternoon,' commanded Fokine. 'We must rehearse with the stairs.' We were alone on the stage except for a flight of stairs that seemed to mount to heaven. It was here that the queen parted from an overbearing lover; she thrusts him from her, he poises one moment with his back to the stairway, then overbalances and rolls down on to floor level. We spent the afternoon working at a relaxed rotation in horizontal position at speed; at last, black, blue, green and slightly bloody, I got it the way Fokine wanted it. 'It must look natural,' he said, 'or it might be funny.' It could never have felt funny....

"The dress rehearsal of *Sémiramis* was full of defeats. On the stage, whilst scenery was being set to rights, whilst musicians practised isolated fragments, whilst dancers crept to and fro trying to find somewhere to warm up, Honegger stood to one side of me and Fokine to the other; Honegger did not like some of the treatment his score had received at Fokine's hands. 'If that part remains in,' he said, 'people will laugh.' Fokine drew himself up to full classic height and beetled his brows. 'I have mounted a hundred ballets, no one has ever laughed.' (I recalled that two of them were comedy ballets.)

"Rubinstein looked very imposing as the Queen of Assyria, the consort of Shamshi-Adad V, the lady Sammuramat, who in her own right was a conqueror of kings and, round about 810 BC, was part builder of Babylon. After Rubinstein had walked over the backs of the captive kings on to her chariot, she was dragged round by other harassed VIPs; it was all soon over, since it was only a formal confirmation of her absolute power. It was then that she noticed me and stood in the centre of the stage staring, as if buying a horse. In the ancient east there is, at moments such as these, a traditional procedure; one casts oneself on one's belly and rubs one's nose in the dust. This slave, however, raises his head and kneels upon one knee. ... At that instant Ida was excellent, for she did nothing but stare at me with serpent's eyes, as if calculating whether she could swallow me or not.

"The next scene was, inevitably, in bed; but on so large a playground the intimate gestures of love were more like long-distance signals. The slave spent most of his time on the floor, whilst Rubinstein, mistress of Valéry's lines, struggled with Fokine's. It was during this scene that she slipped on to my arm one of her bracelets. Cartier had been ordered to supply a suitable object for the occasion. During rehearsals we mimed the gift, so at the first performance I hardly noticed what it was, except that it was strung on elastic. Things seemed to be going nicely ... up to the journey down the stairs. But when the big roll arrived I felt as if I had Brighton beach under me. The bracelet was composed of large, solid cubes of crystal quartz. The next gift of Semiramis was a dagger, which I used appropriately and died, leaving her alone with Valéry."

Keith Lester tells of another incident with Ida at the dress rehearsal of *Perséphone*:

"It was only at the dress rehearsal that I was handed the beaker of temptation; Rubinstein who was near me, uttered a shriek. 'I'm meant to drink from it, not wash in it,' she cried. It was solid silver, Cartier's best and biggest; it weighed a ton. 'Change it,' she ordered. It was never changed; I learned how to resist its centrifugal pull in turns and managed to get rid of it rather earlier than had been intended. At the first performance it behaved very well and, feeling pleased with everything, I mounted the rocky stairway to offer her the wine that could keep her forever in Hell. I found Rubinstein in convulsions of stage fright. Cowering on a palatial lilo, the tongue working overtime to moisten and refresh the fevered lips, if not the fevered brow. What demon drove her to present herself in the difficult and inadequately assembled agglomerations of high art none can explain for certain; but in her utmost need he deserted her. How long she had been there I had not the slightest idea, since she rehearsed her own roles *in camera*. Jooss had sometimes used German at our rehearsals, so I gave her a bright smile and said 'ein, zwei, drei und jetzt zu links' because that was the way it had to go to give her a drink. But her look of glazed horror frightened me. If we had not been through the passage of temptation carefully with Kurt I might have thought that this was a full Stanislavsky rendering....

"The critics were swift to pounce on the lines she spoke early on in the domain of Pluto. 'Where am I?' 'What am I doing here?' They suggested that these sentiments were shared by all."

Apart from *Perséphone* and *Sémiramis* the other new ballet of the season was *Diane de Poitiers* and, in order to make a more varied repertoire, two ballets from her season two years earlier were being rearranged by Fokine. These were Ravel's *Boléro* and *La Valse*.

"In *La Valse,* in resplendent military costumes of an Austro-Hungarian Operetta, we waltzed round the stage with Mme. as lightly as in a dream; we then all changed partners and waltzed back again with her daughter Mlle. X....

"*Boléro* was an enormous, circular table, the size of a skating rink, on which Rubinstein did her utmost to be Andalusian, passionate, flexible, savage and voluptuous. We all crept round and round, crouched over the rim of the table till at last the music ended and the descending curtain released us from what must have looked like a procession of lumbago sufferers at some gypsy Lourdes, conjuring the divinity of Flamingo chorea. We could hardly forgive Ravel for *Boléro*....

"The Gaspoda were in good form: 'Madame's dancing had improved since her sixty-ninth birthday.' They were too kind, it had not. Whatever Rubinstein was with Diaghilev, whatever her performance in *Schéhérazade*, there was little sign of a danseuse of even past merit on the stage of the Paris Opera. As a vision of Maecaenas – for indeed she was that, and could afford, perhaps, too much – she was impressive; as a static goddess she was admirable; but as a dancer, no. What did Fokine hope to make of her with his lessons? Could it have been an answer to Isadora, of whom he said to me, 'A wonderful lot of music but always the same dance.' "

Cléopâtre had proved an enormous success in Paris, and so had Rubinstein. The ballet had suited her. Perhaps her seasons at the Opera were a search for that departed glory, for another such vehicle. How triumphant those first two seasons must have been and how difficult to even equal their success.

In 1929 it was written by a journalist:

"I feel sorry for anyone who did not see the Russian Ballet when Bakst was in the audience studying the effect of his achievements, when Nijinsky leaped and never fell, when Ida Rubinstein resuscitated *Cléopâtre* and when Pavlova, the Oiseau d'Or, crossed the stage shaking a plumed head-dress taller than herself which dragged her head back like that of a stag at bay. A shudder would run through the semi-circle of the audience from top-most gallery to the first row of the stalls, a fevered, exacerbated, electrically tense Paris indulged in a fabulous orgy of music and colour… Ah! how quickly those instants faded…. Nijinsky is mad, Ida Rubinstein acts in plays, Bakst is dead, the sensitivity of the audience is dead too; two or three musicians wander about the house and one yawns."

When Arnold Haskell asked Fokine, "How deep was the influence of Duncan on you?", Diaghilev had written in a letter: "I knew Isadora well in St Petersburg and was present with Fokine at her first debut. Fokine was mad about her dancing and the influence of Duncan on him lay at the base of all his creative work."

Fokine replied: "That is absurd. Diaghilev could never have believed in such a statement nor made it with the slightest degree of sincerity. He watched my rehearsals and saw me compose. He knew perfectly well the differences between my new Russian ballet and Duncan's dancing. I remember going to see her with him. I had already been engaged as Maître de Ballet and had by that time carried out considerable reforms on the Russian stage. The reason for my very great enthusiasm was because I felt that here were so many elements that I was practising and preaching. I found naturalness, expressiveness, and real simplicity. There was a similarity in our aims but an enormous and obvious difference in our methods.

"Her dance is free, mine stylized, and my movements are mechanically highly complex. I was working with dancers with a fixed technique and an old tradition. She for an individual, herself. I am very happy, though, that in the treatment of ancient Greek themes, her speciality, I have something in common with her, just as I am delighted to differ from her, in other modes and styles. She stood for freedom of the body from clothes, while I believe in obedience of the movement to costume and its proper adaptation to period. She had only one plastic conception for all periods and nationalities. While I am essentially interested in the difference of the movement of each individual. She had, for instance, the same form of movement for Wagner, Gluck, Chopin, the Spanish dances of Moszkovsky, and the waltzes of Strauss. The national character is absent; only Greece existed for her, as if it be adapted to all periods. Diaghilev was far too keen an observer not to know all this, especially as his opportunities were better than anyone else's. His statement was made on purpose."

The 1934 season at the Paris Opera ended. Ida was forty-nine, her stagefright was getting worse and her dancing was a constant source of ridicule. Her charisma and stage presence, her androgynous beauty – the strength of her past – had been diluted by age, her fame and notoriety had faded with time, and the innate business acumen she had shown in the past was diluted in the possessive desperation of an ageing narcissistic ambition. For Ida Rubinstein chose to do what she wanted, when she wanted, how she wanted, and Rubinstein "wanted" a lot. But, the one thing she desired more than anything else, the fame, the glory of the prima ballerina, the superstar, which she had had at the very beginning of her career, continued to elude and frustrate her.

Gods; people who leave their own tiny piece of history; people big enough to become pebbles in the sands of time.

Only Gods are immortal. As for the rest, the billions upon billions of souls, who loved and died: what is left for them? "A speck of dust on a great plain." (*Oedipus at Colonus.*)

This was not what Ida had in mind.

17

WORLD WAR TWO

"There are but three events which concern mankind;
birth, life, and death.
All know nothing of their birth,
all submit to die and many forget to live."
La Bruyère (1645–1696)

For almost a quarter of a century Ida Rubinstein had presented Paris with ravishing, sumptuous spectacles in the theatre. She had taken much criticism, but the lavishness and generosity of what she had had to offer was much appreciated.

She also worked unstintingly for charity, often giving not only her time but also her own money. This 'grande dame' would, without reserve, travel miles to do personal appearances in the tiniest venues to raise money for some cause or other. An actor, whom she used in many of these performances, writes in his unpublished memoirs:

"One day … I received a visit from 'The Shadow', smiling as ever! She came to ask me to accompany Mme. Rubinstein to a charity benefit gala for the replacement of the stained glass windows of the cathedral of some small western town.

"I quickly accepted. At the gala she was going to repeat a lecture which she had recently delivered at the Université des Annales on 'The Art with Three Faces'. This lecture was to be followed by the famous scene from *Martyre de St Sébastien* between herself and me."

The actor was given his train ticket, his expenses, his salary, and his orders to wait in his hotel for Ida Rubinstein to arrive.

"At half past eight, according to plan, having dined alone, then having donned my dress suit, someone called me, and the ever-present major-domo escorted me to Mme. Rubinstein's Rolls-Royce where, in driving rain, he opened the door for me, and I quickly got in, making my greetings in the dark, before accepting the fold-down seat opened out for my benefit.

"I had the time, meanwhile, to notice in the back, beside the little black 'Shadow', a white and diaphanous glittering shape, like a magnificent bride.

"Without daring to move my head, with my back turned to the

amazing apparition, I forced myself to take an interest in this small nocturnal journey which led us, guided by a kind local, towards the hotel, through darker and darker streets as far as an indistinct and ancient wooden portal. Quickly on my feet, and replacing the fold-down seat, I stretched out a hand to the white glove of the female traveller who, in turn, descended, followed by 'The Shadow'.

"It was then that, in the rain and in the faint glow of an ancient street light, I was able to admire, stupefied, the stunning splendour of the great lady, dressed, as if for a royal reception, in a rich gold brocade, underneath an immense ermine coat, with her hair entwined in white tulle, whilst costly orchids added a note of refined colour to all that whiteness. One could have said that some Byzantine Blessed Virgin had come to honour with her presence the humble district in which we had disembarked. 'Over here, please, for the artistes' entrance.' And our guide, an open umbrella in his hand, pushed us through a narrow blank space which led us towards the stage door.

"Imagine, fifty metres of bumpy, slippery paving stones between two damp walls … and that fifty metres further divided into two by a rivulet, turned, that night, into a semi-river by the water which fell, without stopping, from the overflowing gutters. Like a timorous and disgusted cat, our queen for the day went from one paving stone to the other, beneath our guide's inadequate umbrella, with me on the other side, supporting her waist, skipping to the same rhythm as hers.

"We halted, at last, before a shabby little door – the artists' entrance – which, at the top of two flights of loose, rickety stairs, opened into a kind of canteen kitchen, where there was scattered some box-seats, illuminated between two ceiling joists by a tiny light bulb, greyish and covered in dust. In these miserable surroundings, and with the constant sound of rain, despite her deep-rooted dignity and her saint-like air, she decided to laugh about it – a nervous laugh certainly, but not one unpleasant word crossed her lips. All those who followed in a second car bustled around her: all had to sit, to tidy themselves, to straighten themselves up!

"During these alterations, and preceded by our obliging guide, we set off to to reconnoitre the surroundings. At the end of the kitchen, a door opened and suddenly, one was on the stage; a dais two metres by three, and behind it, in the faint glow of a fish tank stretched a sad, sad club room, stocked with cane chairs, and, at the back, wooden benches! I fear to describe them, for the chairs and the benches were almost worn out … some scattered groups spoke in lowered voices, and at the back some brats were playing on and under the benches! Again, it wasn't exactly the time for the performance to begin, it is true. Mme. Rubinstein had, to a high degree, the punctuality of kings, and it was raining hard. Perhaps in a few more minutes – and my eyes went again to the little rough wooden dais, to the little conference table, to the little, skimpy rug. All this for 'The Art with Three Faces', and the Prologue of d'Annunzio.

"We waited for some time, the rain seemed to diminish – and, little by little, there arrived, without pushing, amid the the 'Good evenings' and 'What weather!', a few more people. Then, all quietened, a man spoke a few words below the dais, and Mme. Rubinstein made her entrance. I entered at the same time, behind her, and went to seat myself on the far left, awaiting her signal. I then had all the time to study her, and I believe I could say that the moon itself falling upon that humble dais (all decorated with tricolour garlands from the last 14th July) would not have astounded this brave audience more than that unbelievable appearance; it was if everybody had stopped breathing, all with mouths open, a paralysis for several seconds, then a little applause, the others following with an effort – as if it were unseemly to applaud – Blessed Virgin Mary! How many of the little brats at the back dared to believe in such a fairy in their books of fairy tales.

"Had it been wise to hold it here? How could it be appreciated? What was the good? Ida Rubinstein seemed to view these things, or, more precisely, seemed not to see them at all! Completely involved in her subject, her overall duty, this duty which she had taken to herself as a noble cause, she, unshakeable, put down her manuscript on a high table, and sat down on the lowest chair (one which suddenly made her look small), and seriously, wisely began to explain to all those brave, attentive rustics – but hardly ready for it – 'L'Art aux Trois Visages'.

"I must admit that I didn't follow her very well, and I was shocked when, turning to me, she asked me to deliver the Prologue! I don't believe I lie when I say I have never made such an effort to start speaking, knowing that for this audience it might just as well be Chinese!

"As for the scene from *Martyre de St Sébastien* in formal gown and dinner jacket, without the archers and arrows, it merited being something other than curious! Decidedly, the dying Sebastian met with no more luck here than in Milan! As for the takings, I think they barely covered the restoration of a tenth of the stained glass windows, and I have no doubt that this generous benefactor rounded off her artistic contribution with a hefty personal donation to the Cathedral Benefit Fund and the master glass artist.

"Once again we had deceived ourselves; Ida Rubinstein and 'L'Art aux Trois Visages' wasn't a suitable lure for a provincial agricultural town. After this, I would have thought her completely cured of these disastrous events, so little in keeping with her high life-style, and despite appearances, with undoubted blows to her pride! But no, I was astounded to find myself called upon with the same earnestness and the same explanations, a few months later, with the same programme and where? To an enormous, teeming restaurant in Montrouge!"

The actor made many many excuses and tried to avoid involving himself again. After managing to evade a few of these evenings he found himself persuaded to participate once more:

"It was once more in a kitchen that we met again as agreed, to give an evening performance (as always, the ermine, the filmy tulles, the orchids – the charity uniform). But this time immense and squalid, the kitchen for the weddings and banquets of the old Portes de Paris, dark and smelly, with its extinguished stoves, its open cooking pots on a glistening and greasy tiled floor. And from the function rooms came echoes of an orchestra – mandolins, accordions, and trombones – once again to underline the failure of the soul of the actress, for whom luck and the influences had led the way, and rendered childish her really sincere exertions.

"Once again, also, her inbred dignity prevented her from showing anything else but her fixed smile as she plunged into the these disastrous surroundings, into the tobacco smoke and the noise of these *poilus* [soldiers – other ranks] awaiting 'L'Art aux Trois Visages' from their benefactor!"

Ida's last major appearance on stage was the premiere of the Arthur Honegger–Paul Claudel oratorio *Jeanne d'Arc au Bûcher*, in Basle in 1938. She was fifty-three years old. It was a splendid success and hailed as Honegger's greatest triumph since *Le Roi David* in 1921. "Ida Rubinstein portrayed Joan. Her intelligence and her personality fit her for so many exceptional roles that it is scarcely necessary to praise her."

While Arthur Honegger was composing it he had been invited by Gabriele d'Annunzio to his estate:

"D'Annunzio had invited me to visit him at his estate where, looming from the midst of a garden, the whole prow of a cruiser came into view. We climbed the gangway, which was guarded by a marine, arms at order. D'Annunzio took me to admire the magnificent view on Lake Garda, then he said, 'And now to honour the musician who comes to visit the poet, we shall launch the seven notes of the scale into that infinity which has neither number nor limits. Fire!' A terrific explosion of cannon almost threw me flat. Do! Re! Mi! So we climbed the whole scale.

"The next day he took me to the installation of the airbase at Sessinzano, then he conducted me to Milan. I have never seen him since.

"His conversation was a display of fireworks, and one understood how this man of predominantly unattractive physique had such success with women. He was understandably proud of his mastery of the French language. 'Most French writers', he was fond of repeating, 'are satisfied with fifteen hundred words, I know fifteen thousand.' "

Gabriele d'Annunzio, soldier, poet, playwright, womaniser, intellectual and prince died in March 1938.

Since his capture and the siege of Fiume and the relinquishment of the town to the Italian army in January 1921, d'Annunzio had been a problem to the authorities. He was the most popular man in the country. When Mussolini came to power he suddenly became a danger. No one could be more popular than Mussolini. D'Annunzio was showered with honours: in 1924 he was given, by King Victor Emmanuel III in person, the title of Prince of Montenevoso. None of this could hide the fact that he was being kept a virtual prisoner in his villa on the shores of Lake Garda. Mussolini, by giving the 'country's hero' round the clock protection, was, in fact, keeping him under constant surveillance. After his visit to La Scala, Milan, to see Ida in his *Le Martyre de St Sébastien* and his speeches to the audience, he was never again allowed to address his adoring public en masse. Excuses were always found. He was much too charismatic a figure.

He died suddenly on 1st March of a cerebral haemorrhage within a fortnight of his seventy-fifth birthday.

Ida was bereft. She had lost a friend and admirer with whom she had worked and whom she adored for over thirty years. She, and his many other true friends, nursed their grief in private whilst he was given a grand funeral. Against everything d'Annunzio had ever wished, Mussolini delivered an emotional, insincere tribute at the grave.

Ida paid her own tribute to him by giving two private performances of *Le Martyre de St Sébastien* in his memory.

"Perpetually intoxicated, yet ever sober, he used to work twenty-four hours at a stretch when genius burned. His poetry is such a passionate music that its sound alone is enchanting even if the exact meaning escapes foreign ears."

Elisabeth de Gramont

D'Annunzio once wrote: "A greyhound or well-trained racehorse; the legs of Ida Rubinstein; the body of an Ardito folding Prave; the form and structure of my highly polished cranium – these are the most beautiful phenomena in the world."

It was barely three months earlier that Maurice Ravel had died after a debilitating and mysterious illness that seemed to stem from a 1932 crash in a taxi. From that moment he suffered from some kind of cerebral deterioration that prevented him from writing music. After Ida's successful collaboration with him during *Boléro* and *La Valse*, their professional relationship had turned into an enduring friendship. She had commissioned him to write a ballet for her based on the *Arabian Nights*, to be launched in her 1934 season. Ravel had been extremely excited by the idea and had set to work at once. However, after the crash, in which he was knocked unconscious, he did not write another note. His creative genius seemed to be cut off. Friends all tried to encourage him but to little avail. Everyone hoped his condition might be purely temporary.

By 1935 Ravel had hardly put a note down on paper. Even though his thoughts were lucid nothing would seem to translate them into reality. Friends tried to think of any way in which to rekindle his creativity. Ida even arranged for an extended holiday for him to North Africa and Spain, hoping that the sounds and smells and atmosphere would reawaken his atrophied brain, bring back memories, shadows and melodies from the past. Even though the holiday stimulated him and gave him great pleasure he remained unable to write.

Ida had organized a splendid evening for him in Marrakesh at the desert palace of a sultan. Ravel was "enchanted by the oriental splendour of the pageant arranged in his honour, with a hundred dancing girls, a native orchestra and Arab warriors leading magnificent black deerhounds."

Afterwards he was asked if he ever considered writing anything Arabian, to which he replied: "If I wrote anything Arab, it would be far more Arab than all this!"

With his mind still as sharp as ever, it must have been a depressingly frustrating condition, for both himself and his friends.

By the autumn of 1937 Ravel's 'disease' had become worse. His neurosurgeon in Paris, Dr Thierry de Martel, was sure that there was no point in operating on his brain. Ida and many of his friends wanted a second opinion. Ida was determined; she set off by plane to see neurosurgeons and neurologists in Switzerland, Germany, and the United Kingdom. There must be something that could be done. There must be some hope. At last a Dr Clovis Vincent agreed to an exploratory operation to see if there was any sort of brain tumour. The operation took place on 19th December but Ravel sank into a post-operative coma. Ida was permanently at his bedside, praying for his recovery, but on 28th December he died without regaining consciousness.

It took a long time for her to clear the guilt that the operation, on which she had insisted, had shortened his life even though she had been governed by the best motives.

The imminence of war was soon to become the all-preoccupying worry. In Germany the Nazi party was becoming more powerful as the rest of Europe watched in a sort of stupor. The danger signals were flashing and yet very few people seemed to be taking any notice. For Ida, as for millions of others, life was never to be the same again. It was the end of an era, the end of her life in the theatre.

Lord Moyne, luckily, was one of the people who recognized the dangers that were mushrooming in Germany. He and Ida had continued their relationship over twenty-five years. Even though they were most discreet, within Ida's immediate circle and within her companies, it was common knowledge. William Chappell had known all about it when he was interviewed. Lady Moyne died in 1939, leaving Lord Moyne to legitimize his relationship with Ida. There was never any hint of marriage being a possibility, or even their relationship being any less discreet than before; however it was a friendship that was strong enough for Moyne to feel that it was his responsibility to bring her to England, away from the dangers of Paris. Ida took much persuading. She was determined to stay for as long as she could, as she had done in World War I. However by May 1940, when Hitler launched his blitzkrieg against Belgium and the Netherlands, and poured divisions of troops across the French border, she finally decided to go to Algeria, which at least was still French territory. Moyne, realizing the dangers only too well, spent months trying to get her to leave. At last, in the spring of 1941, he was able to arrange a plane to pick her up in Casablanca and take her to Portugal, and finally she made the journey, fraught with danger, from Lisbon to London. There, at last, Moyne arranged a suite for her at the Ritz Hotel. There she stayed at Lord Moyne's expense for the whole of World War Two. He took all financial responsibility for her during her time in England until the end of the war when she could safely return to France, her adopted country. Ida had fled Paris at Moyne's insistence because being Jewish she would have been in greater danger than most. As it was, her magnificent house on the Place des Etats-Unis had been razed to the ground and all her antiques and treasures had been either confiscated or stolen. Built up over three decades, her magnificent library of first editions of Russian, French, English and Italian literature, her collection of manuscripts of all the works she had personally commissioned all disappeared. Her rooms of fine clothes were gone forever. She arrived in London with no money, totally dependent upon Lord Moyne.

Even if they had wanted to marry, politically it would have been unwise. Lady Moyne had been everything that was the best in British society. She was a lady of great beauty, unusual sensibility and had an exceptional pedigree. Ida, on the other hand, in spite of having been extremely well-bred, was everything that was unacceptable to the British aristocracy. Even though her breeding was good, she still had her Russian accent. Also she was Jewish, or at least was born Jewish, even if she didn't practise the Jewish faith, and she certainly looked Jewish. Ida was, in all, quite the opposite of the English rose Lady Moyne. Ida was a divorcee, even though her marriage was one of convenience and not consummated. Her fame in the theatre at the beginning of her career had been close to notoriety. She had appeared nude in public. This was certainly no suitable match for Lord Moyne.

It was a strange liaison; Moyne, the pillar of society, the politician, the public servant; Ida the Jewish Russian actress, or even worse, the Jewish Russian lesbian. Perhaps from his pedestal in British society he needed something more exotic and in Ida he found a woman of culture, an exciting woman who could mirror his own pleasures, his own interests and who would happily share his penchant for travel to strange and uncivilized places. When Ida had first met Lord Moyne, then Walter Guinness, she was a creature of *La Belle Epoque*, a 'New Woman', a 'modern'. It is even more bemusing to wonder what Ida found in Moyne.

After France had fallen and Ida had finally been persuaded to leave Algeria, Sylvia Crawford wrote:

"After the fall of France she succeeded in reaching this country, where she devoted herself to philanthropic activities among the Free French Forces. She shunned publicity and only those close to her knew of the great interest of her benevolence, but many of the Free French Forces, recovering from injury or sickness in different hospitals in the south of England, will surely carry forever in their memories the recollection of her tall elegant figure, not walking but floating along the wards. In particular the French patients accommodated at the British Legion Sanatorium at Preston Hall, Kent and those in her own hospital at Camberley, will know how unsparingly she worked for them, with a rare sympathy, modesty and sensitivity. Despite her great love and knowledge of the theatre she declined to see any play or visit any theatre whilst she was in London during the war years, until eventually she agreed to accompany my husband and myself to see Terence Rattigan's *Flare Path*. She was spellbound and within a few days had adopted an air squadron, a gesture typical of her generosity. Her life will surely be an inspiration to all who knew her."

Once again, as in the First World War, Ida immersed herself in charitable works. It was as if another demon took over. Theatre and her own career appeared entirely forgotten as she worked unstintingly for the war. She began by visiting French pilots who had been shot down around England, ending up in one of the numerous military hospitals near London. There were many stories describing this 'Lady', this 'beautiful fascinating woman' – this 'queen' who came into a ward and silenced these tough, bruised men with much experience of life purely by her presence. Yet when she stayed to talk they found they were not overawed by her, but began pouring out their lives, their troubles and their histories. Ida would spend hours listening, sympathizing, and giving them the courage and determination to carry on.

She even financed and had her own wing in the hospital at Camberley. There she devoted much of her time, not only giving the patients a morale boost by her presence, but physically helping with the nursing itself. All her time was spent on her devotion to the war wounded. She seldom socialized, never appeared at any of the society functions and shunned publicity.

She once and once only gave a huge champagne party for all, including the wounded who could attend, to commemorate the shooting down of a thousand German planes. Then, the ultimate accolade, that was as important to her as any of her theatrical successes: she was made godmother to a Free French Squadron.

Her joy was soon to be shattered. In 1941 Moyne was appointed Secretary of State for the Colonies, where he had to deal with Jewish immigration into Palestine. With the coming of war a flood of European Jews arrived in Palestine and the British Government felt it had to regulate the immigrants. It was an explosive situation.

On 12 December 1941 a converted coal-ship, the *Strima*, set sail for Palestine with 769 Romanian Jews crowded on board. The British Government ordered the Turkish authorities to stop the ship at Istanbul. After two months of delay, and consultations and correspondence the Turks lost patience and towed the ship away out into the Black Sea. There it was hit by a torpedo and sunk. 768 out of the 769 passengers were drowned. The world was appalled, Zionists were outraged, and Abraham Stern, a terrorist leader, demanded revenge. In August 1942 Moyne was appointed Deputy Minister of State in Cairo, and in January 1944 he became Minister Resident in the Middle East. He had been there ten months when, on November 6th, he and his driver were gunned down in the streets of Cairo on their way to work by terrorists from the Stern Gang. Neither survived the attack.

If a graph was taken of Ida's life this would surely have been its nadir. She had only had two loves in her life, one had been the on and off relationship with Romaine Brooks, and the other with Walter Moyne, now gone forever. She was a refugee in London, albeit at the Ritz, with no family to fall back on, the very few friends she could trust dispersed throughout the world, entirely alone. She was desolate. Her career was non-existent, her sensuous and sinewy beauty, on which her career was launched and of which she had remained so proud, diminished with time and age. Her luxurious house in Paris, totally destroyed, her collection of first editions, amassed over thirty years, her important and proud record of the arts in the first half of the nineteenth century, taken by the Germans. Her photos had disappeared forever, and now the man with whom she had shared so much for so long was blown away by an assassin's bullet.

Even then she would not be beaten. Her squadron became her *raison d'être*, her hospital wing at Camberley her strength. Through her own pain, she became godmother extraordinary, giving hope and solace in those dark days.

As soon as the armistice came, Ida returned to Paris. Roland Leblond, Commander of the Légion d'Honneur, was a French pilot who met Ida after the war:

"I never fought in the French Squadron. I was with the English, detached to an English Squadron. My father was in the R.A.F. I flew a Spitfire. I had to bale out offshore off Cornwall and was picked up by the British Navy, and was in hospital from the end of 1942. By the end of 1945 I was back in hospital in France. When I arrived, one of my friends told Madame Rubinstein my story who told him she would like to meet me.

"From the end of 1945 right the way through to 1947 she came to see me in hospital many times. I was young, I was twenty-four, she was about sixty, but we became friends because she was such a giving lady.

"She had charisma. An extraordinary charisma. I don't know why, but there always was this something extra; she seemed to be on another planet. She was always dressed in beautiful clothes, very smart.

"When I left hospital I was still in very bad shape, so we began to write. I didn't see her very often, maybe three or four times. At this time she was all over the place. She had a home in United States Square in Paris. She always seemed to have time for me. We spoke on the phone, and when I was going through particularly bad times she would find time to write very comforting letters.

"She was a mysterious person. There she was, a great star, very rich with great big chauffeur-driven cars, but so kind. She was a one-off. No one could be like her. She was very special. Because she had obviously been such a great artist she had an aura about her. She was very cultivated, and being such a star she knew everybody, all the most famous people, and yet she would devote so much energy and time to the likes of me.

"She was never bitter. From time to time she would reflect about things or some other person, but it was always as if judged by someone outside herself. She was always very calm, happy and full of life. No affectation at all. I was a Parisian pilot and had been in some hard spots. She was a star, an aristocrat and yet she talked to you as if she had always known you. You were never embarrassed but enchanted to talk to her. I saw her a great deal."

M. Leblond has, in his apartment in Menton, a photograph of the Alsace Free French made up of some two hundred young men. Out of these only seventeen survived, and those that did were mostly badly injured. It was to these men that Ida Rubinstein gave her care and devotion.

18

VENCE

"We cannot tear out a single page from our life,
but we can throw the whole book into the fire."
George Sand (1804–1876)

The assassination of Lord Moyne heralded the end of Ida's life in the theatre; she never appeared on stage again. She continued her charitable work but socially became more and more reclusive. She was notably absent from any gala occasions or society functions held in post-war years. She shunned any form of publicity and avoided the spotlight; apart from visiting the sick and wounded in hospitals and convalescent homes, she retired more and more into herself.

In 1951 she left Paris for good to live the life of a semi-recluse just outside Vence, a small, picturesque town on a hillside in the Maritime Alps, twenty two kilometres above Nice in the south of France. There, among the mimosas and lemon trees, in the shadow of the Baous, with some of the loveliest views in France, Ida chose to stay for the remaining years of her life.

Perhaps it was only after World War Two that she realized she had spent too much of her life chasing the glories that had been lavished on her in *Cléopâtre* and *Schéhérazade* at the very outset of her career. Perhaps she had at last succumbed to the realization that she could not succeed in this dream. Her *cause célèbre*, her own ambition, was at last relinquished, as was her former life with all its blatant luxury. There was little left to sustain her. Her one lasting relationship with Walter Moyne having been taken away from her, she turned to a higher plateau. Having always been a zealot devoted to her own artistic ambition, she now became a religious zealot. She had been attracted to religion as far back as the mid-thirties. Having been born a Jew, and raised as a child amongst the society of St Petersburg, with the inevitable influences of Russian Orthodoxy during her years in France, she had turned more and more towards Catholicism.

She formally converted in September 1936, an experience which had made her 'drunk with joy' (Claudel). Now as carefully, as painstakingly and as thoroughly as she had prepared for any of her theatrical productions, her ambition would be devoted to the preparations for the most successful afterlife. Having not sustained the fruits of her success in this world, she devoted her resources to success in the next.

She became more and more of a recluse, but even in this self-imposed life of a virtual hermit she kept herself obsessively thin. She lived on an exceptionally frugal yet extravagant diet. Her housekeeper, Madame Soretto, remembers her being fed only one trout in jelly per day and drinking nothing except herb tea and pink champagne. These days it is clear that she was prone to a type of anorexia nervosa, taking purgatives daily, and her doctor would visit weekly to give her a colonic wash or enema. Amongst society, enemas were much more commonplace in the first part of the twentieth century than they are now, in spite of a small re-emergence of popularity during the late 1980s. In the twenties they were almost one of the "musts" for good health; so Ida may have been continuing the habits of a lifetime.

Liane de Pougy writes in her diary on January 11th, 1920, something that today would be found, at the least, mildly eccentric:

"Like every morning I have had my enema in order to preserve a clear skin and sweet breath. It is a family habit approved by Dr Pinard. One of Mama's old great-aunts, the beautiful Madame Rhones, died at the age of ninety and a half with a complexion of lilies and roses, skin like a child's. She took her little enema, it seems, at five o'clock every evening, so that she would sleep very well. She did it cheerfully in public. She would simply stand in front of the fireplace: her servant would come in discreetly, armed with a loaded syringe; Madame Rhones would lean forward gracefully so that her full skirts lifted, one two three, and it was done. Conversation was not interrupted. After a minute or two my beautiful ancestress would disappear briefly, soon to return with the satisfaction of a duty performed."

Madame Soretto says Ida hardly ate because she remained a dancer until she died. Even if she didn't actually dance she wanted to stay looking like one. She read during the day, or sat on her verandah meditating, looking down the hillside to the distant hazy blue of the Mediterranean. She wanted to cut herself off completely from the world. She wanted to break with her past as a public figure and live in solitude, to meditate and read away her final years.

She occasionally went to Paris to sort out finances with Madame Olivier; most times very little was seen of her. Then out of the blue she would contact one of her few remaining friends, when for an evening she would behave as if she had never left. René Dumesnil tells of a visit:

"For weeks or months we were left without news of her, when suddenly one would receive a basket of fruit or a gigantic box of chocolates with a telegram a hundred words long saying, 'I am a monster! Will you ever excuse my silence?' Or there would suddenly be a telephone call that one had ceased to hope for, and it was not a voice from beyond the grave ... but one full of gaiety, uttering protestations of friendship and promising imminent reunion, 'When I arrive in Paris I will let you know.'

"Days and weeks would pass, and then a call. 'What day will you come to lunch? I'll send Albert to pick you up.' And we would find ourselves, five or six of us, in the suite she occupied at the Georges V hotel. There Ida would be sparkling. 'We must laugh, mustn't we!' With her friends she was like a child, completely spontaneous!

"It was as if she needed these threads from her past to hold onto before she finally let go. Some sort of reassurance that there had been a purpose, a last look back before the next life."

Apart from these occasional 'coffee breaks' she was quietly and thoroughly rehearsing her final exit. In a way, the curtain had already come down, for most of the time she was no longer concerned with the present. She had nothing done to her face, no make-up, no creams, and out of her glorious wardrobe she only wore a long white garment like that of a monk or friar. Every year she spent a month at the medieval Abbey of Hautecombe, near Chambéry, there using every minute for meditation and prayers. The Abbey took in men and women from the outside who wanted to stay there for whatever reasons, for a fortnight, a month, or a year. Ida never once missed. She wore her white robes. All those in the Benedictine order wore white; there was only one difference; Ida's white robes were of the finest silk.

Perhaps through her prayers and meditation Ida found a hint of nostalgia for her roots. For the first time in her life she showed a longing for news of Russia. Maybe her outward serenity was hiding the pain of a lost childhood.

Marguerite Long, a pianist and virtuoso performer, and close friend of some twenty-five years, whom Ida met on those rare trips to Paris, remembered that Ida's happiness at those times bubbled only on the surface:

"I cannot help thinking that, in her retirement ... there was nostalgia for her own country. She loved to recall Russia, and when I returned from Moscow, she wanted to know my impressions and to talk to me of her youth; when I said 'We shall go together', for the first time ever I saw that secret and impenetrable being with tears in her eyes."

But for the remaining eleven months of the year she would remain in her house 'Olivades'. There she would rise early (she was always up and dressed by the time Madame Soretto arrived), have her cup of herb tea, then clean and floss her teeth assiduously every day, a habit ahead of its time. She would spend the morning lying on her couch reading whilst her cook prepared her lunch of one trout in jelly. With lunch she had a glass of champagne. She told Madame Soretto, "The day I stop drinking champagne will be the end!" Ida never cooked.

Often in the afternoon her secretary/companion, Madame Olivier, arrived and they would deal with Ida's accounts and financial matters. Madame Olivier signed all her cheques and had the keys to her many large safe deposit boxes in which were kept her jewellery. They talked a little of the few of Ida's friends who were still alive and then in the evening Ida would sit on her verandah alone, for hours on end, looking at the stars, watching the lights twinkling on the hillside below.

One of the very few occasions that she showed any desire to meet any friends was when she learned that Romaine Brooks was living just outside Nice, not too far away. She sent a loving note saying she would like to meet, but Romaine turned down her invitation. Ida's favourite flowers had always been lilies; she had drunk champagne from the leaves of madonna lilies; Romaine had always compared Ida's beauty to that of a lily. Now she was to turn down Ida's invitation, not for health reasons, nor from any personal animosity, but simply because "She is no longer like a lily."

Perhaps in her harshness Romaine was right. Time had moved on, things had changed. Natalie Barney's 'Fridays' still took place, but something was lacking, the vital energies that were drawn from the faithful few who still came, Colette and Pound, Anna de Noailles, Otto of Hapsburg, Bernhard Berenson, were slowing to a halt. All these people belonged to an era, an epoch that was gone – and Ida more than any.

Ida was of time that had passed and with that passing her fame, that was built on flimsy foundations that had been laid almost half a century earlier, just faded away. Her beauty, her notoriety were only receding echoes of a bygone world.

Ida died quite suddenly at her home, alone, on September 20th 1960, of a heart attack. She was on the telephone. No one knows whom she was calling. The official cause of death was cardiac arrest. Madame Soretto laid her out and dressed her in her silks to be put in her coffin.

On September 29th Ida Rubinstein was buried in a corner of the cemetery at Vence. The cemetery is full of many varieties of tombstones from the Gothic to the Romantic. Ida is buried at the very far end, in the most uncared-for part, where the truly religious are laid to rest. Here is the only place in the cemetery where the tombs are not built on top of the ground. All the stones are quite plain and set into the earth; all ostentation is left to those in the main part of the graveyard.

It was not until a fortnight later that the news of her death reached the Paris press. Her final curtain came down to better reviews than she had had for years.

19

WHISPERS IN THE WINGS

"The Pleasure and consideration that go with realized
ambition, even with boundless power, are nothing
compared with the inner happiness found in affection
and love."

Stendhal (1783–1842)

As soon as M. Roland Leblond learned of Ida's death, he and his wife
immediately went to Vence, where he was shocked to see the utter
frugality of her grave. The tombstone, a plain slab set into the ground
with her name, the date she died, and a small plain cross etched into the
stone. Even the date of her birth was missing. He went straight to Paris to
the Free French Pilots, where they organized and arranged a special
plaque, in honour of Ida, to be put on her gravestone. Translated into
English it reads:

> "Godmother through the War,
> from the Alsace Regiment."

To this day Roland Leblond travels with his wife from his home in
Menton to Vence each All Saints' Day, November 1st, to lay flowers on the
grave of Ida Rubinstein, paying homage to the lady who was so generous
with her time in her concern for the men who fought so gallantly in World
War II.

"I go because of a deep feeling. It is hard to say whether it is sadness or
just emotion. It gives me some idea of the measure of things. I want to
remember, to say my thanks."

The news of Ida's death was now known throughout Europe. There
were obituaries in the French and English newspapers. When Cocteau
heard, he said "With Ida Rubinstein's death a little of my youth has died."

The *Times* obituary ended:

"Around her there clung till the end the atmosphere of a period which
died in the First World War and was buried in the great slump. Her death
sees the passing of a remarkable theatrical personality who became in her
own lifetime a voice from the past."

The Daily Telegraph also spoke of the start of her career:

"Ida Rubinstein's contribution to the theatre was to have been a young
dancer with an exceptional talent, capable of being used to its fullest in

some of the masterpieces of Fokine during his most prolific choreographic phase."

She could never match her initial successes. As Orson Welles said looking back on his life since *Citizen Kane*: "I started at the top of the ladder and have been climbing down ever since."

In the heady moments of those first two Ballets Russes seasons in Paris she was showered with hyperbole. Even Diaghilev, who could barely in the end mention her name without spitting, called her "The mysterious, extravagant, biblical Rubinstein." Léon Bakst, to whom she went when she was still a girl, who with Fokine initially helped get her into the Ballets Russes, and who remained constantly loyal until the day he died, called her "A fabulous being. We are blessed to have her amongst us. I might love the whole of humanity, every living being like a flower of the Lord, but she I adore like a beautiful tulip, insolent and dazzling, proud of herself and shedding pride around her."

She excited the most extravagant praise. Writers of the day fought for adjectives to describe her: "an exotic orchid," "an ibis," "a fatal enchantress in the tradition of the cruel and grasping Astarte" and, as Jean Cocteau found her, "excessively beautiful, like liquor from poison fragrances."

Ida Rubinstein was Art Nouveau. Following directly on from Lois Fuller and Sarah Bernhardt, she appeared to be designed for such an era "as if God had employed an artistic assistant whose sinister hands had let free rein to all his fantasies!"

She was everything the period stood for, and, with the end of that era, that essential magic which was Ida ended too. She continued, still looking for the moonbeams on which to hitch her star, but she was out of time. She was too late. The dedicated, blinkered determination that took her to the top in the beginning was to drag her down in the end; blinkered because she could not, or would not see what was happening around her. She persisted in trying to become a ballerina, dancing in the works she had commissioned long after she was suitable for the roles, towering above her partners in tutus made by Lanvin. "She looked like a sick ostrich – not quite the ibis of before! In *Boléro* she danced on the table and it was said 'Madame falls off every evening into a drum.' "

Ida insisted on thinking that she should become a great dramatic actress, affecting the Bernhardt manner for decades after it became *de trop*. She mounted her own productions of the works of Paul Valéry and Arthur Honegger and Shakespeare's *Antony and Cleopatra*, as translated by André Gide, and played the role in *La Dame aux Camélias* with a pronounced Russian accent. As her style became increasingly irrelevant she was denounced more and more strongly by the critics. Romaine

Brooks described her caustically as "a great deal less than she seemed." Perhaps after the death of Moyne she realized for the first time her ambitions on this earth could not be fulfilled and so she quite purposefully faded into oblivion in her retirement to Vence.

Even though Ida died quietly, without fanfare, prepared as only she knew how to make her entry into the next world, there were still question marks left behind. What happened to her wealth, her jewellery, her magnificent wardrobe? The money that she had invested all went to her Benedictine order. That much is known. But what happened to the remainder?

It seems that Madame Olivier, her long-time secretary, was living under a false name. M. Leblond said: "I don't know what happened with Madame Olivier – blackout – complete blackout. A friend of mine and I tried to track her down, tried to find out anything that had happened, but whenever it was anything to do with Madame Olivier we came to a dead end. It was as if she had never been. Blackout!"

Madame Soretto is much more outspoken, certain she knows what happened:

"Madame Olivier, the secretary woman, the cow! She took everything. She had a young lover who got her to steal the lot, her jewels, her fortune, her clothes. They took the lot. Money, everything, and then skipped town! She had her cheque books, the keys to her safe boxes – everything. They took the lot."

Whatever actually happened has never been discovered. Madame Olivier has never been found and Ida's jewellery, her cash, her wardrobe, all are missing. Perhaps Ida might have even enjoyed the mystery. Once again the enigma, the incomprehensible extravagant being, untouchable, leaving unanswered questions in her wake. For one last time she played the sphinx, leaving an eternal riddle.

If Ida could have rolled back her life as if on film, where would she have stopped? Which moments would she choose to live again? It is doubtful she would have delved into her childhood, into her pre-revolutionary years in St Petersburg, where she had lived amongst the indulged upper classes with her aunt, Madame Horwitz. Perhaps for just a moment she would sit again, as a young girl, on the steps of the Acropolis, under the stars, thinking of her Antigone, dreaming the untroubled dreams of a glorious future in the theatre with the innocence and self-confidence of youth.

Certainly she would stop in those halcyon days at the zenith of her popularity, maybe at that moment when she first stunned Paris entering as Cleopatra, emerging from her twelve veils, this disconcerting and mystical beauty, filling the audience with awe, the echoes of the sublimely terrifying music of Rimsky-Korsakov's *Mlada* still sounding in her ears.

Would it be that moment at La Scala Milan, at the curtain calls of *Le Martyre de St Sébastien*, when Ida stepped forward from the line-up and Gabriele d'Annunzio rose in his box, their eyes met and they smiled, to tumultuous and deafening applause? Or perhaps, one of those private moments on her travels, sitting on the deck of the yacht *Rousalka*, sharing a quiet moment or two with Lord Moyne.

Probably Ida would not look back at all. She would have been devoting all her energies to the future, much too preoccupied preparing for her entry into the next world. There could be no time for what might have been.

She had lived to attract attention; the admiration of distinguished men and women flattered her. Her *cavalieri serventi*, her followers, were amongst the most famous in Europe and were slaves to her power. She had echoed Sarah Bernhardt, bringing back a tiger cub from one of her travels as a pet, drinking her champagne from madonna leaves, fanning the flames of publicity for her bewitching creation.

She who had caused a scandal at the sacrilege of posing naked in a monastic building ended her days in prayer and contemplation, joining the Benedictine monks in the medieval Abbey of Hautecombe to find her peace.

That the light of her career had dimmed long before she finished in the theatre was most probably one of her greatest sadnesses, her ambitions never properly fulfilled. The star that had danced in 1909 and 1910 for Ida was never to be as bright again. But dance it did, and even though she had little personal acclaim for the latter part of her career, her total devotion to the theatre left a legacy that we still enjoy today. The vast number of dancers and musicians, artists, designers, poets and actors who are beholden to her include virtually anyone who was touched by the theatre, in any of its forms, especially ballet.

Ravel wrote his *Boléro* for her, Debussy composed his final score for her, Bakst drew his last design for her, works by Stravinsky, Honegger, Gide, were dedicated to her, Gabriele d'Annunzio wrote *Le Martyre de St Sébastien* for her, Fokine, Massine, Nijinska, Benois all directed and choreographed for her. A world of performers, craftsmen and artisans earned their livelihood in her wake.

If Ida Rubinstein's life had not been so extraordinary, she would have made it so. In many ways Ida Rubinstein invented herself. After all the fanfares, after all the history books have been written, Ida Rubinstein, that "beautiful tulip, insolent and dazzling" (Léon Bakst), is almost forgotten.

The municipal authorities of Vence are fully entitled to dig up her remains. The thirty-year lease on her grave expired in October 1990.

CHRONOLOGY

1866. May. Léon Bakst born in Grodno, as Rosenberg.

1871. Rasputin born in Siberia as Grigori Yefimovich Novykh. 'Rasputin', the name he earned by his behaviour, means 'Debauched One'.

1872. March 19th, Serge Diaghilev born in the Russian province of Novgorod.
        March 21st. Diaghilev's mother dies as a result of the birth.

1874. Diaghilev's father remarries and the family move to St Petersburg.

1876. Margarete Gertrude Zelle (Mata Hari) was born in Holland.

1878. Isadora Duncan was born in San Francisco.

1881. The assassination of Tsar Alexander II. The resulting revival of deep-rooted anti-semitism leads to pogroms in 160 towns and villages.

1882. Laws instituted in Russia restricting Jewish movement and limiting higher education for Jews.

1883. Coco Chanel (first name originally Gabrielle) was born in France.
        Bakst enters the St Petersburg Academy of Arts.
        Commercial theatres are made legal through a new law. Up to then all ballet, opera, and drama was answerable only to the Court and, therefore, entirely governed by its taste which was essentially and culturally restricting.

1884. The Diaghilevs move out of St Petersburg to their family estate.

1885. October 5th. Ida Rubinstein is born to Ernestine and Lvov Rubinstein.

1887/88. Both of Ida's parents die.
        Ida and her sister are taken into the care of their aunt, Madame Horwitz.

1889. Vaslav Nijinsky born to Thomas and Elenora Nijinsky, who are part of a troupe of Polish dancers.

1890. Diaghilev arrives in St Petersburg and enters university to study law.
        Diaghilev meets Alexandre Benois, Léon Bakst, Dima Filosofov, and Walter Nouvel, who are the among the group who will start *Mir Iskusstva (The World of Art)* with him.
        Before entering the university Diaghilev had travelled abroad for the first time with his cousin Dima. Florence, Vienna and Venice impressed and influenced him artistically. He enters university with no interest in law but all in art.
        Diaghilev organizes an exhibition of English and German watercolours, which is sufficiently successful to lead to backing of further exhibitions of a more ambitious nature. Among them were exhibitions of Russian, Scandinavian and, eventually, international artists.
        Diaghilev is responsible for introducing the French Impressionists to Russia.

1895. Diaghilev writes to his beloved stepmother, Elena: "I am firstly a great charlatan, though with 'brio'; secondly, a great 'charmeur', thirdly I have any amount of cheek, fourthly I am a man with a great quantity of logic, but with very few principles, fifthly, I think I have no real gifts. All the same 'I think I have found my true vocation – being a Maecenas.' I have all that is necessary save the money – 'mais ça viendra.'"

1896. Through Bakst's friend, Count Benkendorf, Grand Duke Vladimir Alexandrovich, President of the Imperial Academy of Arts, Bakst's most loyal patron, is instrumental in obtaining a commission for a giant painting of the Russian Admiral Anvellan. This is later displayed at the Naval Museum in St Petersburg.

Léon Bakst returns to Russia from Paris to be appointed "Painter to the Imperial Court".

1897. Diaghilev's first exhibition of English and German watercolours is presented at the Stieglitz Palace. This is followed by a Scandinavian Exhibition later on in that same year.

1898. October. The magazine *Mir Iskusstva (The World of Art)* is first published with Diaghilev as editor.

Prince Volkonsky appointed director of the Imperial Theatres.

Prince Volkonsky engages Diaghilev to edit the Annuals of the Imperial Theatres. Diaghilev later resigns after some altercation with those in authority who do not approve of Diaghilev's overbearing personality. The cover and decorations within the *Year Book 1899/1900* were by Bakst.

Fokine graduates from the Maryinsky School.

1900. Nijinsky is accepted as a day student at the Maryinsky School.

1901. The only book by Diaghilev is published, a scholarly work on the painter Levitsky.

Rasputin converts to the Khlysty religious sect. He then leaves his wife, Proskovia, and their three children for the religious life.

1902. February 22nd. Bakst creates his first theatrical designs at the Hermitage Theatre for a ballet arranged by Marius Petipa.

1903. Léon Bakst marries.

1904. Diaghilev spends most of this year organizing art shows in Russia. *The World of Art* is closed down.

1905. January 22nd. Bloody Sunday. Imperial troops fire upon a delegation of working men who have assembled to petition the Tsar for the redress of certain grievances. About a thousand of them are killed. This incident arouses the sympathy of many who were wavering.

Diaghilev's most impressive exhibition yet, in the Tauride Palace in St Petersburg. Portraits of those famous in Russian history from 1705 onwards have been advertised in the *The World of Art*. The show was in aid of 'War Orphans and Widows' (of the Russo-Japanese War). The Patron was the Czar, who headed an impressive and long list of other patrons.

First appearance in Russia of Isadora Duncan.

Bakst is divorced.

1906. Spring. Diaghilev is introduced to Gabriel Astruc by the Comtesse de Greffulhe (Marcel Proust's Madame de Guermantes) at one of the soirées at her famous salon IV Rue d'Astorg. The musical concerts the following year will be as a direct result of this introduction.

A few months later in 1906 Diaghilev takes his exhibition of Russian Art at the Salon d'Automne to Paris. Part of the success is engendered by the Czar, who lends priceless works from the Imperial collections, which encourages others to do the same.

Josephine Baker was born in St Louis.

Diaghilev organizes a concert in Paris at the Grand Palais des Champs-Elysées.

The magazine *Apollo* devotes an entire issue to Bakst's work.

Bakst opens a school of art in Serquiewskaia Street, where he is living. Chagall and Countess Tolstoy are among his pupils.

1907. Paris. Lois Fuller dances *Salomé* to Schmitt's music.

St Cloud, outside Paris. Léon Bakst's ex-wife gives birth to his son, André, at least two years after their marriage was annulled.

The Paris Opera. Diaghilev puts on five concerts of Russian music, which include compositions by Mussorgsky. The Russian Ambassador and one of the Embassy's youngest diplomats, M. Nelidov, are Diaghilev's patrons.

1908. St Petersburg. *Antigone*. Sets and costumes designed by Léon Bakst. Production by Ida Rubinstein.

Vaslav Nijinsky graduates from the Maryinsky School.

Paris. Diaghilev puts on a complete Russian opera, Mussorgsky's *Boris Godunov*. Decor by Golovin, Benois and Yuon.

Salomé. Choreography by Mikhail Fokine. Sets and costumes designed by Bakst. Production by Ida Rubinstein.

1909. Late April/early May. The Ballets Russes perform for two weeks in Berlin.

May 19th. At 8.30 pm. The Ballets Russes open at the Châtelet Theatre, Paris, with a public dress rehearsal (répétition générale).

The operas, *Ivan the Terrible, Prince Igor, Ruslan and Ludmilla* and *Judith* as well as the dance suite *Le Festin* and the Bluebird pas de deux from *The Sleeping Beauty*.

The second programme of ballets includes *Cléopâtre*, which opens on 2nd June. With music by Arensky, Taneyev, Rimsky-Korsakov, Glinka, Glazunov, Mussorgsky and Tcherepnin.

Choreography by Mikhail Fokine. Sets and costumes designed by Léon Bakst. Idea by Fokine. The principal dancers are Ida Rubinstein, Vaslav Nijinsky, Anna Pavlova, Karsavina, Fokine and Bulgakov.

P. Phillipe sculpts two bronze figures of Ida.

The Ballets Russes season ends with with some of the company appearing in a gala at the Paris Opera House in aid of Messina, the Italian city that had been devastated the year before by a huge earthquake. Amongst the stars are George Robey, Sarah Bernhardt, Nijinsky, Karsavina, Sacha Guitry, Réjane and Felicia Litvin. Described as "one of the most inspiring presentations ever planned" (Bourman).

After the end of the Ballets Russes season Ida performs *à la* Cleopatra at the Olympia in Paris to great acclaim.

27th September–30th September. London Coliseum. Ida performs her Cleopatra-type dances in twice-daily performances.

November 13th. Ida sails to New York to appear at the Metropolitan Opera House.

More Cleopatra-type performances in music-halls in France and Italy. *Mort d'un Cygne (The Dying Swan)* is another of Ida's music-hall offerings.

Bakst paints her portrait sometime between 1909 and 1910.

1910. May 20th. The Ballets Russes perform a two-week season in Berlin with Ida as Cleopatra.

Jacques-Emile Blanche paints Ida. Serov paints a nude of her.

Druet photographs her.

June 4th. *Schéhérazade* opens the 1910 Paris season at the Opera House. Choreography by Mikhail Fokine. With music by Rimsky-Korsakov. Sets and costumes designed by Léon Bakst. Idea by Benois.

Principal dancers, Ida Rubinstein, Vaslav Nijinsky, and Bulgakov, as well as Flore Revalles and Adolf Bolm. Production by Serge Diaghilev for the Ballets Russes Company.

Ida Rubinstein meets Walter Guinness (later Lord Moyne).

Romaine Brooks painted a nude of Ida. *Azalée Blanche.*

Autumn. Ida engrossed in the creation of *St Sébastien.*

1911. March 2nd. D'Annunzio finishes *St Sébastien.*

Nijinsky is dismissed from the Imperial Theatre for appearing in *Giselle* wearing tights without the trunks over them, as the custom is at this time. In the audience were the Dowager Empress and the Grand Duchess Xenia who were to witness a male dancer in only tights, and all his glory, for the first time.

Diaghilev engages Enrico Cecchetti to teach his company in class every day.

After the summer closure of the Imperial Theatres, Diaghilev is able to assemble his company as the dancers are now free to work for him.

April 9th and 10th. Ida is to appear for Diaghilev as Zobeida in *Schéhérazade* in Monte Carlo. Ida lets him down at the last moment by telegram, but Ida does appear for him there on April 24th. This saves Diaghilev from being sued, because he had signed a contract which stipulated that Ida would appear.

May 8th. Cardinal della Volpe authorizes a decree from the Papal Index by which all of d'Annunzio's works are banned. Following this the Archbishop of Paris issues a pastoral letter condemning *St Sébastien* as offensive to the Christian conscience, and all Catholics are forbidden to attend any performances on pain of excommunication.

An invitation to perform *St Sébastien* in Rome as part of the festivities for the fiftieth anniversary of the unification of Italy was cancelled.

May 22nd. *St Sébastien* opens at the Théâtre du Châtelet produced by Ida Rubinstein. Theatre manager Astruc. Sets and costumes by Léon Bakst.

Music by Claude Debussy. Choreography of dance and mime by Mikhail Fokine.

Romaine Brooks paints the nude *Le Trajet*.

June 21. The Ballets Russes has its first London season, following the season in Paris, and opens at the Royal Opera House, Covent Garden, for eight performances.

June 26th. The Ballets Russes takes part in a Royal Gala at Covent Garden, London, to commemorate the coronation of King George V.

In the summer months Romaine Brooks paints Ida as St Sebastian, *The Masked Archer*, subtitled *The Persecuted Woman*, wickedly characterizing d'Annunzio as a masked dwarf.

Rasputin's influence within the Romanov family is at its peak.

1912. May 4th–10th May. A verse-play *Hélène de Sparte* by Emile Verhaeren. Produced by Ida at the Théâtre du Châtelet. Costumes and decor by Léon Bakst. Edouard de Max playing opposite Ida Rubinstein.

May 29th. Nijinsky's choreographic debut with *L'Après-Midi d'un Faune*. With music by Claude Debussy. Choreographed by Vaslav Nijinsky. Costumes and sets by Léon Bakst. Author of plot, Nijinsky. Principal dancers, Nijinsky and Nelidova.

Nijinsky causes a furore and sensation by ending the performance masturbating with the scarf left behind by the nymph.

May 30th. *Le Figaro* calls this a "Loathsome piece of miming." Auguste Rodin and Odilon Redon count themselves amongst Diaghilev's supporters in this battle with and through the press.

June. London. Bakst has the first of two exhibitions of his work at the Fine Art Society in Bond Street.

Fokine resigns from Diaghilev's company because of Nijinsky's new choreographic status in the Ballets Russes.

June 12–19th. *Salomé*. Produced by Ida at the Théâtre du Châtelet. Choreography by Mikhail Fokine. Costumes and decor by Léon Bakst. Edouard de Max as Herod.

1913. March 12th. D'Annunzio's fiftieth birthday. He finishes *La Pisanelle*.

June 10th. *La Pisanelle*, or *La Mort Parfumée*, premiered at the Théâtre du Châtelet, with a cast of 212 actors. The male lead is Edouard de Max. Sets and decor by Léon Bakst. Ida's costumes designed by Worth. Choreography by Mikhail Fokine. Music by Pizzetti, conducted by Desiré-Emile Inghelbrecht. It runs for ten days.

Diaghilev presents Karsavina in *Salomé*.

Robert de Montesquiou commissions a painting of Ida from Antonio de La Gandara, who is in fashion at the time. The painting was to be exhibited at the Spring Salon of 1914.

June/July. Léon Bakst has another exhibition of his work at the Fine Art Society in Bond Street. Purchasers include Lady Duff, Vaslav Nijinsky, Charles Ricketts, James de Rothschild, Lady Sackville, Sir Philip Sassoon, and Lady Mond. Although both this exhibition and that of the previous year hang some hundred and forty drawings each, only twenty-seven works in all are sold.

August 15th. The Ballets Russes sets sail on the S.S. *Avon* for its South American Tour.

October. D'Annunzio sues for the cancellation of *St Sébastien* in Rome during 1911 and wins the case.

Ida sets out on her travels to places such as Constantinople, then to the Red Sea, and continuing to Nairobi, where she goes off on a lion-hunting expedition.

1914. July. Ida is in Switzerland with Romaine Brooks.

July 28th. The Austro-Hungarian Empire declares war on Serbia. The beginning of the First World War. Ida and Romaine return immediately to Paris.

Ida finances and sets up her own hospital for war wounded in the Carlton Hotel, where she works as hard at nursing the soldiers as any of the medical staff. Such altruism was carried out in a nurse's uniform designed for her by Bakst.

September 10th. Nijinsky marries Romola de Pulszky in the Town Hall of the Argentine capital and and later in the Catholic church of San Miguel.

Ida continues to be involved with L'Association Générale des Combattants et Mutilés for many years after the war.

1915. Ida's sexual relationship with Romaine is ended.

D'Annunzio returns to Italy just before Italy enters the war. Ida notes that he "immediately fulfilled the triple destiny dreamt of by Leonardo da Vinci, that of being poet, tribune of the people and soldier."

The sinking of the *Lusitania*.

19th December. Edith Piaf was born.

1916. D'Annunzio is badly wounded and is in danger of losing his sight. Ida visits him in Venice, braving the dangers of such a journey, to be by his side.

February 22nd. Sarah Bernhardt has her leg amputated. Ida pays all her clinical and surgical expenses and is a constant visitor. Ida looks after Sarah Bernhardt after the tragedienne's amputation.

17 December. Ida misses a rehearsal, "being prudent for the first time in my life," for a matinee recital of selected patriotic war poems by Robert de Montesquiou at the Théâtre Sarah Bernhardt, wearing her famous nurse's uniform designed by Bakst.

December 29–30. Rasputin is murdered by a group of concerned noblemen headed by Prince Feliks Youssupov, the husband of the Tsar's niece. Rasputin had told the Tsarina that were he ever to be killed by any of her family, then the family itself would not survive more than two years. Two years later the Romanovs would be assassinated.

1917. Ida is seriously considering mounting the play *Sappho Désespérée* by Lucie Delarue-Mardrus. She was not to do so, perhaps because of the possible reaction to the androgynous Ida portraying Sappho.

Picasso makes his first designs for Diaghilev, the ballet *Parade*.

March 13th. The Tsar abdicates.

Late spring. Ida plans *Antony and Cleopatra*.

Summer. Ida gives one performance of the fourth act of *Phèdre* at the Paris Opera House for impoverished Russians. It actually turns out to be for impoverished Romanians. Sets and costumes by Léon Bakst. With Edouard de Max.

Ida is to use the same costumes later in another production of *Fedra* by d'Annunzio.

July 25th. Mata Hari was shot.

November 6th. The October Revolution. Ida loses all her wealth and property in Russia, income from these sources ceases, but her riches are so great that it makes little difference to her.

Ida buys a private aeroplane and a yacht larger than the British royal yacht.

Ida's husband arrives in Paris and requests a divorce. Ida refuses. Vladimir puts a private detective on her tail, but thanks to her discretion he cannot prove any grounds for a divorce and disappears forever out of her life. No scandal about Ida with Romaine or Walter Guinness could be proved.

Ida gives several poetry recitals of Robert de Montesquiou's second volume of *Offrandes Blessées* entitled *Sabliers et Lacrymatoires*. Several performances of which are cancelled because of the German bombardment of Paris.

1918. Walter Guinness is mentioned three times in despatches and awarded a bar to his Distinguished Service Order.

Romaine Brooks paints Ida in her nurse's uniform in which, Cocteau says, she appears "like the penchant perfume of some exotic essence, ethereal, otherworldly, divinely unattainable."

November 11th. The armistice is signed.

1919. Early March. *Le Roi Errant* by Imroulcais, at the Théâtre des Alliés.

April 1st. Gala charity matinee performance at the Paris Opera. Ida dances *La Tragédie de Salomé*, a ballet based on a poem by Robert d'Humières, music by Florent Schmitt, newly choreographed for Ida by Nicola Guerra. Herodias played by Christine Kerf and Herod played by Georges Wague (Colette's former actor colleague). Also performing are Sarah Bernhardt reciting the poem *Triomphe* by Fernand Gregh, and Luisa Tetrazzini in arias by Rossini, Ambroise Thomas and Ignace Paderewski.

Ida's *La Tragédie de Salomé* included in the repertoire of the Paris Opera until June 27th.

Late August. Ida flies to Venice in her new aeroplane, to bring d'Annunzio a copy of Montesquiou's poems *Un Moment du Pleur Eternel*. D'Annunzio "baptized" the plane *St Sébastien*. The plane's fuselage bears Sebastian's words "Je viens, je monte, j'ai des ailes!"

Ida visits d'Annunzio a few days later and witnesses his historic stand against the Allies for the town of Fiume. Just before the expedition set out, d'Annunzio takes Ida out on to the balcony of her hotel, the Danieli. Gazing out over the lagoon, he tells her about his secret plan to capture the town. "I am feverish for mortal adventure", he confesses. According to Tom

Antongini, who heard the story from the poet's own lips, Ida's response is equally feverish. She embraces him, with the words "I love you."

1920. Filming of *St Sébastien* is started, produced by Vidult Haut. It would be abandoned after only the dance sequences were shot. Fragments of these survive.

May 4th. Ida appears at the Opera (whilst in rehearsals for *Antoine et Cléopâtre*) at a grand gala in aid of Russian refugees in France, in a dramatized recitation of *La Nuit de Mai* by Alfred de Musset. Ida plays the role of the Muse and Sarah Bernhardt plays the Poet. Ida also rejoined the Ballets Russes for the night to play the role she created, Zobeida, in *Schéhérazade*, with Massine playing the Golden Slave and Enrico Cecchetti as the Chief Eunuch.

On the same night the actress Réjane dies.

Ida recuperates by resting at the Trianon Palace Hotel in Versailles. Then she flies to Venice to film *La Nave* by d'Annunzio for Arturo Ambrosio and Armando Zanotto, produced by d'Annunzio's son Gabriellino who is also artistic director.

June 14th. Ida puts on *Antoine et Cléopâtre* at the Paris Opera. Translated by André Gide; music by Florent Schmitt; costumes designed by Jacques Dresa, except Ida's costume, which is designed by the fashion house of Worth. Edouard de Max plays Antony, with Armand Bour and Georges Wague playing other leading roles.

1921. Ida makes another film, *San Giorgio*, with Giulio Artiste Sartorio.

After nearly two years of preparations, Ida's house, 7 Place des Etats-Unis, is ready. Ida leaves the hotels where she has lived, and gives up her studio at 54 Rue Vaneau.

December 11th. Robert de Montesquiou dies, one day before Ida's return to France after two months of travel.

19th December. A service for de Montesquiou is held at Saint-Pierre-de-Chaillot.

21st December. De Montesqiou is buried in the Cimetière des Gonards at Versailles, where his lover Gabriel Yturri is also buried. Ida attends, as do Elisabeth de Gramont, Natalie Barney, Frédéric de Madrazo, Louise Breslau, and Dr Couchaud.

1922. May 1st. The premiere of *Artémis Troublée* at the Paris Opera House. Costumes, decor and, for the first time, libretto by Bakst. Choreography by Nicola Guerra. Music by Paul Paray.

June 15th. Dress rehearsal for a revival of *St Sébastien*.

June 16th. The conductor, André Caplet, who participated in the orchestration, walks out the day before the opening because of the "state of disorder on stage". This is due to the inadequate amount of time allotted to Ida by the Opera House.

June 17th. Saturday. A charity performance for a monument to those who fell at the Battle of the Somme. Henri Defosse steps in at the last minute as conductor.

June 23rd. Last performance of *St Sébastien* which is now officially made a part of the Paris Opera's repertoire.

June 24th. Ida appears again at the Paris Opera for yet another charity event. In a tableau representing the marriage of the Doge, Ida appears with Edouard de Max. Their last public appearance together.

August. André Doderet, translator of d'Annunzio's *Fedra*, visits d'Annunzio, at Ida's behest, in Gardone. D'Annunzio has just made his famous speech on the balcony in Milan, preventing civil war in Italy.

November. The discovery of Tutankhamun's tomb.

Sarah Bernardt schools Ida in *La Dame aux Camélias*, in the part which she herself had made famous.

Ida performs as Marguerite Gautier, in the last act, at a charity gala for needy Russians. Sarah wishes Ida to take on her own mantle, and is in the audience.

1923. March 26th. Sarah Bernhardt dies.

June 6th. An afternoon dress rehearsal of *Phaedre* at the Paris Opera.

Premiere of *Phaedre* by d'Annunzio. Sets and costumes by Léon Bakst.

June 8th. Jacques Rouche, the director of the Paris Opera, publishes in *Le Figaro* a letter from d'Annunzio explaining his reasons for not being there with all the many other celebrities.

St Sébastien, the last production in Ida's 1923 season of d'Annunzio. Unlike last year's production, there is ample time to rehearse, with the Opera being more fair, professional, and cooperative. Music conducted by Philippe Gaubert.

27th November. Ida fulfills a promise to Sarah with a gala performance of *La Dame aux Camélias* at the Théâtre Sarah Bernhardt for soldiers wounded in the war. Sets and decor by Alexandre Benois. Ida goes on to give fifty performances.

For the next few years Ida travels extensively with and without Walter Guinness. Her yacht is always ready at a moment's notice.

1924. Gabriele d'Annunzio is made Prince of Montenevoso by Mussolini.

February. Ida appears once again at the Théâtre Sarah Bernhardt in *Le Secret du Sphinx*, playing the Spirit of the Sphinx. A verse play by Maurice Rostand. Costumes by Romain de Tirtoff.

Late February. A more "polished" *St Sébastien* is once again revived at the Paris Opera House.

May. *St Sébastien* at the Théâtre de la Monnaie in Brussels.

July 10th. Ida dances in a ballet season at the Paris Opera House, in which she performs the name role of *Ishtar*. Music by Vincent d'Indy. Decor and costumes by Léon Bakst. His last creation.

October 28th. Edouard de Max dies.

December 27th. Léon Bakst dies in a clinic at Rueil-Malmaison, outside Paris, alone.

December 31st. Bakst is buried in Paris.

1925. April 1st. Ida appears at the Théâtre de Vaudeville as Natasha Filippovna Barashkov in *The Idiot* by Dostoievsky. Adapted by Vladimir Bienstock and Fernand Nozière. Sets and costumes by Alexandre Benois. The play runs for the whole of April.

Ida has no more theatre performances, and spends most of the rest of this year on her exotic, long-haul travels.

November. A memorial exhibition is held in Paris for Léon Bakst.

1926. March. Ida performs *St Sébastien* at La Scala, Milan, in the presence of d'Annunzio with Arturo Toscanini conducting.

April. Ida takes her repertoire to Rome, to the Teatro Constanzi. The planned gala performance of *Le Martyre de St Sébastien* is cancelled on short notice.

April 9th. Ida replaces *St Sébastien* by a gala performance of *La Dame aux Camélias* in aid of charities and in memory of Queen Margherita of Italy, mother of King Victor Emmanuel III, who had recently died.

This is followed a few days later with a second performance of *La Dame aux Camélias*, then two performances of *The Idiot*, and then one performance of *Phaedre* for which Ida has had new incidental music especially commissioned from Arthur Honegger.

Strangely, apart from including *St Sébastien* in her Covent Garden season in 1931, Ida is never to perform any works by d'Annunzio again.

At the end of the season Ida spent two weeks visiting d'Annunzio before returning home.

June 11th. The much delayed public dress rehearsal for *Orphée* at the Paris Opera.

On the same day she appears at the Odeon Theatre in a charity gala production of *La Dame aux Camélias*. It was for her favourite cause, the war wounded soldiers of the Association des Ecrivains. It raised a record amount of money.

June 12th. The official unveiling of a memorial statue of Sarah Bernhardt. The statue, by François Sicard, stands in the Place Malesherbes.

Ida gives a second performance of *La Dame aux Camélias* the day before the first night of *Orphée*.

June 13th. Premiere of *Orphée* at the Paris Opera, a mime-drama by Cocteau, originally from a work by Roger-Ducasse. Decor and costumes by Alexander Golovin. Incidental music by Arthur Honegger. (This work was first created in 1913, and a concert performance by Alexander Ziloti was given in St Petersburg in 1914. Since then it had been forgotten.)

November 11th. The anniversary of the armistice. A charity gala for all holders of the Croix de Guerre. The star of the gala was Ida in *Ishtar*, by Vincent d'Indy.

1927. Isadora Duncan was tragically strangled when her scarf was caught in her car wheel at Nice.

17th February. The public dress rehearsal of *L'Impératice aux Rochers* by Saint Georges de Bouhelier at the Paris Opera. Sets and costumes by Alexandre Benois, incidental music by Arthur Honegger, directed by

Alexander Sanin.

18th February. Premiere of *L'Impératice aux Rochers.*

March 15th. Ida gives a lecture on d'Annunzio at the Université des Annales. This is later to be published in both French and Italian.

28th April. Ida again performs *Ishtar* in a charity concert organized by *Paris-Midi.*

1928. Ida forms her "Les Ballets Ida Rubinstein" with Bronislava Nijinska as main choreographer and ballet mistress, and Alexandre Benois as chief designer of sets and costumes. The male dancer is Anatole Vilzak, who will later become a star in the United States. The company includes: Ludmilla Schollar (Vilzac's wife) who has second billing after Ida; Nina Verchina; David Lichine; Frederick Ashton; Joyce Berry; Alexis Dolinoff; Rupert Donne; Nadeja Nikolaeva; Eugen Lapitzky; Unger; Singayevsky; Nijinska's husband, and William Chappell. Léonide Massine comes over from America to choreograph two of the ballets.

August 1st. The company begins rehearsals from 9am to 11pm daily. Ida has separate and private rehearsals.

November 22nd. Les Ballets Ida Rubinstein opens at the Paris Opera, with *Les Noces de Psyché et de l'Amour* as the first ballet of the season, newly commissioned from Arthur Honegger. *La Bien-Aimée*, newly commissioned from Milhaud; *David*, newly commissioned from Henri Sauguet. The opera *Tsar Saltan*, by Rimsky-Korsakov, was adapted into the ballet *La Princesse Cygne* for Les Ballets Ida Rubinstein; and Borodin's music was arranged by Nicolas Tcherepnin for the light ballet *Nocturne. Boléro*, commissioned from Ravel, was the much awaited final ballet of the first evening.

November 27th. *Le Baiser de la Fée* is premiered, music by Igor Stravinsky.

November 28th. *Nocturne* is premiered.

December 4th. The premiere of *David*, choreographed by Massine, and part of the final night of Les Ballets Ida Rubinstein season.

In all there were nine new ballets offered for the new Les Ballets Ida Rubinstein season 1928/9, which also included *L'Oiseau de Feu.*

1929. May. *Les Enchantements d'Alcine*, newly commissioned from Georges Auric.

May 23rd. Premiere of *La Valse*. Composed by Ravel. Choreography by Nijinska. Sets by Benois.

May 30th. Les Ballets Ida Rubinstein moves from the Paris Opera House to the Théâtre Sarah Bernhardt, to give one final performance of *Le Baiser, Les Enchantements,* and *Boléro.*

May 30th, afternoon. Ida is taken to court by Sammy Brill, a film maker, for non-payment of 20,000 francs which Ida owed him and had refused to pay because she had felt that his work was unsatisfactory. She is sued under her legal married name of Madame Horwitz. Ida loses the case.

August 19th. Diaghilev dies in Venice, in essence "on water", as predicted, to his terror, many years before. With him are Serge Lifar, Boris Kochno, and Misia Edwards (Misia Sert, his friend from the early days in Paris).

October. The Wall Street crash.

1930. Natalie Barney privately publishes a novel entitled *The One Who is Legion* or *A.D.'s After-Life*, about a rematerialized ectoplasmic suicide resulting in an androgynous hermaphrodite.

1931. Ida reassembles her company.

May. The launch of Sadler's Wells Ballet.

Ida arrives in London followed by her cast of one hundred artistes and seventy tons of luggage and much "hype".

June 23rd. Ida's London season opens at the Covent Garden Opera House with a repertoire consisting of two French plays and ten ballets. Bronislava Nijinska is artistic director and choreographer. Ida had collaborated on the selection of music with composers Honegger, Tcherepnin, and Milhaud who orchestrated works by Bach, Borodin, Schubert and Liszt for her. For the performances of his *Boléro* and *La Valse*, Ravel conducts the orchestra, as does Stravinsky for the premiere of his new ballet *Le Baiser de la Fée*. Léonide Massine comes over from New York to choreograph *David and Goliath* and *Alcine*.

Ida's season at Covent Garden opens on July 6th with *Le Martyre de St Sébastien*, a performance in aid of the French Hospital in London. Written by Gabriele d'Annunzio, with music by Claude Debussy. Costume and scenery by Léon Bakst

July 7th. The second night at Covent Garden. Ida presents three ballets. *La Princesse Cygne*, taken from one of Rimsky-Korsakov's operas: *David*, libretto by Doderet, music by Henri Sauguet, choreographed by Léonide Massine, and *Boléro*.

July 8th. Ida's programme is *Nocturne, La Valse*, which was rechoreographed by Mikhail Fokine, and *La Princesse Cygne*.

July 9th. *La Dame aux Camélias*, by Dumas.

July 10th sees the premiere of *Amphion*. Choreography by Massine. Sets and costumes by Benois. Libretto by Paul Valéry. Composed by Arthur Honegger. Also on the same bill is *Boléro*, conducted by Ravel.

Other ballets are *Les Enchantements d'Alcine*. Music by Georges Auric, scenario taken from Ariosto by Lois Lalory. *Les Noces de Psyché et de l'Amour* by Alexandre Benois, music by Arthur Honegger. *La Bien-Aimée*, also by Alexandre Benois, with music by Darius Milhaud. *Nocturne*, music by Borodin. *Le Baiser de la Fée*, music by Stravinsky. The season ends with *Les Noces de Psyché et de l'Amour, La Bien-Aimée* and *David*.

1932. Walter Guinness is elevated to the peerage as Lord Moyne.

Ida continues to work at future plans for her productions interspersed with "sudden secret journeys to distant lands".

October. Ravel is injured in a Paris taxi.

1934. April 30th. Premiere at the Paris Opera of *Perséphone*, by André Gide, with music by Stravinsky, choreographed by Mikhail Fokine.

Premiere of *Diane de Poitiers*, libretto by Elisabeth de Gramont, music by Jacques Ibert, choreographed by Fokine, sets and costumes by Benois. *Boléro* is the final offering of the evening.

May 4th. *Perséphone, Diane de Poitiers,* and *La Valse,* choreographed by Fokine.

May 6th. Dress rehearsal of *Sémiramis.* Libretto by Paul Valéry, music by Arthur Honegger, choreographed by Fokine.

May 9th. *Perséphone.*

May 21st. The end of Ida's 1934 season and the last time she would dance for Paris audiences.

Ida sails off in her yacht for more of her exotic travels.

July 21st. Ida is appointed to the Légion d'Honneur.

Ida and her company are nominated as the "Representatives of French Artistry" at the 1934 Salzburg Festival.

1935. January 27th. Ida dances, for the very last time, in Brussels at the Palais des Beaux-Arts, at a gala charity concert in aid of Russian mothers resident in Belgium. In this final performance Ida dances her roles in *Perséphone, Diane de Poitiers,* and *Sémiramis.*

March 27th. Ida appeared as Clytemnestra in *Les Choréophores,* translated by Paul Claudel, score by Darius Milhaud, costume and decor by Audrey Parr.

November 28th. London. Ida as reciter only in *Perséphone* at a Sir Henry Wood Stravinsky concert in the Queen's Hall. The French tenor René Maison sings the part of Eumolopus. The concert is broadcast by the BBC.

1936. September. Ida converts to Catholicism. Soon after she becomes one of the Dominican Order's tertiary sisters, a lay person committed to an altruistic life of charity.

1937. December. Maurice Ravel's health is deteriorating. Ida flies off around Europe to find a neurosurgeon who can help him, after Dr Thierry de Martel tells her that nothing can be done. Finally a Dr Clovis Vincent agrees to an exploratory operation. This is performed on December 19th. Ravel sinks into a coma and eventually dies on December 28th.

1938. March 1st. Gabriele d'Annunzio dies of a cerebral haemorrhage; he was seventy-four.

Summer. In memory of d'Annunzio, Ida gives two private performances of *Le Martyre de St Sébastien.*

Ida goes off on a retreat to Tournai, at the Dominican Convent of Saulchoir, to prepare herself for *Jeanne d'Arc.*

May 12th. Ida plays Joan of Arc in the premiere of the concert-oratorio *Jeanne d'Arc au Bûcher,* by Honegger, at Basle. A German translation by Hans Reinhardt.

Ida tours little towns and hamlets throughout France, appearing in tatty halls and rooms, with lectures on "The Art with Three Faces" and scenes from *St Sébastien.*

Ida books the Paris Opera House for *Jeanne d'Arc au Bûcher* and *La Valse* for November 29th and 1st and 6th of December, and other dates for some unspecified productions, presumably from the many commissions she has not yet staged.

1939. May. Ida appears in the French premiere of *Jeanne d'Arc au Bûcher* in Orleans, conducted by Louis Fourestier. Sets are by Benois and choreographed section by Boris Romanov.

May 24th. Ida is awarded the grand cross of an Officer of the Légion d'Honneur.

June 15th. Ida appears again as *Jeanne d'Arc au Bûcher* in the new theatre of the Palais de Chaillot.

September 3rd. France and Britain are at war with Germany.

Lady Evelyn Hilda Stuart Erskine, daughter of the fourteenth Earl of Buchan, Lady Moyne, Lord Moyne's wife, dies.

Ida sets up a hospital in a wing of Etioles, close to Corbeil, where she nurses wounded French soldiers.

In between her nursing duties she gives several money-raising charity and morale-boosting performances of *Jeanne d'Arc au Bûcher* in France and abroad.

1940. February 22nd. Ida as *Jeanne d'Arc au Bûcher* is broadcast on Radio Paris as a live performance.

The transcript of a pre-recorded interview with Ida by Germaine Dacaris had been printed in *L'Oeuvre* two days before and had attracted much attention. In it she outlined her many plans for the future.

Ida begins a Belgian tour of *Jeanne d'Arc au Bûcher*, in Liege, in Antwerp, and, on February 29th, in Brussels at the Palais des Beaux-Arts with Queen Elizabeth of the Belgians in the audience.

1941. May. Ida has to flee to the south of France, where she and her secretary, Madeleine Koll, cross the Mediterranean to Algeria. Lord Moyne, Secretary of State for the Colonies, arranges for Ida and Madeleine to get from Algeria to Casablanca, and onto an aeroplane waiting to fly them to Lisbon. From Lisbon they are able to get to the comparative safety of England.

June. Ida arrives in London with no financial resources whatsoever. Lord Moyne takes responsibility for Ida in every way. He installs her in a suite at the Ritz and totally finances her throughout the war years.

Ida continues with nursing of the Free French Forces in England in the sanatorium at the British Legion headquarters in East Grinstead. She will eventually acquire her own hospital in Camberley.

Ida totally gives up all social activities.

Persuaded by Sylvia Crawford, Ida attends a performance of *Flare Path* by Terence Rattigan, after which she adopts an air squadron.

December 12th. The *Strima*, a converted coal ship, crowded with 769 Romanian Jews is denied entry to Palestine by the British, and is eventually sunk with the loss of all but one on board. Abraham Stern demands revenge.

1942. August. Lord Moyne is appointed Deputy Minister in Cairo.

1944. January. Lord Moyne becomes Minister-Resident in the Middle East.

November. Lord Moyne and his driver are gunned down in the streets of Cairo by the Stern Gang. Both die.

Ida is not invited, neither does she attend any public or private ceremony for her lover. Their relationship will remain discreet until the end.

1945. May 8th. The war ends.

Ida returns to Paris, where her house had been razed to the ground.

Ida goes to stay in Biarritz.

1947. Roland Leblond at last leaves the hospital where he has been visited and cared for by Ida continuously throughout his lengthy confinement.

1950. Ida moves to Vence in the south of France and becomes a virtual recluse.

For one month every year, until her death, Ida retreats to the medieval Abbey of Hautecombe, near Chambéry, to pray and meditate.

April 8th. Vaslav Nijinsky dies in a hotel in London, in the arms of his wife Romola.

1953. June 6th. The ashes of Nijinsky are taken to Paris and buried in the Montmartre Cemetery.

1954. The Diaghilev Exhibition at the Edinburgh Festival, and later at Forbes House in London; each had to be extended twice.

1960. September 20th. Ida dies.

October. A month later Ida's death is publicly reported.

1967. The Diaghilev costumes are put up for auction at Sotheby's in Bond Street, and attract record prices.

1971. Coco Chanel dies in her Paris apartment at the Ritz.

1990. October. The lease on Ida's grave expires and the municipal authorities are fully entitled to dig up her remains.

PRINCIPAL SOURCES

Alexander, Sidney, *Marc Chagall*
Antongini, Tom, *D'Annunzio*
Bade, Patrick, *Femme Fatale*
Balanchine, George and Mason, Francis, *Balanchine's Festival of Ballet*
Barnes, Patricia, *The Children of Theatre Street*
Benois, Alexandre, *Reminiscences of the Russian Ballet*
Bernhardt, Lysiane, *Sarah Bernhardt – My Grandmother*
Bland, Alexander, *A History of Ballet and Dance*
Bourman, Anatole, *The Tragedy of Nijinsky*
Brooks, Romaine, *Between Me and Life*
Brown, Frederick, *An Impersonation of Angels – A Biography of Jean Cocteau*
Bruckner, Christine, *Desdemona – If Only You Had Spoken*, (tr. Eleanor Bron)
Buckle, Richard, *Nijinsky*
Buckle, Richard and Taras, John, *George Balanchine – Ballet Master*
Busoni, Ferruccio, *Letters To His Wife*
Chagall, Marc, *My Life*
Chalon, Jean, *Portrait of a Seductress – The World of Natalie Barney*
Clarke, Mary and Crisp, Quentin, *The History of Dance*
Craft, Robert (ed.), *Stravinsky – Selected Correspondence*
De Cossart, Michael, *Ida Rubinstein, A Theatrical Life*
Doolittle, Hilda, *Bid Me To Live*
Faderman, Lilian, *Surpassing the Love of Men*
Gramont, Elisabeth de (Duchesse de Clermont-Tonnerre), *Years of Plenty*
Gregory, John and Vladmikova, Alexander, *Leningrad's Ballet*
Grey, Beryl (ed.), *My Favourite Ballet Stories*
Hanlon, Emily, *Petersburg*
Harris, Ann Sutherland and Nochlin, Linda, *Women Artists 1850–1950*
Haskell, Arnold, *Balletomania – Then and Now*
Haskell, A. L. and Clarke, M. (eds), *Ballet Manual 1901–1962*
Hemingway, Ernest, *Death in the Afternoon*
Honegger, Arthur, *I am a Composer*
Howell, Georgina, *"VOGUE", 75 Years of Style*
Humphries, Steve, *A Secret World of Sex*
Johnston, Jill, *Lesbian Nation*
Kessler, Count Harry, *The Diaries of a Cosmopolitan*
Kochno, Boris, *Diaghilev and the Ballets Russes*
Kurth, Peter, *Anastasia*

Lawson, Joan, *A History of Ballet and its Makers*
Lester, Keith, *Rubinstein Revisited*, (Article in "Dance Research", Vol. 1, No 2, 1983)
Levinson, André, *Bakst – The Story of the Artist's Life*
Lewis, Edward, *The French on Life and Love*
Libman, Lillian, *And Music at the Close*
Lieven, Prince Peter, *The Birth of the Ballets Russes*
Lifar, Serge, *Serge Diaghilev. His Life. His Work. His Legend*
Martin, Del, *Lesbian/Woman*
Massine, Léonide, *My Life in Ballet*
Milhaud, Darius, *Notes Without Music*
Moyne, 2nd Baron, *Lord Moyne (1st Baron)*
Nardelli, Federico and Livingston, Arthur, *D'Annunzio: A Portrait*
Nijinska, Bronislava, *Early Memoirs*
Nijinska, Romola, *Nijinsky*
Nijinsky, Vaslav, *The Diary of Vaslav Nijinsky*
Painter, George D., *Marcel Proust*
Percival, John, *The World of Diaghilev*
Ponse, Barbara, *Identities in the Lesbian World*
Pougy, Liane de, *My Blue Notebook*
Propert, Walter, *The Russian Ballet 1921–1929*
Richardson, Joanna, *Sarah Bernhardt and Her World*
Rose, Sir Francis, *Saying Life*
Sarde, Michèle, *Colette*
Secrest, Meryle, *Between Me and Life. A Biography of Romaine Brooks*
Sinowjewa, Annibal, *Thirty-Three Monsters*
Spencer, Charles, *Léon Bakst*
Steegmuller, Francis, *Cocteau*
Stravinsky, Igor, *An Autobiography*
Stravinsky, Igor and Craft, Robert, *Dialogues*
Summers, Antony and Mangold, Tom, *The File on the Tsar*
Tanner, Donna, *The Lesbian Couple*
Troyat, Henri, *Catherine the Great*
Tuchman, Barbara W., *The Proud Tower – A Portrait of the World Before the War*
Vaughan, David, *Frederick Ashton and his Ballets*
Wickes, George, *The Amazon of Letters*
Woolf, Vicki, *Shape Up For Sex*

Grove's Concise Dictionary of Music
Romaine Brooks (1874–1970) Exhibition June–September, 1987. Catalogue published
    by Musée de la Ville, Poitiers
The Penguin Guide to Popular Music 1989. Donald Clark (ed.)
The William Morris Scrapbooks. The Theatre Museum, London

INDEX

Other titles in the Choreography and Dance Studies series:

This book is part of a series. The publisher will accept continuation orders which may be cancelled at any time and which provide for automatic billing and shipping of each title in the series upon publication. Please write for details.